DIGITAL TECHNOLOGY AND THE FUTURE OF BROADCASTING

ELECTRONIC MEDIA RESEARCH SERIES
Sponsored by the Broadcast Education Association
Robert K. Avery, Series Editor

SPORTS MEDIA
Transformation, Integration, Consumption
Edited by Andrew C. Billings

New in Paperback

MEDIA MANAGEMENT AND ECONOMICS
RESEARCH IN A TRANSMEDIA ENVIRONMENT
Edited by Alan B. Albarran

MEDIA AND THE MORAL MIND
Edited by Ron Tamborini

MEDIA AND SOCIAL LIFE
Edited by Mary Beth Oliver, Arthur A. Raney

DIGITAL TECHNOLOGY AND THE FUTURE OF BROADCASTING

Global Perspectives

Edited by
John V. Pavlik

Routledge
Taylor & Francis Group

NEW YORK AND LONDON

First published 2016
by Routledge
711 Third Avenue, New York, NY 10017

and by Routledge
2 Park Square, Milton Park, Abingdon, Oxon, OX14 4RN

*Routledge is an imprint of the Taylor & Francis Group, an informa
business*

Library of Congress Cataloging in Publication Data
Digital technology and the future of broadcasting : global
perspectives / [Edited by] John V. Pavlik.
pages cm. — (Electronic media research series)
Includes bibliographical references and index.
1. Broadcasting—Technological innovations. I. Pavlik, John V. (John
Vernon) editor.
HE8689.4D55 2016
384.51—dc23
2014045613

ISBN: 978-1-138-89122-7 (hbk)
ISBN: 978-1-315-70977-2 (ebk)

Typeset in Sabon
by Swales & Willis Ltd, Exeter, Devon, UK

CONTENTS

FIGURES

TABLES

CONTRIBUTORS

Robert Alan Brookey	Ball State University, USA
Michael Brouder	Ball State University, USA
Michael D. Bruce	University of Alabama, USA
Naeemah Clark	Elon University, USA
Dwight DeWerth-Pallmeyer	Widener University, USA
Miao Guo	Ball State University, USA
Michael Holmes	Ball State University, USA
Tim Hudson	Point Park University, USA
YoungChan Hwang	DanKook University, South Korea
Joe F. Khalil	Northwestern University in Qatar, Qatar
Randolph Kluver	Texas A&M University, USA
EunKyung Lee	Social Innovation Center, The Hope Institute, South Korea
Joon Soo Lim	Syracuse University, USA
John V. Pavlik	Rutgers University, USA
Peter B. Seel	Colorado State University, USA
Mitchell Shapiro	University of Miami, USA
Fei Shen	City University of Hong Kong, Hong Kong
Mike Z. Yao	University of Illinois, USA
Zhi'an Zhang	Sun Yat-Sen University, China

SERIES EDITOR'S FOREWORD

Since its inception in 1948, the Broadcast Education Association (BEA) has fostered a serious commitment to scholarly research, though that commitment became more formalized with the publication of its first scholarly journal, *Journal of Broadcasting* (later *Journal of Broadcasting & Electronic Media*) in 1957. Over the BEA's rich intellectual history, its annual meetings have afforded both academics and professionals with a wide range of opportunities for the presentation of important scholarship focusing on broadcasting and the electronic media.

In 2008, BEA launched a new series of programs designed to advance original research initiatives under the direction of the Association's Research Committee. The name of this new scholarly venture within the framework of the annual conference is the BEA Research Symposium Series, and over the past seven years it has served to advance the research agendas of our discipline and provide a forum for some of the leading scholars and latest ground-breaking research in our field. The first Research Symposium in 2008 was orchestrated by Professor Jennings Bryant with a focus on Media Effects. This was followed in 2009 with a Research Symposium on the subject of TechnoPolitics, under the direction of Professor Linda Kaid.

In response to these two highly successful symposia, discussions began in 2010 between BEA and Routledge, of the Taylor & Francis Group, to form a partnership to enable the publication of an annual volume resulting from the yearly BEA Research Symposium. That new scholarly publication venture is the Electronic Media Research Series, and is intended to serve as cutting-edge seminal publications that offer an in-depth cross section of significant research topics. The 2010 Research Symposium Chair was Andrew C. Billings and hence the first volume in the new series edited by Professor Billings is *Sports Media: Transformation, Integration, Consumption*, published in 2011. The 2011 Research Symposium Chair, Ron Tamborini, edited the second volume, *Media and the Moral Mind*, released in 2012. The third volume growing out of the 2012 Research Symposium, published in 2013, was edited by Alan B. Albarran and is titled, *Media Management and Economics Research in a Transmedia Environment*. The fourth volume, *Media and Social Life*, was co-edited by Arthur A. Raney and Mary Beth Oliver and was published in 2014.

The present volume, titled *Digital Technology and the Future of Broadcasting: Global Perspectives*, resulted from the 2014 Research Symposium chaired by Professor John V. Pavlik, Rutgers University. This volume has been edited by Professor Pavlik and contains both selected papers from the Symposium and essays written especially for this collection. Together, the chapters contained in this volume offer a unique perspective on questions about how digital technologies are reshaping the broadcasting industries around the world. The chapters address the numerous forces that pervade the emerging technologies, structures, content changes, and the newly developing economic and regulatory models required by the evolving media environment. The BEA and Routledge are proud to make this important volume available to scholars across the entire communication discipline and beyond.

Robert K. Avery
BEA Research Committee Chair
Symposium Series, Executive Editor

PREFACE

Digital technologies are ushering in a sea-change in broadcasting in the United States and around the world. These changes are transforming virtually every aspect of broadcasting, including the content, means of production and distribution, structures, economics, and means of public engagement in broadcasting. The international perspectives offered in this edited volume provide both an agenda for future research as well as insight into the dynamics of twenty-first-century broadcasting on an increasingly global stage.

Acknowledgements

The editor thanks all those individuals who have contributed to the development of this book. To begin, thanks to Prof. Robert K. Avery, Professor in the Department of Communication at the University of Utah. As chair of the Research Committee of the Broadcast Education Association (BEA), Bob's leadership and vision made the BEA2014 Research Symposium and subsequent book possible. Also, thanks to Linda Bathgate, publisher, Communication and Media Studies, Routledge/Taylor & Francis Group. Linda's commitment and that of Routledge/Taylor & Francis Group are of particular importance in the publication of this book. Thanks as well to Heather Birks, Executive Director of the BEA, for all her efforts in support of the Symposium and the book. Thanks as well to other BEA leadership, including previous Research Symposium chairs Art Raney, Florida State University, Mary Beth Oliver, Pennsylvania State University, and Donald G. Godfrey, Professor Emeritus, Arizona State University. Finally, thanks to BEA2014 Research Symposium paper reviewers, Byung S. Lee, Elon University; EunKyung Lee; Dwight DeWerth-Pallmeyer, Widener University; Antonio Brasil, Federal University of Santa Catarina, Rio de Janeiro; Tim Hudson, Point Park University, and Mitchell Shapiro, University of Miami. Without their extraordinary help, neither the symposium nor the book would have been possible.

INTRODUCTION

Digital technology is fundamentally reshaping broadcasting and the media in the United States and around the world. Based on the BEA2014 Research Symposium, this book features distinguished scholars whose research spans domestic and international issues of technological change and the implications for broadcasting and related media in a global context. Topics considered include the impact of digital technology on: (1) the structure of broadcasting organizations and regulation, (2) the nature of broadcast content or media programming and how it is delivered at home and abroad, (3) engagement and interaction of the public with broadcasting and social and mobile media, and (4) the reshaping of revenue models for broadcasters and media organizations in the US and globally. Chapters help set an agenda for research on the implications of digital technology for broadcasting and broadcasting education in the US and internationally.

The book features 14 original chapters organized into three parts. The first two parts contain chapters based on competitively reviewed research papers that were originally presented at the BEA2014 Research Symposium. The third part features chapters based on presentations by a panel of distinguished broadcasting scholars from around the US and internationally, as well as chapters authored by the paper discussants at the BEA2014 Research Symposium. While the chapters in the first two parts provide empirically based scholarship on directions and issues in broadcasting in an increasingly global, digital arena, the third part provides reflection on the problems and prospects for research, education, and public policy that arise in this era of rapid and continuing change.

Part I

The book opens with a series of three chapters developed from original research investigations. The theme of Part I is research challenges in a changing broadcast environment, in particular, social media, eye tracking, and audience measurement.

Chapter 1 is "Motivations for Viewers Using Social Media During the Olympic Games: Implications for the Future of Sports Broadcasting." This top student paper in the BEA2014 Research Symposium paper competition is authored by Joon Soo Lim, Syracuse University, and YoungChan Hwang, SBS (Seoul Broadcasting System).

Chapter 2 is "Double Vision: An Eye-Tracking Analysis of Visual Attention Between Television and Second Screens." Authors of this chapter are Miao Guo, Ball State University, and Michael Holmes, Ball State University.

Chapter 3 is "Twitter and Television: Broadcast Ratings in the Web 2.0 Era." Authors of this chapter are Michael Brouder, Ball State University and Robert Alan Brookey, Ball State University.

Part II

Part II also features research investigations originally presented at the BEA2014 Research Symposium. The theme of Part II is research issues and advances in global broadcasting, in particular, international broadcasting developments, visual structure, and digital displays.

Chapter 4 is "Broadcast and New Media Use in China: Findings from a National Survey." Authors of this chapter are Fei Shen, City University of Hong Kong, Zhi'an Zhang, Sun Yat-sen University, and Mike Z. Yao, University of Illinois.

Chapter 5 is "Sensational Pictures: An Analysis of Visual Structure on Five Transnational Arab News Channels," authored by Michael D. Bruce, University of Alabama.

Chapter 6 is "Telepresence and Immersion with Ultra-High-Definition Digital Displays: Background and Future Directions for Research," authored by Peter B. Seel, Colorado State University.

Part III

Part III of the book provides international perspectives on broadcasting in the digital age. Through a series of commentaries and essays, a distinguished group of scholars expand on their remarks originally offered at the BEA2014 Research Symposium or developed uniquely for this volume.

Chapter 7 is "The Future of Television: An Arab Perspective" authored by Joe F. Khalil, Northwestern University in Qatar. An associate professor at Northwestern University, Dr Khalil is an expert on Arab television production and programming and has more than 15 years of professional television experience as director, executive producer, and consultant with major Arab satellite channels (Orbit, MBC, MTV, CNBC Arabiya) and has conducted workshops on behalf of USAID, IREX, and the University of Pennsylvania. He received an MA from Ohio University and a PhD from Southern Illinois University, Carbondale.

Dr Khalil is the recipient of the 2008 SIUC Excellence in Commitment Graduate Student Research Award and a research grant from the Smith Richardson Foundation. His scholarly interests revolve specifically around Arab youth, alternative media, and global media industries. As consultant, Dr Khalil has conducted or supervised corporate research related to production and programming. He has authored a policy monograph on Arab satellite entertainment television and public diplomacy and is also co-author of *Arab Television Industries* (2009, with Marwan Kraidy). He is currently working on a book project based on his dissertation, *Youth-generated Media in Lebanon and Saudi Arabia*, which examines alternative media cases in both countries.

Chapter 8 is "Tourism as a Mediated Practice in a Global Media Context: The Gaze of Female Korean Tourists to New York City and the Meaning of Their Practices," authored by EunKyung Lee, Social Innovation Center, The Hope Institute. This chapter examines tourists who are female and from a non-Western country, and the role of digital media, including broadcast sources, in shaping their cultural gaze. Most of those studied are active consumers of global media products including *Sex and the City*. These women participate in, and are also affected by, the contemporary globalization process as well. On the internet, these women collect and appreciate various images of and scenes from the world's tourist spots and register various meanings into those images. In particular, Dr Lee examines the experience of Korean female tourists to New York City. By analyzing personal travelogues on the web and in-person interviews she illuminates in what ways these women's tourist practices are mediated and what kinds of gazes they carry toward their destination. Also, this study examines the ways in which their tourism experience creates hybrid cultures after they return home. Dr Lee finds that these women challenge the taboo and perception of danger for lone female travelers while they try to gaze back at Western (American) culture and images from their media experience.

Chapter 9 is "Assessing the Role Audience Plays in Digital Broadcasting Today and Tomorrow," authored by Dwight DeWerth-Pallmeyer, Widener University. Dr DeWerth-Pallmeyer builds off the classic 1996 *The Audience in the News* project and examines the ways social media interact with broadcast news.

Chapter 10 is "Confronting the Central Paradox of Media Studies: The Network Society, Digital Technologies, and the Future of Media Research," authored by Randolph Kluver, Texas A&M University. The Media Monitoring System is a real time international broadcast transcription and translation system built on computerized algorithms. Dr Kluver is Executive Director of Global Partnerships and Projects (GPP), and Associate Professor in the Department of Communication at Texas A&M University. He has been PI or co-PI on over $4 million for international research and educational grants and contracts. In 2007, Dr Kluver led the campus initiative to establish the Confucius Institute at Texas A&M, and served as the Director of the CI until 2012.

Currently, he is co-PI (with Stephen Balfour) of the MMS/CAMMI Project, a real-time international broadcast transcription and translation system, and is actively engaged with university faculty to develop research protocols and educational applications for this pioneering technology, especially through the Global Networked Media Archive, an initiative to create online, searchable databases of online media.

Dr Kluver's research agenda focuses on international communication and the political and geopolitical implications of new media technologies. He was one of the principal investigators of the international Internet and Elections project, a comparative analysis of the use of the internet in the 2004 election cycle. He serves on the editorial boards of the *Journal of Communication*, the *Journal of Computer-mediated Communication*, the *Asian Journal of Communication*, *New Media and Society*, *China Media Research*, and the *Western Journal of Communication*. Dr Kluver's current research interests include digital and cultural diplomacy, the role of the internet in Asian societies, Asian political communication, globalization, and the political and social impact of information technologies.

Dr Kluver's book *Civic Discourse, Civil Society, and Chinese Communities* won the Outstanding Book Award from the International and Intercultural Division of the National Communication Association in 2000. His essay "The Logic of New Media in International Relations" received the 2003 Walter Benjamin Award from the Media Ecology Association as the outstanding research article in media ecology.

Chapter 11 is "Connecting in the Scandalverse: The Power of Social Media and Parasocial Relationships," authored by Naeemah Clark, associate professor in the School of Communications at Elon University. She has edited the book, *African Americans in the History of U.S. Media*, co-authored a textbook *Diversity in U.S. Media*, published work in *Journalism History* and *American Behavioral Scientist*, and has presented numerous papers at various conferences. Dr Clark is interested in studying and teaching about economic, programming, and diversity issues related to the media and entertainment industries. Before coming to Elon in 2009, Dr Clark worked at the University of Tennessee-Knoxville and Kent State University. She has a PhD and MA in mass communication from the University of Florida and a BS in English Education from Florida State University. Since coming to Elon in 2009, Dr Clark has led student groups to Vietnam, Berlin, and Central Florida.

An authority on diversity in media, Dr Clark recently wrote a column for the (Burlington, NC) *Times-News* that centers on the anti-gay comments of Phil Robertson, the star of A&E's "Duck Dynasty." Clark writes that, while she agrees with A&E's decision to suspend Robertson, she also understands why the network put him back on the air:

A&E was right to suspend Robertson from the program. The network will also be right when it allows the daddy of "Duck Dynasty" back on the show . . . Why? Well, to quote that awful Mr Potter in *It's A Wonderful Life*, the "building and loan is a business not a charity ward." Television is a business.

Chapter 12 is "The Legacy of Dr. Horrible: Potential Research into Second-Screen Intrusion, Coordination, and Influence" by Tim Hudson, Point Park University. Dr Hudson's essay examines the technological developments that have led to the transformation of network television.

Chapter 13 is "Changing Paradigm?" by Mitchell Shapiro of the University of Miami (Florida). Dr Shapiro offers a high-level view of the changing broadcasting landscape at home and abroad. Across time and space, broadcasting has undergone dramatic change over the past half century, and the time has come to ask new research questions to guide the scholarly examination of broadcasting in the twenty-first century.

Chapter 14 is "Immersion: Implications of Wearable Technologies for the Future of Broadcasting" by John V. Pavlik, professor in the Department of Journalism and Media Studies at the School of Communication and Information at Rutgers University, the State University of New Jersey, and Chair, BEA2014 Research Symposium. Dr Pavlik has written widely on the impact of new technology on journalism, media, and society.

Part I

RESEARCH CHALLENGES IN A CHANGING BROADCAST ENVIRONMENT

1
MOTIVATIONS FOR VIEWERS USING SOCIAL MEDIA DURING THE OLYMPIC GAMES

Implications for the Future of Sports Broadcasting

Joon Soo Lim and YoungChan Hwang

Introduction

In an article published in the *International Journal of Human–Computer Interaction*, Stefan Agamanolis stated, "Broadcasting is all about creating shared experiences" (Agamanolis, 2008, p. 121). Agamanolis suggested that the concept of broadcasting was destined to change as the digital television platforms were introduced and they were "coupled with a broadband back-channel" (p. 127). He also suggested that the new mode of interactive television would enable people to communicate with "different groups of people that were not possible before" (p. 121), which could "create a sense of community" (p. 127). Although Twitter was not fully fledged to be used as a major backchannel communication tool to talk about live television programming when Agamanolis published the article, he seemed to be ascertaining that the future of broadcasting would be evolving to convey shared experiences among virtually connected people powered by backchannel communication.

Indeed, the concept of interactive television that Agamanolis envisioned has become a reality in both television production and consumption. Accordingly, an increasing amount of research has emerged to explain diverse aspects of the social television (social TV) phenomenon, such as motivations for social TV (Han & Lee, 2014; Schirra et al., 2014), the effect of social TV on sports channel loyalty (Lim et al., 2015), prevalent use (e.g., information, attention-seeking, emotion, etc.) of social TV

(Giglietto & Selva, 2014; Iannelli & Giglietto, 2015), the effect of second-screen use on recall and comprehension of television news (Van Cauwenberge et al., 2014), and the effect of second-screen use on program engagement measured by brain activity (Pynta et al., 2014).

We note that there is a need to refine the user motivations for engaging in backchannel communication while watching live televised sporting events—those motivations that are well aligned with traditional uses and gratifications (U&G) research, while stressing the unique characteristics of new communication-related behaviors that take place on two screens. In addition, we also note a research need to connect the motivation factors to other psychological attitudes associated with the viewing experience. A few researchers have noted that feelings of social presence are important in order to understand the current social TV phenomenon. This phenomenon has even created the social TV ratings called "Nielsen Twitter TV Ratings" in a partnership with Nielsen and Twitter Inc. Researchers asserted that social TV has much to do with social presence (Lim et al., 2015; Shin, 2013; Xu & Yan, 2011).

Sports television producers also have a keen interest in the future of social TV and want to take advantage of this phenomenon. A few researchers of both industry (Goel, 2015; Proulx & Shepatin, 2012) and academia (Hechelmann, 2012; Lim et al., 2015; Pynta et al., 2014) started to present some empirical evidence regarding the positive outcomes of viewer engagement through social TV. It is notable that such positive outcomes, such as viewer commitment to the broadcasting brand or the sports channel (Hechelmann, 2012; Lim et al., 2015; Proulx & Shepatin, 2012), are often preceded by enhanced feelings of social presence (Hassoun, 2012; Hutchins, 2010; Lim et al., 2015). The current study attempts to connect viewer motivations for engaging in social TV to their sports channel commitment during the televised 2014 Sochi Winter Olympics.

Literature Review

Social TV in Viewing Mega-Sporting Events

There is increasing scholarly investigation into the latest trend in audiences' television consumption, from a linear format to non-linear viewing and interactive engagement and even to a co-production of the content. In particular, audiences' second-screen use while viewing television has become a new norm during consumption of television content. This new phenomenon is called social TV, defined as "real-time backchannel communication on social networking sites (SNSs) during a live television broadcast" (Lim et al., 2015, p. 158). An industry report claimed that, in 2013, "about one in six Americans posted comments about the shows during their broadcasts" (Goel & Stelter, 2013).

This latest trend in viewing television content has made a greater impact not only on audience viewing habits but also on broadcasters' programming of live events. These days, broadcasters and sports program producers set it as a priority to engage the audience in their programming. For instance, most live televised sports programs incorporate selected tweets back into the show to increase audience engagement with their programs and the sportscasters (Harrington et al., 2012). Being aware of the importance of viewer engagement in sports viewing, producers of sports programs invest in technologies and systems that enable people to engage with the sports programs and sportscasters (Bodhani, 2012).

Television industry professionals wondered whether social TV conversation could lift viewership of particular television shows (Goel & Stelter, 2013; Proulx & Shepatin, 2012). It is not conclusive whether or not Twitter chatter during shows makes a positive impact on conventional TV ratings, and recent industry data revealed that social TV conversation tends to get more intensive as the audience becomes more engaged with the segment of a show (Goel, 2015). We believe that an intense social TV conversation will eventually boost television program ratings by generating more excitement, curiosity, and social-ness. In particular, being involved with social TV during live televised sports events, viewers have several different motives to gratify their needs for using backchannel communication with other viewers. Backchannel communication during televised sports games allows viewers to satisfy their needs of seeking information, being thrilled in victory, and talking with others either vicariously or directly. It also enables them to experience the feeling of being together, although other social TV viewers are not physically present at the same place—this is known as the feeling of social presence.

The Uses and Gratifications Perspective: Motivations for Social TV

The U&G perspective for audience research into mass communication has provided media scholars with a theoretical framework that guides ever-changing audience behavior in the consumption of televised sports. Wenner and Gantz (1998) asserted that audience research in media sports "has come from a uses and gratifications perspective" and "has generally focused on the factors that motivate audience consumption and enjoyment of mediated sports" (p. 48). The U&G perspective is a relevant and meaningful framework that explains viewer motivations for live sports on television since "viewing sports on television is more often than not an intentional action by an active audience" (Raney, 2006, p. 326).

A body of research (Gantz, 1981; Raney, 2006; Wann, 1995; Wenner & Gantz, 1998) has examined motivational factors that underlie sports media consumption. Raney (2006) identified various motivational factors in a few psychological perspectives: cognitive, emotional, social, and behavioral motivations. While Raney considers viewing televised sports as a primary "function of affect" (p. 325), he also emphasizes that it requires some cognitive activity to process game-related statistics. Notably, group affiliation motives were identified to explain viewing mega-sporting events such as the World Cup and Olympics, in which people can feel a sense of national pride or belonging (Raney, 2006).

An earlier explorative study by Gantz (1981) identified four factors of television sports viewing: (1) to thrill in victory, (2) to let loose, (3) to learn, and (4) to pass time. Gantz (1981) also asserted that viewing sports on television can be perceived as communicative behavior that motivates people to interact with others and be vocally responsive to statements made by sportscasters.

An emerging question is whether motivations for social TV during live sports events would be different from the aforementioned motivations for sports television viewing. To answer this question, we attempted to integrate traditional motivations for televised sports viewing with the motivations for communicating with others on social media platforms, particularly during television viewing. The literature review allowed us to propose the following four motivations that can account for social TV during live mega-sporting events such as the Olympics.

Information Motives

Sport fans seek out information about their team and players online (Ha et al., 2013; Hur et al., 2007; Stavros et al., 2014). Researchers (Han & Lee, 2014; Wohn & Na, 2011) who explored viewer motivations for social TV have identified that audiences have motivations to seek and share information through communication on second screens while viewing television shows. Those sports fans seek various sports information, including team performance, player profiles, and schedules through the Internet, and want to know more about things happening in their favorite sports (Ha et al., 2013; Hur et al., 2007; Kang et al., in press). Before the social TV era, sports fans had to rely on proprietary information that was tightly controlled by the media and broadcasters (Sutera, 2013). Hence, Sutera (2013) explains that television and radio stations were "the only ways fans not in attendance at the actual event could know what was happening while the game was still being played" (p. 41). In the age of social TV, however, the information sources for the game, team, and players have been greatly diversified, and those traditional information hubs are competing with numerous individuals and amateurs who post game-related information in real time (Sutera, 2013). A unique trend in this social media age is that the fans like to share the information they have collected through the internet with others (Kang et al., in press), which forms the fanship across the social media platforms.

6

Excitement Motives

Enjoyment or hedonic motives have been identified as important for using television (Ferguson & Perse, 2000), social networking sites (Lin & Lu, 2011; Park et al., 2009), and sports-related mobile apps (Kang et al., in press). When it comes to spectators' motives for enjoying sporting games, however, previous research has documented excitement motives (Gantz, 1981; Mehus, 2005; Raney, 2006; Westmyer, DiCioccio, & Rubin, 1998). Sports spectators or sports television viewers have intrinsic motives to express their emotions when they are thrilled in victory. These excitement motives are also the main motivation for social TV users. It is reported that viewers of televised sporting games use backchannel communication to share emotions about a game and players, or to express their feelings of the moment (Han & Lee, 2014).

Social Interaction Motives

According to Wenner and Gantz (1998), social interaction motives for watching televised sports are concerned with conversational utility (e.g., something to talk about) and companionship (something to do with family or friends). These social interaction motives also exist in the consumption of new media content such as YouTube (Haridakis & Hanson, 2009). Social interaction motives for social TV focus more on cyber-interaction than on real-life companionship, as Haridakis and Hanson (2009) suggested. Some sample items that reflect social interaction motives include (1) to belong to a group with the same interests as mine, (2) because I enjoy answering other people's questions, and (3) because it makes me feel less lonely (p. 325).

Convenience Motives

The use of the internet and smartphones to find sports-related information is much faster and more convenient than ever before. In a study of online sports consumption, Hur and his colleagues (2007) identified that convenience was the most important motive for internet consumption, since the internet makes it easier and faster to find useful information and consume sports-related content.

Users of social TV tend to believe social media empowered them to be more effective and efficient in generating, sharing, and searching for content and information, in addition to communicating and interacting with others (Han & Lee, 2014). In particular, sports fans who are well adapted to using their second-screen devices that are powered by social apps or sports-related apps involve themselves in social TV behavior. This is because communicating with others and finding information is quick, easy, and convenient (Kang et al., in press).

The perception of convenience in engaging in social TV is primarily derived from the attributes of mobility and brevity of Twitter messages (Hull & Lewis, 2014). In other words, social TV users can easily obtain the desired information without being constrained by time and space. Researchers (Ha et al., 2015), who highlighted convenience attributes in using mobile SNSs, noted that mobility enables users to acquire information fast by reducing the time constraint and the amount of effort for information access. Accordingly, the convenience motive can be important for using social TV during televised sports viewing. For instance, fans during a live sporting event can use their smartphone apps and conveniently access self-tailored information (Gantz & Lewis, 2014). Gantz and Lewis (2014) describe how accessing this tailored information in real time can be done easily by making an example of using an ESPN app by which "fans can tailor ESPN's newsfeed to include their favorite sports and favorite teams filtering those stories first" (p. 4).

Social Presence Theory

Social presence refers to "the degree of salience of the other person in the interaction and the consequent salience of the interpersonal relationships" (Short et al., 1976, p. 65). In a mediated communication setting, the concept of social presence was proposed to explain how much the mediated communication environment could create the sense of the real or physical presence of the other communication actor(s). However, there has been considerable scholarly debate on whether media communication through telecommunication can provide the sense of social presence (Flanagin & Metzger, 2001; Rice & Love, 1987; Schroeder, 2010; Short et al., 1976; Walther, 1992; Williams, 1977). Some critics (Collins, 2014) argue that the mediated communication environment cannot provide the same level of vividness, excitement, and/or sense of involvement that the participants of live events can feel. Those critics point out that mediated communication through telecommunication cannot simulate the spatial environment in which real participants of communication can process the whole verbal and nonverbal information through all five senses during face-to-face interaction.

Walther (1992) challenged the critics' views that computer-mediated communication (CMC) environments have innate disadvantages in offering the feeling of propinquity with others and social presence because of lack of social context cues. On the basis of the media richness theory, Walther (1992) argued that CMC has evolved enough to become rich media by which users can convey "socioemotional content" (p. 66), even in text-based mediated communication. He also raised a possibility that the initially low level of social presence could change as "interaction history develops" (Walther, 1992, p. 74).

We note that backchannel communication in ever-evolving social apps and instant messaging services such as KakaoTalk (a free mobile instant messaging application primarily used in South Korea) enables social TV users to create what Walther called "socioemotional content" that is rich in social context cues. All participants in Kehrwald's (2008) interviews agreed that "text-based online messages contain cues that indicate the social presence of the individual who sends them" (p. 95). Earlier, it was reported that participants of an online forum who had a higher sense of social presence were more satisfied with the virtual platform when they used emoticons to express their feelings (Gunawardena & Zittle, 1997), which indicates that it is possible to use certain social context cues and convey socioemotional experience online to express missing nonverbal cues in written form.

Sports viewers' increasing use of second screens to share game-related information and/or emotional feelings about televised games allows them to interact with other viewers who are geographically dispersed around the nation. In this new virtual co-viewing experience, sports television viewers who are involved in backchannel communication experience a sense of togetherness with those who are not physically co-present, as mentioned earlier, which is called a sense of "social presence" (Biocca et al., 2003; Lee, 2004; Lim et al., 2015).

A few recent studies (Han & Lee, 2014; Lim et al., 2015; Wohn & Na, 2011) have suggested that audiences of televised sporting events can develop a feeling of social presence while they virtually interact with other television viewers through their second screens. Users of social TV can feel a sense of being together with others who are geographically dispersed (Han & Lee, 2014; Lim et al., 2015). A user in Han and Lee's (2014) qualitative study exactly reflected this kind of feeling of social connectedness: "Even though my buddy and I watch sports programs at different places, we can cheer for and yell out via KakaoTalk. So, I feel like I am there at the sports arena with my friend" (p. 239). Han and Lee suggested that the feelings of social presence tend to be strong because "dramatic emotions can be exchanged through cheering and similar activities" (p. 240).

Some research (Garramone et al., 1986; Perse & Courtright, 1993) has suggested that feelings of social presence may not entirely hinge on the media attributes and that it can be influenced by the audience's goals and motivations. From a motivation perspective, excitement motives of using social media can drive individuals to increase their engagement thinking about the reward from the feelings of being together with others (Mäntymäki & Riemer, 2014). When viewers have a stronger need to root for their favorite team or player with other fans, therefore, they will experience more feelings of social presence when they engage in social TV conversations.

Therefore, the following hypothesis was posited:

H1: The excitement motives for social TV will be positively correlated with the perceived social presence.

Today, viewers of live sporting events use Twitter to learn more about game-related information. Viewers are involved in backchannel communication for various reasons, but they are more inclined to scan Twitter's opinion stream to see other viewers' opinions or reactions to referee decisions and/or sportscasters' and commentators' comments. Social media-based backchannel communication also helps users to find game-related information and links to the video materials for the athletes they are interested in (Hutchins & Rowe, 2012). In addition, some social TV users use Twitter to share "the progress of a game promptly, or to relay details about a game" (Han & Lee, 2014, p. 240). The significant amount of information and feedback can facilitate the perceived interactivity, which can increase the feelings of social presence (Garramone et al., 1986).

The social TV setting is a kind of collaborative virtual environment that allows users to have real-time information access and immediate feedback, which can cause a greater sense of social presence (Bente et al., 2008). A qualitative study (Kehrwald, 2008) of online learning environments proposed a new definition of social presence derived from users' own experience: "Social presence is an individual's ability to demonstrate his or her state of being in a virtual environment and so signal his or her availability for interpersonal transactions" (p. 94). Apparently, this perspective of social presence highlights the importance of individual motivation to engage in communicative exchanges. Kehrwald (2008) found that users of virtual learning environments develop the feelings of social presence as they have their own presence as well as initial interactions with others. In the development process, individuals' motivations to engage in relational exchanges affect their sense of social presence. Therefore, Kehrwald (2008) concluded that users of virtual platforms "need a motive which makes the interactions purposeful and, ultimately, beneficial for themselves" (p. 97). During sports television viewing, users having a goal to seek information can develop a sense of social presence since information richness is an antecedent of social presence (Cyr et al., 2007; Fulk et al., 1987).

Unlike motives for traditional media use, social media users tend to believe SNSs are quite effective and efficient as they allow them to find and share the information they are interested in without being constrained by time and space. This motive for seeking convenience was well documented in literature with regard to internet use (Ko et al., 2005; Papacharissi & Rubin, 2000) and SNS use (Gibbs et al., 2014; Hicks et al., 2012; Kim et al., 2011; Whiting, 2013). Social TV activity during live sporting events is gaining popularity among sports fans. This is due to the convenience of obtaining most self-tailored information faster and efficiently. In particular, smartphone apps for social media and social TV enable viewers of televised events to get "immediate access to convenient, self-tailored content" (Gantz & Lewis, 2014, p. 4). The utilitarian motivations such as information and convenience motives can stimulate social TV users to enhance the feelings of social presence by fulfilling their gratification to find relevant information fast and in an easy fashion.

Therefore, we proposed the following hypotheses:

H2: The informative motives for social TV will be positively correlated with the perceived social presence.

H3: The convenience motives for social TV will be positively correlated with the perceived social presence.

Researchers of social learning have suggested that the sense of social presence could foster online social interaction, which affects social learning (Kehrwald, 2008; Kreijns et al., 2004; Tu, 2000). From a different perspective, however, one may wonder how people's conscious use of a certain computer platform to make a greater social interaction can allow them to experience feelings of social presence when they enter the mediated communication environment. This approach to social presence comes from the so-called relational view of social presence (Gunawardena, 1995; Kehrwald, 2008; Walther, 1992). In this perspective, the feelings of social presence can stem from relational motivators, accrued experience, and distinctive impressions of other interactants, rather than coming from the characteristics of the media.

A conceptual essay that delineated the multidimensionality of social presence (Biocca et al., 2003) suggests that "symbolic representation of others" or "sensory awareness of the embodied other" should be prerequisites for experiencing feelings of being with others in a virtual space. Social TV users can develop this sense of awareness through the artifacts of mediated text messages, user handles and selfies, and the number of retweets or favorites, etc.

We assume that the degree of social presence one feels can increase as the mediated social interactants or artifacts become more salient. Since social presence is based on each user's subjective perception, the level of intimacy and immediacy of social interactants can influence the degree of social presence (Sung & Mayer, 2012). Consequently, social TV users' need to belong with other sports fans can play a big role in the perceived social presence while viewing the live Olympic Games.

Based on the review of literature, we posit the following hypothesis:

H4: The social interaction motives for social TV will be positively correlated with the perceived social presence.

Social TV Motives and Sports Channel Commitment

A surfacing question for the emergence of the social TV phenomenon is how sports media companies can adapt to this rapidly changing social and ambient media environment. Sports managers have sought answers for whether social TV conversations really help sports television channels to increase more viewership and loyalty to the sports channel. To find answers to such questions, we believe that sports television channels need to look into viewer motivations to use social TV and how they can lead to commitment to the sports channel that the audience consumes.

Sports channel commitment is an important concept to professional broadcasters, who try to build long-lasting relationships with their audiences (Kim et al., 2013). Channel commitment is critical because it is an antecedent to viewers' channel loyalty (Lim et al., 2015). We examine what motivations for viewers' social TV are connected with their commitment to a sports television channel.

Following the literature on affective commitment (Kim et al., 2013; Konovsky & Cropanzano, 1991; Lövblad et al., 2012) and engagement motives for social TV (Kim et al., 2013; Nee, 2013), sports channel commitment in this study is defined as "a sense of positive regard for and attachment to a sports channel" (Konovsky & Cropanzano, 1991, p. 699).

Previous research suggested that information motives and utilitarian motives in terms of convenience would be good predictors of consumer commitment to a brand or an organization (Nee, 2013). Equally important is the role of hedonic motives of Twitter users in their affect for a certain sports channel. A recent study by Nielson indicates that the greater the excitement with the segment of TV programming, the higher the level of social TV activity (Goel, 2015). Hence, it can be assumed that viewers who have motivations of thrill in victory with others tend to engage more deeply in backchannel communication. We also assume that the more social TV users have excitement motives for social TV activity, the more positive affect they will have for the broadcasting channel they are watching. Kim et al. (2013), in their conceptual paper, postulated that the hedonic motives of social TV would have a positive impact on channel commitment.

In addition, Kim and his colleagues (2013) postulated that social interaction motives and sports channel commitment would be correlated highly. In social media, sports fans have a natural tendency to find and interact with other people who root for the same team. Consuming a sports channel is more than viewing the live game. A recent study (Lim et al., 2015) that examined the relationship between social TV activity and sports channel commitment revealed that social TV users' social interaction with others to share opinions and feelings about the channel has ultimately increased channel commitment.

On the basis of this review, we propose the following hypotheses:

H5: The information motives for social TV will be positively correlated with sports channel commitment.

H6: The convenience motives for social TV will be positively correlated with sports channel commitment.

H7: The excitement motives for social TV will be positively correlated with sports channel commitment.

H8. The social interaction motives for social TV will be positively correlated with sports channel commitment.

Social Presence and Sports Channel Commitment

To retain consumers and make them come back to buy is the final, but the most important, step in consumer relationship marketing. In the sports media business, retaining ever-fragmenting fans is not an easy job for the managers and producers of sports broadcasting companies. In particular, it is a more challenging task for those producers in major network television channels in Korea, since the exclusive right for broadcasting a mega-sporting event such as the World Cup or the Olympics is not possible in practice. To those producers of the main three network stations (SBS, KBS, MBC) that simultaneously broadcast the same mega-sporting event, being ahead on the fierce ratings battle requires them to employ effective strategies in terms of added content value and featuring more popular sportscasters and commentators. Today, sports producers also take viewer engagement seriously, since viewers can be fans or critics of their channel and social media chatter can be an important opinion barometer (Cameron & Geidner, 2014).

Researchers of e-commerce suggest that a trust perception toward an organization's e-commerce site can only be built over a long period of time through ongoing interpersonal interaction and that it is mediated by affective commitment a consumer feels toward the organization (Turri et al., 2013). Indeed, Ogonowski and his colleagues (2014) found that the enhanced feelings of social presence from an e-commerce website tended to increase an initial trust perception. This trust perception is closely related to a brand's consumer commitment. A recent study by Lim and his colleagues (2015) revealed that the sense of social presence had a positive impact on channel commitment.

Therefore, we posit the following hypothesis:

H9: The perceived social presence will be positively correlated with sports channel commitment.

Method

Context of the Study

Broadcasting channels in the United States usually hold exclusive rights to sporting events. For instance, NBC holds the exclusive rights to broadcasting the Olympics in the US. In today's Korean media market, where numerous cable channels and digital media compete for securing fragmented television audiences, three nationally syndicated television channels are facing stiff competition to win the ratings battles for live mega-sporting events that all three networks telecast at the same time.

The current study was conducted during the 2014 Sochi Winter Olympic Games. Three of South Korea's national network television channels were competing to win the ratings war in the highly anticipated figure skating event with Kim Yuna. The competition among those networks was driven not so much by fiduciary incentives, but rather by maintaining sports fans' commitment to their channel. Since each game-broadcasting television station for the Olympics merely plays a role of retransmitting the televised screen from the OBS (Olympic Broadcasting Services), created by the IOC (International Olympic Committee) to serve as the Host Broadcaster Organization for all Olympic Games, viewership ratings were believed to be dependent on the sportscasters and added content in the form of game-related records and other public relations efforts. This is why sports producers are interested in the motivations of television viewers' social media and their relationships with viewers' channel commitment.

Sample and the Survey Procedure

The data for this study were collected through an online survey of a sample drawn from national panel data. Participants of the main survey were randomly drawn from the national panel pool of Korea Research Inc., a leading South Korean consumer research firm. The total sample size for the completed responses was 500. The potential panel participants were randomly selected and asked if they had been involved in using social media platforms such as Facebook, Twitter, or KakaoTalk/KakaoStory to communicate with others while watching the 2014 Sochi Winter Olympic Games. Those who said "Yes" for the filtering question were selected as panel respondents for the survey and asked about their experience related to backchannel communication. A total of 276 males (55.2 percent) and 224 female panels participated in the main survey. The average age was about 29 years old, and about 58 percent of the participants were college graduates. The average television viewing time was 3.48 hours during the weekend and 2.31 hours on weekdays. The amount of time that participants spent on viewing the Winter Olympics was 2.83 hours on average. When it comes to the media used to watch the Olympic Games, television was the most used with 51 percent of participants, followed by smartphone (41 percent) and computers (8 percent).

Before conducting the main survey, a pilot study was administered after the Korean gold-medalist Sang-Hwa Lee's long-track speedskating race, which was the second most viewed among all the televised Winter Olympic Games. This pilot study helped the researchers enhance validity and reliability of the key questions such as motivations for backchannel communication while watching the Olympic Games, different types of engagement behaviors, channel commitment, and so on. A main survey was administered by Korea Research Inc. for three days right after the 2014 Sochi Winter Olympic Games' finale.

Measures

Backchannel communication motives

Based on the review in the previous section, we assumed that backchannel communication motives for live televised sporting events could be identified with four dimensions: information seeking, excitement, convenience, and social interaction motives. All items used to measure each of the four motives are presented in Table 1.1.

Information motives concern the motivations to learn about players, teams, and games (Gantz, 1981; Raney, 2006) through backchannel communication. One item addresses the unique ability of television media in conveying information about a specific situation (Frandsen, 2008).

Convenience motives were measured by four items adapted from previous research that identified convenient *information-seeking motives* (Haridakis & Hanson, 2009), the utility of game-related information (i.e., ease of access and timeliness) (Kim et al., 2011), and saving time in sharing information (Parra-López et al., 2011).

Four items were used to measure social interaction motives. Social interaction motives concern one's motivation to have group affiliation in watching the games and interacting with other fans (Wann, 1995) and to enjoy sharing the opinions about the player one is rooting for (Ha et al., 2013).

All of the motive items were assessed on a seven-point Likert-type scale anchored by "not agree at all" (1) to "entirely agree" (7).

Social presence

The social presence measure was based on Biocca and his colleagues' conceptual and operational definition (Biocca et al., 2003; Nowak & Biocca, 2003), and thus was composed of three items that were related to perceived salience of other social TV users. These three items reflect the sense of co-presence (e.g., I feel like many people were watching at the same time) (Biocca et al., 2001, 2003; Lee, 2004; Lee & Nass, 2003), psychological involvement or immediacy (e.g., I feel like I was watching the game

Table 1.1 Testing the Measurement Model: A Confirmatory Factor Analysis

Factor & Items	CFA item loading[a]	S.E.	t	CR[b]	AVE
Information Motives (M = 3.86, SD = 1.22, α = 0.94)				0.94	0.80
INFO1: It helps me to obtain more knowledge about the sports games.	0.87	0.01	70.47***		
INFO2: It provides useful information about athletes and their performances in sports games.	0.94	0.01	120.22***		
INFO3: It increases my understanding of the televised sport.	0.91	0.01	93.96***		
INFO4: It helps me to receive specific information about a situation while watching the game.	0.85	0.01	59.96***		
Convenience Motives (M = 3.58, SD = 0.97, α = 0.88)				0.88	0.64
CONV1: It allows me to find what I want to know with less effort.	0.87	0.02	55.04***		
CONV2: It is easy to receive game-related information through SNSs.	0.89	0.02	58.93***		
CONV3: It helps me transmit and share game-related information fast and expediently.	0.76	0.02	33.01***		
CONV4: It is the most effective way to receive answers for game-related questions.	0.66	0.03	22.78***		
Excitement Motives (M = 3.99, SD = 0.97, α = 0.94)				0.94	0.80
EXCI1: It is exciting to root for my country's player/team with other fans.	0.86	0.01	64.95***		
EXCI2: I can express my excitement as though I were shouting in a stadium.	0.93	0.01	105.95***		
EXCI3: It is exciting to interact with others on SNSs while watching televised Olympics.	0.91	0.01	93.15***		

Item				
EXCI4: I enjoy reading the reactions of other viewers, which peps me up.	0.87	0.01	66.52***	
Social Interaction Motives (M = 4.54, SD = 1.40, α = 0.85)				
SOCI1: I want to belong to other sport fans who watch the Olympic Games.	0.75	0.03	29.16***	0.85	0.58
SOCI2: I like the group affiliations I get from interacting with others.	0.76	0.03	30.46***	
SOCI3: I enjoy watching the sports games more when I am with a larger group.	0.74	0.03	29.44***	
SOCI4: I like to share my opinions about the player whom I am rooting for.	0.80	0.02	35.79***	
Social Presence (M = 4.95, SD = 1.13, α = 0.79)				
SP1: I feel like I was physically communicating with others.	0.84	0.02	40.48***	0.79	0.57
SP2: I feel like I was watching the game with friends.	0.81	0.02	36.75***	
SP3: I feel like many people were watching at the same time.	0.59	0.03	17.24***	
Commitment (M = 4.42, SD = 1.14, α = 0.81)				
COMT1: I am emotionally attached to the current sports channel.	0.90	0.02	40.98***	0.82	0.60
COMT2: I am emotionally connected to the current sports channel.	0.81	0.02	34.16***	
COMT3: I am emotionally committed to the current sports channel.	0.59	0.03	16.98***	

Notes: All items were measured on a 7-point Likert scale ranging from 1 (strongly disagree) to 7 (strongly agree).
SP = social presence, COMT = commitment to the sports channel, INFO = information motives, CONV = convenience motives, EXCI = excitement motives, SOCI = social interaction motives.
χ^2/df = 2.24, CFI = 0.97, TLI = 0.96, SRMR = 0.04, RMSEA = 0.04. *p<0.05, **p<0.01, ***p<0.001.

[a] Standardized estimates.
[b] Composite reliability = (Σ std. loadings)2/(Σ std. loading)2 + Σ measurement error.

with friends) (Kim & Biocca, 1997), and behavioral engagement (e.g., I feel like I was physically communicating with others) that one felt in relation to the social presence of others during the social TV experience. The three statements were asked on a Likert-type scale anchored by "strongly disagree" (1) to "strongly agree" (7).

Channel commitment

The commitment toward a sports television channel was measured based on the items asking commitment toward the other related electronic channels such as mobile channels (Pihlström, 2007) or cable news channels (Penn, 2011; Pihlström, 2007). Items for channel commitment were composed of three questions on a seven-point Likert-type scale: "I am emotionally attached to the current sports channel," "I am emotionally connected to the current sports channel," and "I am emotionally committed to the current sports channel."

Results

Correlations among Latent Variables

Table 1.2 presents the mean and standard deviation and correlations among latent variables. The mean of social interaction motives was the highest (M = 4.54, SD = 1.40) on a seven-point Likert scale. All four dimensions of backchannel communication motives bar convenience motives were positively correlated with social presence. It is noteworthy to see that the correlation coefficient of social interaction motives ($r = 0.79$, $p < 0.001$) is very high for the latent factor of social presence. All four dimensions of backchannel communication motives were positively correlated with channel commitment. Notably, information motives were most highly correlated with channel commitment.

Table 1.2 Mean and Standard Deviation and Correlation Matrix for the Latent Variables

	Mean	SD	1	2	3	4	5	6
1 SP	4.95	1.13	1					
2 COMT	4.42	1.14	0.36**	1				
3 EXCI	3.99	0.97	0.32**	0.21**	1			
4 INFO	3.86	1.22	0.35**	0.40***	0.34**	1		
5 CONV	3.58	1.10	0.05	0.25**	0.16**	0.38**	1	
6 SOCI	4.54	1.40	0.79***	0.24**	0.13**	0.16**	−0.03	1

Note: SP = Social Presence, COMT = channel commitment, EXCI = excitement motives, INFO = information motives, CONV = convenience motives, SOCI = social motives. *** Correlation is significant at the 0.001 level; ** Correlation is significant at the 0.01 level.

An EFA and CFA of Backchannel Communication Motives for Televised Olympic Games

To identify the best factor solutions for backchannel communication motives, an exploratory factor analysis (EFA) was performed using maximum likelihood (ML) estimation with Geomin rotation using Mplus version 7 (Muthén & Muthén, 1998–2012). The model comparisons by model fit information suggest that the motivation for backchannel communication can be best explained by a four-factor solution (χ^2 = 189.638, df = 62, χ^2/df = 3.06, CFI = 0.98, TLI = 0.96, SRMR = 0.02, RMSEA = 0.07). Since we have refined the motivation-related questions through a pilot study, the factors extracted from the main survey were well loaded on four dimensions we identified as a priority.

After identifying four factors of backchannel communication motives, we employed a confirmatory factor analysis (CFA) to confirm the four-factor structure of the social TV motivation. The CFA indicated a good model fit, χ^2 = 244.906, df = 98, χ^2/df = 2.50, CFI = 0.97, TLI = 0.97, SRMR = 0.04, RMSEA = 0.06.

Results of the Measurement Model

Based on the two-stage approach of model validation (Anderson & Gerbing, 1988), the measurement validity was assessed for each construct appearing in the structural model. A CFA was conducted through using Mplus version 7 (Muthén & Muthén, 1998–2012) prior to estimating and testing the hypothesized structural model. An analysis of the fit indices of the measurement model indicated high fit indices, confirming that the proposed model is highly appropriate for analyzing the data. The ratio of the χ^2 to the degrees of freedom (χ^2/df = 2.24) and the goodness-of-fit indices (SRMR = 0.04, RMSEA = 0.04, CFI = 0.97, TLI = 0.96) were within the recommended cutoff ranges (SRMR ≤ 0.10, RMSEA ≤ 0.08, CFI ≥ 0.90, and TLI ≥ 0.90) by Hu and Bentler (1999).

The measurement model also checked the validity for items representing each latent construct (Fornell & Larcker, 1981). Table 1.1 (on page 15) presents the measurement model results, including items of key concepts, standardized factor loadings and average variance extracted (AVE). The convergent validity was assessed through checking whether the path coefficients from latent constructs to their corresponding indicators were statistically significant. All items loaded significantly (p < 0.001) on their corresponding latent constructs. Reliability of the measures was confirmed with the composite reliability index being higher than the recommended level of 0.60 (Bagozzi & Yi, 1988).

The AVE showed a range from 0.57 to 0.80, which exceeded the recommended 0.50 thresholds. These results showed the evidence of convergent validity (Anderson & Gerbing, 1988; Bagozzi & Yi, 1988). In conclusion, the measurement model of this research showed satisfactory reliability and convergent validity.

Results of Hypothesis Testing

Structural equation modeling (SEM) was conducted using Mplus version 7 (Muthén & Muthén, 1998–2012) to test the research hypotheses. Figure 1.1 displays the results of testing the SEM. We obtained a good model-fit between the data and the proposed structural model (χ^2/df = 1.75, CFI = 0.98, TLI = 0.98, SRMR = 0.04, RMSEA = 0.04).

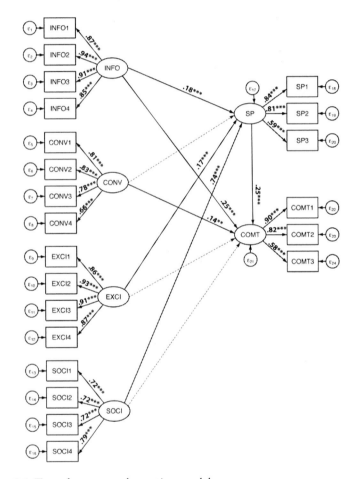

Figure 1.1 Test of a structural equation model.

Note: Solid lines represent significant standardized coefficients; dotted lines represent non-significant paths.* $p < 0.05$, ** $p < 0.01$, *** $p < 0.001$. χ^2/df = 1.75, CFI = 0.98, TLI = 0.98, SRMR = 0.04, RMSEA = 0.04.

We proposed four hypotheses regarding the relationships between each dimension of social TV motives and social presence. The results from the SEM showed that social interaction motives are the strongest predictor of social presence (β = 0.74, t = 22.21, p < 0.001). This result indicates that those who have higher motivations to belong with other sports fans and those who watch the sports game with a large body of people tend to have great feelings of social presence. The results support H4.

The excitement motives had a positive impact on social presence (β = 0.17, t = 3.96, p < 0.001), which corroborates H2. Information motives were positively correlated with social presence (β = 0.18, t = 4.09, p < 0001). In other words, the higher the information motives for social TV, the greater social presence is perceived. Thus, H2 was supported. However, convenience motives for social TV did not yield a statistically significant result in predicting social presence. Therefore, H3 was not supported.

In testing H5 to H8, we examined how each dimension of social TV motives relates to sports channel commitment. In H5, we predicted that, if the information motives for social TV were higher, then the sports channel commitment would be greater. As predicted, information motives for social TV have a positive impact on channel commitment (β = 0.25, t = 4.37, p < 0.01). Therefore, H5 was supported. In H6, we predicted that the higher the convenience motives for social TV, the sports channel commitment would be greater. The data yielded a positive standardized coefficient for the structural relation (β = 0.14, t = 2.69, p < 0.01), which supports H6. However, we did not find a significant standardized coefficient from excitement motives to sports channel commitment. Thus, H7 was not supported. The path between social interactive motives and social presence was not statistically significant either. So, H8 was rejected.

Finally, the endogenous variable of sports channel commitment was regressed on social presence to test H9. We found that social presence had a positive correlation with channel commitment (β = 0.25, t = 2.08, p < 0.05), which supports H9.

Overall, the structural equation model predicted approximately 69 percent of the observed variance for social presence and about 23 percent of variance for channel commitment.

Discussion

The current research attempted to identify the motivations of social TV use among the television viewers of the 2014 Winter Olympic Games and connect these motivational factors to social TV users' feelings of social presence and affective commitment to the sports channel. We have identified four motivations: information, excitement, social interaction, and convenience. The first three motivations are well aligned with motivations for viewing sports on television as reviewed in previous research (Gantz, 1981; Raney,

2006; Wenner & Gantz, 1998). Although the factor labels sound similar, we must take note that the specific items comprising each motivational factor for social TV are different from those for sport television viewing. For instance, excitement motives for social TV users are driven to such feelings when they virtually interact with other viewers and/or root for their country's players/teams through social media. It is also noteworthy that participants of the current study rated their social interaction motives higher than any other motives. In other words, social TV users have motivations to belong with other sports fans and share their opinions about the players they root for. Lastly, convenience motives are somewhat unique motivations that have not been identified in traditional sport viewing.

As reported in this study, the motivations underlying social TV users' backchannel communication are multifaceted. Therefore, the study rejects the idea that users would not watch live sports casts. People do not simply stop viewing live streaming sporting events simply because they read the entire game on Twitter stream as Hull and Lewis (2014) assumed.

Fans are turning to Twitter to get the desired information in a more convenient manner, but they still enjoy television viewing because of the thrill of sharing victory with other social TV users and getting along with other fans who are rooting for the same team. This is why sporting events, which comprise about 2 to 3 percent of TV programming in any given month, can generate about 50 percent of the Twitter activity around TV, as told by an executive of Nielsen's SocialGuide unit (Goel & Stelter, 2013).

When it comes to the relationships between social TV motives and social presence, we found that all except convenience motives were positively correlated with social presence. Notably, social interaction motives have a substantial impact on the sense of social presence. Although two other motivations, for information and excitement, also influence the feelings of social presence, social interaction motives were the strongest in predicting social presence. This high correlation between social interaction motives and social presence indicates that social presence can be greatly affected by one's motivations to interact with other viewers, which supports the relational views of social presence theory (Kehrwald, 2008; Walther, 1992). In particular, the results support Kehrwald's (2008) suggestions that the development of social presence in a virtual space cannot occur unless participants have a motive to make their interactions meaningful and beneficial for themselves. These results also support Perse and Courtright's (1993) view that higher perceived social presence is associated with individuals' social motivations.

Furthermore, we found that the higher the feelings of social presence, the greater the commitment to the channel. While we have not detailed the mechanism in which social presence leads to channel commitment, the findings provide broadcasters and marketers with important managerial implications. The implications are discussed in the following section.

22

Finally, results also showed that utilitarian as opposed to hedonic motivation directly affects viewers' channel commitment. These findings need to be read with caution since the path results also imply that the effects of hedonic (i.e., excitement) and social interaction motivations might lead to channel commitment via perceived social presence. The implications are also provided in the following section.

Managerial Implications

As sports fans' engagement in backchannel communication while viewing a televised mega-sporting event is likely to increase (Gantz & Lewis, 2014), the results from the current study provide some managerial implications. The first takeaway is that social TV users of live sporting events have higher social interaction motives than any other motives. Sports producers can nudge viewers' social media engagement with the channel by displaying a sample thread of social media discussion over the live show or sportscasters' comments.

Second, sports television channels need to present their game- or player-related information in a "Twitter bite" so that other social TV viewers can retweet it easily. This study suggests that social TV users who have higher motivations for information showed higher channel commitment as well. Television sports channels own tremendous amounts of information and related video materials. In preparing for any mega-sporting event, those sports television channels can effectively transmit their materials through social media, which can satisfy the sports fans' need for shareable and memorable information.

Third, television sports channels should make great endeavors to transform individual viewers' channel commitment into building a channel-based viewer community (See Lim et al., 2015). In this regard, those broadcasters can learn from the BBC's effort to build and maintain relationships with the social TV viewer community generated by committed viewers of a specific program such as *Up For Hire* (see van Dijck & Poell, 2015).

Fourth, marketers who sponsor popular sporting events started to realize the importance of getting people to converse through their second screens during live television programming. This is why companies try to take advantage of social TV by hijacking the most exciting moment of mega-sporting events such as the United States Open. For instance, Heineken sponsored tweets from the official Twitter account of US Open Tennis (@usopen), in which video highlights were posted including a remarkable 54-stroke rally between Novak Djokovic and Rafael Nadal (US Open Tennis, 2013). When an executive of Heineken made it clear that the company wanted to "bring people to the event who weren't there" (Goel & Stelter, 2013), it apparently indicated the power of social TV conversations in generating the sense of social presence and its connection to potential consumers' commitment to the brand.

Lastly, sports channels must satisfy the viewers' desire for useful information about the games and players. As mentioned earlier, broadcasters have been the major source of sports-related information before the social media age. Still, they are the most reliable and effective information providers to sports fans and television viewers. They also have the most powerful and exclusive game-related resources and assets that can make social TV users most engaged—that is, game-related videos. A segment or excerpt of a game-related video, or highlights of the game, or interviews with popular players, coaches, and commentators can engage their viewers and increase their channel commitment.

Limitations and Suggestions for Future Research

Like common limitations of other U&G studies, we also need to note that the current work does by no means provide the definitive or exhaustive motivational factors. We note that the items for social TV motivations in this current study were limited by the existing pool of motivations from previous research on sports television viewing and a couple of exploratory studies on social TV (e.g., Han & Lee, 2014; Wohn & Na, 2011). Future research should expand the inventories of social TV motives so that they can encompass the newly emerging communication behaviors among the viewers of live television shows. For instance, social TV users have motivations to interact with their favorite players/sportscasters (Lim et al., 2015) or television hosts/guests (Iannelli & Giglietto, 2015).

Another limitation is that the results of this study may be limited only to Korean social TV users' motivations and their attitudes. This limitation can open a door for future research that may examine the different U&G of social TV among users of different cultures.

Conclusion

At the 2012 Social TV conference, executives from major sports television channels in the United States agreed that social TV would be ever changing the sports fields and the future of sports broadcasting (Pardee, 2012). These executives of major sports television channels apparently have a rosy view with regard to the future of sports broadcasting. This is assuming that the increasing social TV trend for sporting events will bring in greater opportunities for broadcasters, since people will keep watching sports on large screens and using second screens as "just complementing viewers' traditional experience" (Pardee, 2012). It is also believed that the social media chatter for sporting events will draw more viewers to a television station.

A recent report from Nielson also added another positive outlook for the future of social TV: It found that the deeper the viewer engagement with the moment of the televised event, the more tweets were posted (Goel, 2015).

The results indicate that the level of social TV activity increases as the intensity of viewers' engagement with the TV segment increases. Goel (2015) points out that the study by Nielson and Twitter still does not provide the most important question posed by marketers and broadcasters alike: Will social TV increase the viewership of television shows?

While the results of the current study do not provide a definitive answer to this question, the findings can add another positive outlook for the future of sports broadcasting in the age of social TV. As discussed earlier, broadcasters need to understand what motivations drive viewers to engage in social TV and how different motivations can generate positive affects to the channel.

References

Agamanolis, S. (2008). At the intersection of broadband and broadcasting: How interactive TV technologies can support human connectedness. *International Journal of Human-Computer Interaction, 24*(2), 121–135.

Anderson, J. C., & Gerbing, D. W. (1988). Structural equation modeling in practice: A review and recommended two-step approach. *Psychological Bulletin, 103*(3), 411–423.

Bagozzi, R., & Yi, Y. (1988). On the evaluation of structural equation models. *Journal of the Academy of Marketing Science, 16*(1), 74–94.

Bente, G., Rüggenberg, S., Krämer, N. C., & Eschenburg, F. (2008). Avatar-mediated networking: Increasing social presence and interpersonal trust in net-based collaborations. *Human Communication Research, 34*(2), 287–318.

Biocca, F., Harms, C., & Burgoon, J. K. (2003). Toward a more robust theory and measure of social presence: Review and suggested criteria. *Presence: Teleoperators and Virtual Environments, 12*(5), 456–480.

Biocca, F., Harms, C., & Gregg, J. (2001). The networked mind's measure of social presence: Pilot test of the factor structure and concurrent validity. Paper presented at the 4th annual International Workshop on Presence, Philadelphia.

Bodhani, A. (2012). Olympics up close and social. *Engineering and Technology, 7*(7), 35–37.

Cameron, J., & Geidner, N. (2014). Something old, something new, something borrowed from something blue: Experiments on dual viewing TV and Twitter. *Journal of Broadcasting & Electronic Media, 58*(3), 400–419.

Collins, R. (2014). *Interaction ritual chains.* Princeton, NJ: Princeton University Press.

Cyr, D., Hassanein, K., Head, M., & Ivanov, A. (2007). The role of social presence in establishing loyalty in e-Service environments. *Interacting with Computers, 19*(1), 43–56.

Ferguson, D. A., & Perse, E. M. (2000). The World Wide Web as a functional alternative to television. *Journal of Broadcasting & Electronic Media, 44*(2), 155.

Flanagin, A. J., & Metzger, M. J. (2001). Internet use in the contemporary media environment. *Human Communication Research, 27*(1), 153–181.

Fornell, C., & Larcker, D. F. (1981). Evaluating structural equation models with unobservable variables and measurement error. *Journal of Marketing Research, 18*(1), 39–50.

Frandsen, K. (2008). Sports viewing: A theoretical approach. *International Journal of Sports Communication, 1*(1), 67–77.

Fulk, J., Steinfield, C. W., Schmitz, J., & Power, J. G. (1987). A social information processing model of media use in organizations. *Communication Research, 14*(5), 529–552.

Gantz, W. (1981). An exploration of viewing motives and behaviors associated with television sports. *Journal of Broadcasting, 25*(3), 263–275.

Gantz, W., & Lewis, N. (2014). Sports on traditional and newer digital media: Is there really a fight for fans? *Television & New Media, 15*(8), 760–768.

Garramone, G. M., Harris, A. C., & Anderson, R. (1986). Uses of political computer bulletin boards. *Journal of Broadcasting & Electronic Media, 30*(3), 325–339.

Gibbs, C., O'Reilly, N., & Brunette, M. (2014). Professional team sport and Twitter: Gratifications sought and obtained by followers. *International Journal of Sport Communication, 7*(2), 188–213.

Giglietto, F., & Selva, D. (2014). Second screen and participation: A content analysis on a full season dataset of tweets. *Journal of Communication, 64*(2), 260–277.

Goel, V. (2015). Study of TV viewers backs Twitter's claims to be barometer of public mood. *The New York Times*, March 9, p. B5.

Goel, V., & Stelter, B. (2013). The battle for the second screen. *The New York Times*, October 3, p. B1.

Gunawardena, C. N. (1995). Social presence theory and implications for interaction and collaborative learning in computer conferences. *International Journal of Educational Telecommunications, 1*(2), 147–166.

Gunawardena, C. N., & Zittle, F. J. (1997). Social presence as a predictor of satisfaction within a computer-mediated conferencing environment. *American Journal of Distance Education, 11*(3), 8–26.

Ha, J.-P., Ha, J., & Han, K. (2013). Online sport consumption motives: Why does an ethnic minority group consume sports in a native and host country through the internet? *International Journal of Sport Management, Recreation and Tourism, 11*, 63–89.

Ha, Y. W., Kim, J., Libaque-Saenz, C. F., Chang, Y., & Park, M.-C. (2015). Use and gratifications of mobile SNSs: Facebook and KakaoTalk in Korea. *Telematics and Informatics, 32*(3), 425–438.

Han, E., & Lee, S.-W. (2014). Motivations for the complementary use of text-based media during linear TV viewing: An exploratory study. *Computers in Human Behavior, 32*, 235–243.

Haridakis, P., & Hanson, G. (2009). Social interaction and co-viewing with YouTube: Blending mass communication reception and social connection. *Journal of Broadcasting & Electronic Media, 53*(2), 317–335.

Harrington, S., Highfield, T., & Bruns, A. (2012). More than a backchannel: Twitter and television. *Participations: Journal of Audience & Reception Studies, 10*(1), 405–409.

Hassoun, D. (2012). Tracing attentions: Toward an analysis of simultaneous media use. *Television & New Media*, December 12, doi:10.1177/1527476412468621.

Hechelmann, C. B. (2012). Social media engagement in a dedicated Facebook channel: An analysis of relationships to emotional attachment, self-brand connection and brand commitment towards sports sponsoring brands. Doctoral dissertation, University of Technology, Sydney.

Hicks, A., Comp, S., Horovitz, J., Hovarter, M., Miki, M., & Bevan, J. L. (2012). Why people use Yelp.com: An exploration of uses and gratifications. *Computers in Human Behavior, 28*(6), 2274–2279.

Hu, L.-T., & Bentler, P. M. (1999). Cutoff criteria for fit indexes in covariance structure analysis: Conventional criteria versus new alternatives. *Structural Equation Modeling, 6*(1), 1–55.

Hull, K., & Lewis, N. P. (2014). Why Twitter displaces broadcast sports media: A model. *International Journal of Sport Communication, 7*(1), 16–33.

Hur, Y. J., Ko, Y. J., & Valacich, J. (2007). Motivation and concerns for online sport consumption. *Journal of Sport Management, 21*(4), 521–539.

Hutchins, B. (2010). The acceleration of media sports culture. *Information, Communication & Society, 14*(2), 237–257.

Hutchins, B., & Rowe, D. (2012). *Sport beyond television: The internet, digital media and the rise of networked media sport.* New York: Routledge.

Iannelli, L., & Giglietto, F. (2015). Hybrid spaces of politics: The 2013 general elections in Italy, between talk shows and Twitter. *Information, Communication & Society* (ahead of print), 1–16.

Kang, S. J., Ha, J.-P., & Hambrick, M. E. (in press). A mixed method approach to exploring the motives of sport-related mobile applications among college students. *Journal of Sport Management.*

Kehrwald, B. (2008). Understanding social presence in text-based online learning environments. *Distance Education, 29*(1), 89–106.

Kim, J. W., James, J. D., & Kim, Y. K. (2013). A model of the relationship among sport consumer motives, spectator commitment, and behavioral intentions. *Sport Management Review, 16*(2), 173–185.

Kim, T., & Biocca, F. (1997). Telepresence via television: Two dimensions of telepresence may have different connections to memory and persuasion. *Journal of Computer-Mediated Communication, 3*(2).

Kim, Y., Sohn, D., & Choi, S. M. (2011). Cultural difference in motivations for using social network sites: A comparative study of American and Korean college students. *Computers in Human Behavior, 27*(1), 365–372.

Ko, H., Cho, C.-H., & Roberts, M. S. (2005). Internet uses and gratifications: A structural equation model of interactive advertising. *Journal of Advertising, 34*(2), 57–70.

Konovsky, M. A., & Cropanzano, R. (1991). Perceived fairness of employee drug testing as a predictor of employee attitudes and job performance. *Journal of Applied Psychology, 76*(5), 698–707.

Kreijns, K., Kirschner, P. A., Jochems, W., & van Buuren, H. (2004). Determining sociability, social space, and social presence in (a)synchronous collaborative groups. *CyberPsychology & Behavior, 7*(2), 155–172.

Lee, K. M. (2004). Presence, explicated. *Communication Theory, 14*(1), 27–50.

Lee, K. M., & Nass, C. (2003). Designing social presence of social actors in human computer interaction. Paper presented at the Proceedings of the SIGCHI Conference on Human Factors in Computing Systems, Fort Lauderdale, Florida.

Lim, J. S., Hwang, Y., Kim, S., & Biocca, F. A. (2015). How social media engagement leads to sports channel loyalty: Mediating roles of social presence and channel commitment. *Computers in Human Behavior, 46*, 158–167.

Lin, K.-Y., & Lu, H.-P. (2011). Why people use social networking sites: An empirical study integrating network externalities and motivation theory. *Computers in Human Behavior, 27*(3), 1152–1161.

Lövblad, M., Hyder, A. S., & Lönnstedt, L. (2012). Affective commitment in industrial customer–supplier relations: A psychological contract approach. *Journal of Business & Industrial Marketing, 27*(4), 275–285.

Mäntymäki, M., & Riemer, K. (2014). Digital natives in social virtual worlds: A multi-method study of gratifications and social influences in Habbo Hotel. *International Journal of Information Management, 34*(2), 210–220.

Mehus, I. (2005). Sociability and excitement motives of spectators attending entertainment sport events: Spectators of soccer and ski-jumping. *Journal of Sport Behavior, 28*(4), 333.

Muthén, L. K., & Muthén, B. O. (1998–2012). Mplus user's guide (7th ed.). Los Angeles: Muthén & Muthén.

Nee, R. C. (2013). Social TV and the 2012 election: Exploring political outcomes of multiscreen media usages. *Electronic News, 7*(4), 171–188.

Nowak, K. L., & Biocca, F. (2003). The effect of the agency and anthropomorphism on users' sense of telepresence, copresence, and social presence in virtual environments. *Presence: Teleoperators and Virtual Environments, 12*(5), 481–494.

Ogonowski, A., Montandon, A., Botha, E., & Reyneke, M. (2014). Should new online stores invest in social presence elements? The effect of social presence on initial trust formation. *Journal of Retailing and Consumer Services, 21*(4), 482–491.

Papacharissi, Z., & Rubin, A. M. (2000). Predictors of internet use. *Journal of Broadcasting & Electronic Media, 44*(2), 175.

Pardee, T. (2012). How social TV is changing the field for sports. *Advertising Age,* May 9. Online at http://adage.com/article/special-report-social-tv-conference/social-tv-changing-field-sports/234664/ (retrieved April 10, 2015).

Park, N., Kee, K. F., & Valenzuela, S. (2009). Being immersed in social networking environment: Facebook groups, uses and gratifications, and social outcomes. *CyberPsychology & Behavior, 12*(6), 729–733.

Parra-López, E., Bulchand-Gidumal, J., Gutiérrez-Taño, D., & Díaz-Armas, R. (2011). Intentions to use social media in organizing and taking vacation trips. *Computers in Human Behavior, 27*(2), 640–654.

Penn, K. (2011). Organizational identification, commitment, and imagined community among the audience of the Fox Cable news channel. MA thesis, West Texas A&M University, Canyon.

Perse, E. M., & Courtright, J. A. (1993). Normative images of communication media mass and interpersonal channels in the new media environment. *Human Communication Research, 19*(4), 485–503.

Pihlström, M. (2007). Committed to content provider or mobile channel? Determinants of continuous mobile multimedia service use. *Journal of Information Technology Theory and Application, 9*(1), 1–23.

Proulx, M., & Shepatin, S. (2012). *Social TV: How marketers can reach and engage audiences by connecting television to the web, social media, and mobile.* Hoboken, NJ: Wiley.

Pynta, P., Seixas, S. A., Nield, G. E., Hier, J., & Millward, E. (2014). The power of social television: Can social media build viewer engagement? A new approach to brain imaging of viewer immersion. *Journal of Advertising Research, 54*(1), 71–80.

Raney, A. A. (2006). Why we watch and enjoy mediated sports. In A. A. Raney & J. Bryant (Eds.), *Handbook of sports and media* (pp. 313–329). Mahwah, NJ: Lawrence Erlbaum Associates.

Rice, R. E., & Love, G. (1987). Electronic emotion: Socioemotional content in a computer-mediated communication network. *Communication Research, 14*(1), 85–108.

Schirra, S., Sun, H., & Bentley, F. (2014). Together alone: motivations for live-tweeting a television series. Paper presented at the Proceedings of the 32nd annual ACM Conference on Human Factors in Computing Systems, Toronto, Ontario, Canada.

Schroeder, R. (2010). *Being there together: Social interaction in shared virtual environments.* Oxford, UK: Oxford University Press.

Shin, D.-H. (2013). Defining sociability and social presence in social TV. *Computers in Human Behavior, 29*(3), 939–947.

Short, J., Williams, E., & Christie, B. (1976). *The social psychology of telecommunications.* London: John Wiley & Sons.

Stavros, C., Meng, M. D., Westberg, K., & Farrelly, F. (2014). Understanding fan motivation for interacting on social media. *Sport Management Review, 17*(4), 455–469.

Sung, E., & Mayer, R. E. (2012). Five facets of social presence in online distance education. *Computers in Human Behavior, 28*(5), 1738–1747.

Sutera, D. M. (2013). *Sports fans 2.0: How fans are using social media to get closer to the game.* Plymouth, UK: Scarecrow Press.

Tu, C.-H. (2000). On-line learning migration: From social learning theory to social presence theory in a CMC environment. *Journal of Network and Computer Applications, 23*(1), 27–37.

Turri, A. M., Smith, K. H., & Kemp, E. (2013). Developing affective brand commitment through social media. *Journal of Electronic Commerce Research, 14*(3), 201–214.

US Open Tennis (@usopen). (2013). IN CASE YOU MISSED IT: The stunning 54-shot rally between #Djokovic & #Nadal. Presented by @Heineken_US. WATCH (tweet), September 9. Online at https://twitter.com/usopen/status/377226961984450560 (retrieved April 9, 2015).

Van Cauwenberge, A., Schaap, G., & van Roy, R. (2014). "TV no longer commands our full attention": Effects of second-screen viewing and task relevance on cognitive load and learning from news. *Computers in Human Behavior, 38*, 100–109.

van Dijck, J., & Poell, T. (2015). Making public television social? Public service broadcasting and the challenges of social media. *Television & New Media, 16*(2), 148–164.

Walther, J. B. (1992). Interpersonal effects in computer-mediated interaction: A relational perspective. *Communication Research, 19*(1), 52–90.

Wann, D. L. (1995). Preliminary validation of the sport fan motivation scale. *Journal of Sport & Social Issues, 19*(4), 377–396.

Wenner, L. A., & Gantz, W. (1998). Watching sports on television: Audience experience, gender, fanship, and marriage. In L. A. Wenner (Ed.), *MediaSport* (pp. 233–251). New York: Routledge.

Westmyer, S. A., DiCioccio, R. L., & Rubin, R. B. (1998). Appropriateness and effectiveness of communication channels in competent interpersonal communication. *Journal of Communication, 48*(3), 27–48.

Whiting, A. (2013). Why people use social media: A uses and gratifications approach. *Qualitative Market Research: An International Journal, 16*(4), 2.

Williams, E. (1977). Experimental comparisons of face-to-face and mediated communication: A review. *Psychological Bulletin, 84*(5), 963–976.

Wohn, D. Y., & Na, E.-K. (2011). Tweeting about TV: Sharing television viewing experiences via social media message streams. *First Monday, 16*(3).

Xu, H., & Yan, R.-N. (2011). Feeling connected via television viewing: Exploring the scale and its correlates. *Communication Studies, 62*(2), 186–206.

2

DOUBLE VISION

An Eye-Tracking Analysis of Visual Attention Between Television and Second Screens

Miao Guo and Michael Holmes

Television audiences now have greater control over how they consume television. They can time-shift content and choose the viewing screen which best meets their needs: a traditional television screen, a computer monitor, or a mobile device. As second-screen devices such as smartphones, tablets, and laptops proliferate, consumers' interaction with television content through an additional screen has emerged as a noteworthy phenomenon known as second-screen viewing. Second-screen usage has empowered television viewers, giving them unprecedented access to, and interaction with, television programming and related content. This "double vision" is especially meaningful for broadcasters, program producers, and advertisers in their justification of investment in content, retaining and acquiring customers, enhancing brand affinity and program loyalty, and identifying and marketing to the most valuable audiences.

The traditional mass-oriented, liner-structure media are aggressively aligning with personal and mobile media to exploit the second-screen viewing trend. Major broadcast/cable networks (e.g., eighteen of NBC Universals' channels, nine of Time Warner's, and six of News Corp.'s and Disney's) have mobile companion apps to make viewing more accessible and enjoyable (Hall, 2013). Cross-network "umbrella" apps such as Zeebox and Shazam are exploding in popularity due to their diverse content options and interaction functions. Most importantly, the rise and ubiquity of social media have significantly enhanced television viewing activities, transforming second-screen usage into a social television viewing experience. The second-screen social television experience enhances viewer engagement, extends the value of brands and content properties, and opens up new advertising opportunities for media industries.

Engagement with second-screen devices is driven by increasing cross-platform and multi-tasking audience behavior. Recent research shows multiplatform consumption, especially interacting with mobile devices and enhancement apps while watching television, is becoming the norm. According to a Nielsen cross-platform report, 85 percent of tablet and smartphone owners report using their devices while watching television at least once a month, while 41 percent of tablet owners and 39 percent of smartphone owners do so daily (Nielsen, 2013). Another industry survey revealed that viewers report switching their attention from one screen to another as many as 27 times an hour (Bokenham & Hughes, 2013). However, questions remain about how much second-screen usage is related to content type (television programming and commercials), and how the potential distraction of mobile devices influences primary screen program consumption and advertising message absorption. Accordingly, the purpose of this study is to examine how television viewers distribute their visual attention between the "first" screen (the television screen) and "second" screen devices (e.g., smartphones, tablets, and laptops) during television programming and commercials.

Literature Review and Research Questions

Visual Attention to Television

In the visual attention research fields, there are two traditional but opposing approaches to explain the relationship between attention and the formal features of television content (Hawkins et al., 2005). Specifically, the reactive approach posits "television's features demand viewer attention," while the active approach asserts "the viewer strategically uses features as cues to learned associations with expectations of content" (Hawkins et al., 2005, p. 163). Studies tend to hold that the individual's visual orientation results from diverse factors, and viewers' perceptions of a scene are developed by a combination of attention, eye movement, and memory (Anderson & Burns, 1991; Schmitt et al., 2003).

Cognitive attention is presumed to be reflected in eye movement and point of gaze. Prior research revealed the average length of an uninterrupted gaze at television content (i.e., the duration of a continuous series of gaze points all located on the television screen) is about 7 seconds, with the median gaze less than 2 seconds in length (Hawkins et al., 2005). The authors proposed a "hazard function" to describe the short glance phenomenon. They suggested that once a look at television begins, the glance tends to terminate during the first second or so. The hazard (of looking off-screen) typically peaks at 1–1.5 seconds and then decreases, at first quickly but then more slowly, to reach a very low asymptote after around 15 seconds (Hawkins et al., 2005). Several studies confirm this attentional inertia and offer a variety of explanations from different perspectives, including cognitive engagement and distractability (Anderson & Lorch, 1983; Burns & Anderson, 1993; Hawkins et al., 1991).

Based on the length of a look, there are four styles of visual attention to television content (Anderson & Lorch, 1983; Hawkins et al., 2005; Huston & Wright, 1983). "Monitoring" refers to the shortest look with little inertia (less than 1.5 seconds), reflecting an active, informed monitoring of content; the brief look can confirm or disconfirm an already-formed expectation of television content. If people do not follow the content, they tend to engage in an "orienting" viewing style (ranging from 2 to 5 seconds) afterwards to further evaluate their viewing decisions (Burns & Anderson, 1993). Moderate-length looks, classed as "engaged," range from 6 to 15 seconds, reflecting substantial attention engagement and deep comprehension of television content (Hawkins et al., 2005). The fourth viewing style, "stares," includes gazes longer than 15 seconds, reflecting continued engagement with television but less involvement than a mix of looks of various lengths (Hawkins et al., 2005).

Visual Attention to Television with Second-Screen Apps

There are few studies of visual attention to mobile devices during television or video content consumption. As more television viewers engage in two-screen viewing, scholars and industry practitioners are eager to learn the possible impacts on visual attention to television. When examining how consumers use the second-screen app, Zeebox, to interact with advertising, The Pool (2013) found that during program content 69.3 percent of visual attention was primarily focused on television, while 23.5 percent was distributed to the companion app. However, when a commercial break begins, the pattern reverses and viewers focused heavily on Zeebox.

Holmes et al. (2012) investigated viewers' visual attention via eye-movement patterns as they watched two television shows while interacting with show-specific tablet apps providing content synchronized to show content. The study showed that these enhancement apps garnered considerable visual attention, accounting for around 30 percent of the total viewing session. The findings also indicated that, even without a "push" of interactive content to the tablet, viewers still tended to distribute some of their attention to their tablets. The authors found that gaze time on the television screen and off-screen fell during commercials, while gaze time on the tablet increased. The study also found that the presence of the second screen significantly decreased the average gaze length on television, leading the researchers to suggest that second-screen viewing may create a fundamental shift in how viewers direct visual attention to the television screen.

Visual Attention and Memory

There are multiple research traditions to address the relationships among visual attention, visual situations, and memory. Baddeley (1986, 1992) argued two types of memory constitute working memory: a visual-spatial memory and an auditory-textual memory. According to cognitive load theory, each type of working memory is limited by its capacity; cognition can be overloaded under certain circumstance due to split-attention effects (Sweller, 1988, 1994). Prior research found that audio combined with text seemed to overwhelm the individual channels, whereas the combination of audio with a relevant visual demanded less time to process the information (Chandler & Sweller, 1992). Paivio (1986) further proposed a dual-coding theory and asserted that memory can be enhanced when corresponding visual and verbal information are paired in working memory simultaneously. These theories imply that enhancement apps used by second-screen device users while watching television may be overwhelmed or a distraction, depending upon the alignment between the two content sources.

Several eye-tracking studies showed that more attention leads to more opportunity to encode and store advertising messages, and found a positive relationship between visual attention and memory (Goodrich, 2011; Lee & Ahn, 2012; Pieters et al., 2002). When examining attention to banner ads and their effectiveness, Lee and Ahn (2012) further found animation in banner ads not only attracted less attention than static ads but also reduced the positive effect of attention on memory. Drawing upon the aforementioned theories and diverse approaches, this study examined how television viewers distribute their visual attention to television and companion mobile devices, including smartphones, tablets, and laptops. The following research questions are proposed:

RQ1: Is the "hazard function" for gaze length at television valid in a multi-screen viewing environment?

RQ2: What is the typical distribution of visual attention to the television screen and the second screen?

RQ3: Are there differences in distribution of visual attention to the television screen and the second screen between television programming and commercial breaks?

Methods

Eye Tracking

Visual attention to television can be observed with eye tracking, a process of measuring eye movements, such as point of gaze, fixations, saccades (movement from fixation to fixation), and smooth pursuit. This study is focused on point of gaze (i.e., which screen is the focus of visual attention) rather than saccades and smooth pursuit. While the information from the scene is mainly acquired during fixations (gaze events long enough to support high-quality information processing), it should be noted that visual fixation is "a readily-observed indicator, but not directly a measure of attention itself" (Hawkins et al., 2005, p. 165). Nonetheless, most previous research has evidenced that visual fixation has important relationships to cognitive attention, and the length of a fixation is a valuable indication of information processing or cognitive activities (Hawkins et al., 2005).

This study used the Tobii eye-tracking system (www.tobii.com), which includes hardware for unobtrusive tracking of eye movement and software for data analysis. The eye-tracking hardware used in this study was Tobii Glasses, a comfortable and unobtrusive device looking much like a large pair of sunglasses. Infrared "markers" placed around the television screen and the stand for the mobile device allowed the glasses to calculate the coordinates of each point of gaze, in 0.033-second intervals. The target "area of interest" (AOI) for each gaze point (television, mobile device, or unknown/other) was assigned according to the eye-gaze coordinates for each sampling interval.

Subjects

Aided by a professional marketing research firm, this study recruited nineteen participants from New York City during March 2013. The primary recruitment filter was a criterion that the participant typically used a second-screen device to access television-related content while viewing, at least once per week. Among the 19 participants, 11 were female (57.9 percent). Caucasians and white Hispanics accounted for 73.7 percent of the sample and 26.3 percent were African Americans. The subjects' ages ranged from 18 to 60 years. Participants were asked to bring their own preferred mobile device. Two participants were tablet users, two used laptop computers, and 14 were smartphone users.

Media Use Situation

The eye-tracking sessions were conducted in a media research facility located in New York City. After a participant signed a consent form (describing the research procedures, risks, and their rights) and completed a short Tobii Glasses calibration process, he or she was ushered into a simulated home living room equipped with a 55-inch HD television, a sofa with side tables, and a coffee table equipped with a stand for the mobile device. When seated on the sofa in a comfortable position, the participant could view the television on the front wall and interact with the second-screen device on the coffee table.

The nineteen participants were eye tracked while watching approximately 30 minutes of a television show of their choice and interacting with content of their choice on their mobile device (e.g., social media sites, television network companion apps, show websites, or unrelated online content). The participant-chosen program genres included reality shows, talk shows, local news, sitcoms, and live sports events. After the eye-tracking session, a brief post-session interview was conducted and video recorded. The interview questions focused on the participant's experience of the television and mobile device, whether the lab experience was significantly different from his or her normal "two-screen" viewing behavior, and what second-screen activities the participant engaged in during the session.

Results

Of the 19 participants in the eye-tracking portion of the study, three were excluded from the analysis due to system calibration problems resulting in high rates of missing data. "Missing" gaze coordinates in the remaining cases (i.e., data points below the default coordinate confidence threshold of the Tobii software) presumably resulted from the challenge of two scene planes (the television and the mobile device) at such disparate distances from the viewer (eight feet and two feet). A gap in the data of less than 0.10 seconds was filled by assigning it the AOI (target screen) value of the preceding record.

To address the problem of missing (low-confidence) data for intervals longer than 0.10 seconds, frame-by-frame manual coding of the point of gaze in Tobii video recordings of the eye-tracking sessions was performed to identify entry and exit time values for gaze events in each AOI. Comparison of the original and manually coded data revealed that most of the low-confidence data points were in the mobile device AOI. In the original eye-tracking data for the approximately 8.5 hours of viewing in this study, 57.6 percent of viewing time was spent with the television as the point of gaze, 28.8 percent with the mobile device as the point of gaze, and 13.5 percent with an off-screen or unknown point of gaze. In the manually coded data, 60.7 percent of viewer time was spent with the television as the point of gaze, 36.7 percent with the mobile device as the point of gaze, and 2.6 percent with an off-screen or unknown point of gaze.

The distribution of the point of gaze across areas of interest varied considerably across cases (see Figure 2.1). The manually coded data are used in gaze maps shown below; the original data are used in analysis of gaze lengths as the manual coding may have an artifact of missing some very short gazes.

The first research question addressed whether the hazard function for gaze lengths at television holds in a multi-screen viewing environment. The

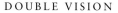

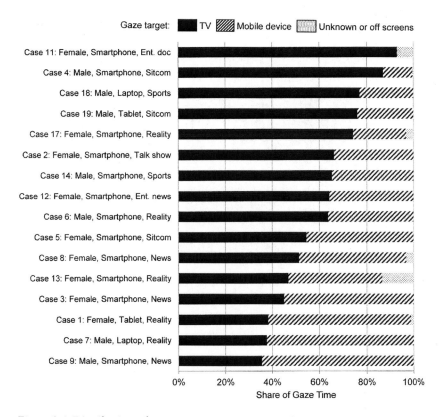

Figure 2.1 Distribution of gaze time across screens, with participants rank-ordered by share of gaze given to the television screen.

eye-tracking data showed that the short glance phenomenon still holds true in the cross-media television consumption context. The majority of gaze events (97.7 percent) were of less than 1 minute's duration (as reflected in the average gaze length). A small number of long gazes (less than 1/3 of one percent of all gaze events) accounted for over 14 percent of total gaze time (Table 2.1).

Table 2.1 Share of Gaze Events and Share of Total Gaze Time

Length (minutes)	Share of Gaze Events (%)	Share of Total Gaze Time (%)
< 1	97.7	57.4
1–2	1.7	19.7
2–3	0.3	5.9
> 3	0.3	14.4

The second research question addressed the distribution of gaze time across screens. Examination of viewer gaze distribution between the television "big screen" and the second-screen devices suggests two patterns: (1) viewers looking mostly at television with periods of extended gaze to the mobile device; and (2) viewers looking mostly at television with shorter periods of gaze to the second screen. Only one case showed clear second-screen dominance. The timelines in Figure 2.2 show the distribution of gaze time to the television screen, mobile screen, and off-screen or unknown/ missing gaze. The time axis labels are in 1-minute increments and the mapping is for 5-second intervals. The map can be read left to right as a map of shifts in the primary target of visual attention. The timeline above the gaze map indicates the placement of ad pods within program content.

The average length of a gaze event (continuous gaze points within a single screen without interruption) was almost 5 seconds for the television but less than 2 seconds for the mobile device (see Table 2.2). Alternating rapid gazes between the television and mobile screen tended to be interspersed with longer gaze events on a single screen, as reflected in the standard deviation values in Table 2.2. The length of the longest gaze event varied across participants in this study from 202.5 seconds to 820 seconds, with an average of 465.7 seconds.

The third research question explored if visual attention distribution between television and the second screen differed during television programming and commercial breaks. The timing of periods of extended or

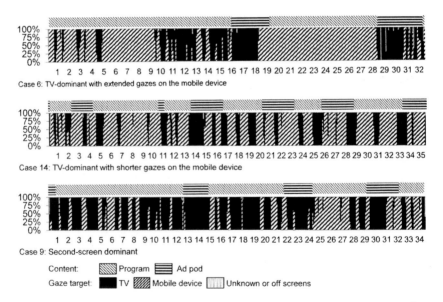

Case 6: TV-dominant with extended gazes on the mobile device

Case 14: TV-dominant with shorter gazes on the mobile device

Case 9: Second-screen dominant

Figure 2.2 Example timelines of gaze distribution across screens (gaze ratios within 5-second intervals).

Table 2.2 Gaze Event Length by Target Screen

	Gaze Event Length	
	Mean	*SD (standard deviation)*
Television	4.71	(47.65)
Mobile	1.64	(32.97)
Other/unknown	0.51	(8.49)

multiple gazes to the smartphone suggests a tendency of some viewers to shift to the mobile device during commercials. While 65.7 percent of gaze time was to the television during program content, only 44.6 percent of gaze time was dedicated to the television during ad pods.

The variability of relationships between advertising and attention to the second screen is apparent in the gaze maps. Figure 2.3 displays simplified gaze timelines which show only the most-viewed screen in each 5-second interval for the example cases. The first participant in Figure 2.3 (case 2) watched an episode of the *Ellen* talk show. In her post-session interview she reported (as did many participants) that she tended to use her device during commercials. She looked for information on show guests during ad pods but also used her device during program content. Overall, her style implies less engagement with advertising content but enhanced engagement with the show itself.

Ad pod placement is less predictable and commercial breaks shorter during live sports, which may influence the pattern of relatively frequent shifts seen for case 14 in Figure 2.3. This participant reported he tended to use his phone to check scores of other games (often through a Google

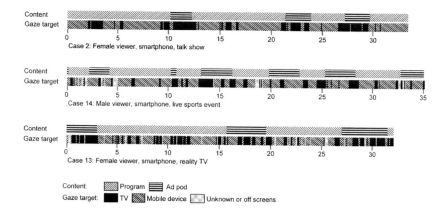

Figure 2.3 Examples of contrasting alignment of mobile device gaze events with ad pods and program content.

search), to check his basketball fantasy leagues, and occasionally to follow up on something featured in a commercial. This is an example of distraction by the second screen: his use is sports-related but not directly connected with the game he is watching.

The third gaze map in Figure 2.3 reflects a different kind of television–second screen relationship, based on social television viewing. This participant reported only a handful of favorite shows have her undivided attention; during these favored shows she will only make social media posts during commercials. For other shows (such as this reality show, which she tends not to watch mid-season), "It's background noise to my phone. I'll watch and message or comment on Facebook or Twitter." Nevertheless, she frequently glanced at the television during the second and third commercial breaks. She also noted a preference for social viewing with friends: "I don't feel a need [to post] if people I care about aren't watching."

As noted, the two viewing patterns each had multiple examples in the sample. Another logically expected pattern (second screen dominant with brief gaze episodes on the television screen) was only found in one case, in which a woman watching a reality television show made extensive use of the stars' Instagram sites to view celebrity, product, and hairstyle images. While her visual attention pattern alone would suggest she was distracted by the second screen, she was reported as being deeply engaged with the show. She was apparently using her mobile device in support of parasocial interaction and identity attributes of that engagement.

Discussion

The first finding of this study is that the hazard function/extended gaze phenomenon still holds true in a second-screen viewing environment. This "long tail" of extended gazes has been seen in numerous prior eye-tracking studies of television viewing (Anderson & Lorch, 1983; Burns & Anderson, 1993; Hawkins et al., 1991, 2005). However, one related study of visual attention to television with a second-screen device tablet found it absent when using researcher-selected, show-specific synchronized apps (Holmes et al., 2012). The show-specific companion apps may have been a "demand effect" for the tablet application, which in turn may have reduced the likelihood of extended gazes to the television screen. Their results may imply that the rapid-shift pattern is specific to synchronized apps or was an artifact of the novelty of such apps to participants. However, the present study allowed participants to use their preferred mobile device and select their online applications, as a regular television viewer watches television at home. The findings here showed that extended gazes were present in a second-screen viewing situation, as commonly found in single-screen television viewing studies. This important finding here significantly contradicts the implication of the prior study that second-screen usage may fundamentally alter how people view television, even though total gaze time on the big screen may be reduced.

In terms of the typical pattern of visual attention across screens, it is not surprising that the distribution of gaze time favors the television rather than the second screen. However, the distribution of gaze time across screens differed depending on whether the television content was programming or commercials. This finding resonated with the study of two-screen viewing using specific apps (e.g., Holmes et al., 2012; The Pool, 2013). During commercials, the share of time on the television fell and the share of gaze time on the second screen increased. This tendency to look at the second screen during commercials was a recurrent theme in post-section individual interviews, where it tended to take the form of a simple cause-and-effect relationship, i.e., "I use my phone/tablet/computer during commercials." However, no participant attained complete "ad avoidance" at the visual level.

The second screen would garner considerable visual attention during commercials in this study, which may be associated with lower engagement with television commercials. The implication is that companion devices can act as a distraction or reinforcement, having negative or positive impacts for television advertisers and program producers. Practitioners and scholars have suggested various benefits of cross-media engagement for advertisers and broadcasters. From the advertisers' perspective, engaged viewers in the multimedia environment are more likely to remember an advertisement, internalize the message, and be motivated by it than those who are less engaged (Epps, 2009). In addition, advanced web-based technologies and their online applications, especially social media platforms, are useful in nurturing customer relationships with brands among those who are most tightly engaged with the program. Because more involved viewers tend to engage in cross-media activities, advertising campaigns utilizing cross-media platforms might increase the likelihood of targeting the most involved viewers (Harris Interactive, 2008; Networked Insights, 2010). Hence, the value of advertising grows as viewers connect television programming and marketing message in multimedia platforms.

In summary, interview responses and eye-tracking results suggest a variety of forces act upon participants to engage their visual attention with one screen or the other: interest in the content (whether ads or programming), program events triggering social media use or other online activity, and motivations for mobile device use unrelated to viewing television (though these may reflect content interest levels). Viewers have always had the opportunity and motivations to look away from the television screen, as the hazard function demonstrates; now, however, they have a particularly attractive alternative point of gaze, the second screen provided by the mobile device. This screen can either reinforce or distract from engagement with program and advertising content. The participants' range of uses for the second screen and variety of patterns of visual attention to it suggest that we should be cautious in referring to what is sometimes labeled "the second-screen experience" and instead consider the label "second-screen experiences."

Limitations and Future Research

The ecological validity of this study could be improved in future research. First, this study did not include audio cues as a variable in the eye-tracking analysis. Several participants mentioned that audio cues could drive shifts in where they were looking; for example, mobile device alerts for incoming text messages or social media postings draw attention to the second screen, while a program soundtrack clue can trigger a shift back to the television. Second, the research was carried out in a realistic living room but nevertheless in a lab setting. The lab lacks the familiarity and distractions of a person's own home. The setting also has a "demand" component, which means that participants may show greater attention in the special setting than they would in an unprompted session of viewing at home. Third, the sample size of the research is limited and more valid results may be drawn from a larger sample size. Lastly, the current study is restricted by its non-random sample (drawn from an existing research participant panel). Caution is needed in judging the representativeness of the results. Future research could address the visual attention in a second-screen setting using field research as second-screen viewing becomes more widely adopted. In addition, studies that systematically examine different program genres (as opposed to participant-selected genres) might offer new insights on visual attention distribution across screens, as attentional demands vary across program genres.

References

Anderson, D. R., & Burns, J. (1991). Paying attention to television. In J. Bryant & D. Zillmann (Eds.), *Responding to the screen* (pp. 3–25). Hillsdale, NJ: Lawrence Erlbaum Associates.

Anderson, D. R., & Lorch, E. P. (1983). Looking at television: Action or reaction? In J. Bryant & D. R. Anderson (Eds.), *Children's understanding of television: Research on attention and comprehension* (pp. 1–30). New York: Academic Press.

Baddeley, A. D. (1986). *Working memory*. Oxford University Press.

Baddeley, A. D. (1992). Working memory. *Science, 225*, 556–559.

Bokenham, N., & Hughes, B. (2013). *The second screen fallacy: What it all really means.* Online at http://ipglab.com/wp-content/uploads/2013/10/The_Second_Screen_Fallacy_Sept_20131.pdf (retrieved November 15, 2013).

Burns, J., & Anderson, D. R. (1993). Attentional inertia and recognition memory in adult television memory. *Communication Research, 20*(4), 327–352.

Chandler, P., & Sweller, J. (1992). The split-attention effect as a factor in the design of instruction. *British Journal of Educational Psychology, 62,* 233–246.

Epps, S. R. (2009). *What engagement means for media companies.* Online at www. dynamiclogic.com/na/research/whitepapers/docs/Forrester_March2009.pdf (retrieved December 12, 2010).

Goodrich, K. (2011). Anarchy of effects? Exploring attention to online advertising and multiple outcomes. *Psychology & Marketing, 28*(4), 417–440.

Hall, G. (2013). Why TV network have decided they are completely cool with the second-screen revolution. *L.A. Biz,* October 28. Online at www.bizjournals. com/losangeles/news/2013/10/28/tv-everywhere-apps-take-advantage-of.html (retrieved December 12, 2013).

Harris Interactive. (2008). The next wave in media measurement and engagement: Multi-screen engagement study finds greatest advertising value among audiences that cross platforms and are the most engaged. *BusinessWire.com,* June 25. Online at www.businesswire.com/news/home/20080625006000/ en/Wave-Media-Measurement-Engagement-Multi-Screen-Engagement-Study (retrieved June 29, 2009).

Hawkins, R., Kim, Y., & Pingree, S. (1991). The ups and downs of attention to television. *Communication Research, 18*(1), 53–76.

Hawkins, R. P., Pingree S., Hitchon, J., Radler, B., Gorham, B. W., Kahlor, L., Gilligan, E., Serlin, R. C., Schmidt, T., Kannaovakun, P., and Kolbeins, G. H. (2005). What produces television attention and attention style? Genre, situation, and individual differences as predictors. *Human Communication Research, 31*(1), 162–187.

Holmes, M. E., Josephson, S., & Carney, R. E. (2012). Visual attention to television programs with a second-screen application. In *Proceedings of the Symposium on Eye Tracking Research and Applications* (pp. 397–400), New York.

Huston, A., & Wright J. (1983). Children's processing of television: The information functions of formal features. In J. Bryant & D. R. Anderson (Eds.), *Children's understanding of television: Research on attention and comprehension* (pp. 35–65). New York: Academic Press.

Lee, J. W., & Ahn, J. H. (2012). Attention to banner ads and their effectiveness: An eye-tracking approach. *International Journal of Electronic Commerce, 17*(1), 119–138.

Networked Insights. (2010). *Social sense TV: Networking ratings report.* Online at http://networkedinsights.com/NI01tv17979d53-a071-491e-a37a-9a8346c2e491. pdf (retrieved December 10, 2010).

Nielsen. (2013). *A look across screens: The cross-platform report.* New York: Nielsen. Online at www.nielsen.com/content/dam/corporate/us/en/reports-downloads/2013%20Reports/Nielsen-March-2013-Cross-Platform-Report.pdf (retrieved December 10, 2013).

Paivio, A. (1986). *Mental representation: A dual coding approach.* Oxford: Oxford University Press.

Pieters, R., Warlop, L., & Wedel, M. (2002). Breaking through the clutter: Benefits of advertisement originality and familiarity for brand attention and memory. *Management Science, 48*(6), 765–781.

The Pool. (2013). *Two screen TV lane*. Online at http://yaffacdn.s3.amazonaws. com/live/adnews/files/dmfile/zeebox.pdf.pdf (retrieved November 15, 2013).

Schmitt, K. L., Woolf, K. D., & Anderson, D. R. (2003). Viewing the viewers: Viewing behaviors by children and adults during television programs and commercials. *Journal of Communication, 53*(2), 265–281.

Sweller, J. (1988). Cognitive load during problem solving: Effects on learning. *Cognitive Science, 12*, 257–285.

Sweller, J. (1994). Cognitive load theory, learning difficulty and institutional design. *Learning and Instruction, 4*, 295–312.

3

TWITTER AND TELEVISION
Broadcast Ratings in the Web 2.0 Era

Michael Brouder and Robert Alan Brookey

On July 11, 2013, Mia Farrow tweeted a picture of herself and Philip Roth captioned, "We're watching #Sharknado." As Christopher Rosen has noted, the tweet was a hoax, but it blew up on the internet because of the humor inherent in the prospect that such a noted actress and author would be "watching a movie where Tara Reid and Ian Ziering fight tornado sharks" (2013, para. 3). Although Farrow's tweet was a hoax, as the *Hollywood Reporter* would observe, *Sharknado* was a trending topic among the industry, with Will Wheaton, Patton Oswald, Olivia Wilde, and Elizabeth Banks all tweeting about the SyFy cable channel movie (THR Staff, 2013). It would appear where this Twitter trend was concerned, Hollywood was not alone; Danny Sullivan tracked tweets for the show and observed, "at its peak, #Sharknado was doing 5,032 tweets per minute, which is about 84 tweets per second" (2103, para. 5). A high rate, but as Sullivan avers hardly a record. For the SyFy channel's purposes, however, *Sharknado* did not need to set any records. Paul Vinga, writing for the *Wall Street Journal's Money Beat* offered this observation about the *Sharknado* phenomenon: "(V)iewership came almost wholly from the buzz on Twitter, and that little frenzy is exactly what advertisers are looking for . . . which is simply the ability to capture the viewer's attention. Any company advertising during *Sharknado* hit on a mini-windfall" (2013, para. 4).

The twitter trending on *Sharknado* might have been as easy to dismiss as the movie itself, except for what would happen a month later. In August of 2013, Nielsen Media Research released data for the first time that seemed to address a question many television broadcasters had about a possible two-way causal influence between Twitter activity and television ratings (Finn, 2013). Although media and advertising executives were still reluctant to accept the data as fact, it was a seminal moment for legacy media. From the perspective of television broadcasters it was especially important, as all broadcast television networks have seen their steepest declines ever in households watching television across all dayparts (Carter, 2012). The current fragmentation of television viewership is also well documented (Webster, 2005), as is the exodus of traditional television viewers to alternative media, including streaming outlets such as Netflix, on-demand services, and DVR recordings (Pisharody, 2013). These new data, however, are the first of their kind from Nielsen, or any other source, that suggest that Twitter has become one of the top three factors for generating increased television viewership (Nielsen Holdings, 2013a).

Yet, a few months later, during the spring upfronts, major networks were extolling their plans to maximize audience engagement through content especially designed for Twitter (Poggi, 2014b). Indeed, in anticipation of the upfronts, advertisers were already suggesting that multiple data streams would inform the ad buys that they would make (Poggi, 2014a). Given the reluctant attitude that media and advertising executives had displayed a few months earlier, attitudes toward social media, and Twitter in particular, had changed significantly.

While Nielsen's data are intriguing, and clearly media companies see value in Twitter, there is little scholarly published work examining the relationships formed at the crossroads of legacy and new media. Because of the lack of research in the area of Twitter and its effect on television viewership, we will argue for an aggressive, scholarly study of social media, particularly Twitter. Indeed, it is Twitter's rapid growth as a communication and data gathering tool that is prompting Nielsen to create new measurement methodologies for the broadcast television industry. To provide the proper context, we will review the history of Nielsen's methodologies and the television industry's vocal opposition to the shortcomings in accounting for new media's influence on viewership. Next, we will consider the existing literature on social media's effect on television viewership. From there, Twitter's symbiotic relationship with television will be explored, particularly as a cross-promotion platform. Finally, we will identify critical issues that should be considered as the relationship between Twitter and television viewership evolves.

Television Ratings: A History

Well before the emergence of television as a medium in the early 1900s, the measurement of consumers of traditional media has been a fundamental tool for marketing, advertising, and programming decision makers. In the mid 1980s, media researcher Hugh Beville crafted an important source book on broadcast television and radio ratings, systematically breaking down the history of audience measurement beginning with radio in the

1930s, the emergence of television audience measurement, and then the measurement methodologies developed by several competing companies in subsequent years. Notably, he explored the history and emergence of no fewer than 14 qualitative research models established by competing research companies, as well as an outline of modern cable audience measurement (Beville, 1985). Perhaps the oldest, and most notorious, method involves the maintenance of viewer diaries. Beville outlines both strengths and weaknesses for this system, but in subsequent years since his book was published, weaknesses have been compounded. In fact, a recent longitudinal study released by the Council for Research Excellence has found that both the inaccuracies and biases of diary reporting are greater than was originally assumed (Marszalek, 2013).

In the face of fierce competition from US and European companies, Nielsen Media Research emerged victorious in its systematic drive for dominance in the television ratings marketplace by developing the *peoplemeter* (Buzzard, 2002). Peoplemeters expanded the capabilities of traditional household meters by allowing viewers to enter information about who was watching television at a particular moment in time. These meters were also expected to solve some of the problems associated with the older diary system. Yet, even the peoplemeters are a problematic means of measuring television viewership (Asaravala, 2004).

Ratings research was, and continues to this day, to be imperfect and occasionally biases emerge that gave an advantage to some and disadvantaged others. Because the peoplemeter system does a better job of measuring small, demographically targeted audiences, advertiser-supported cable networks are likely to be beneficiaries of skewed numbers. Both broadcasters as well as cable programmers felt this discontent with Nielsen. If peoplemeter data allow cable to compete more effectively with the major networks for advertiser dollars, it might ultimately have an impact on the kinds of programming appearing on television. The point is, not only does industry demand shape the nature of ratings data, but the availability of certain kinds of data can shape the industry too (Buzzard, 2002).

A study by Timothy Moreland (1995) noted the discontent with Nielsen research methodologies grew among both broadcasters and advertisers just prior to the emergence of widespread internet use by consumers. The results of Moreland's study indicated skepticism in Nielsen ratings by the respondents, but neither advertisers nor broadcasters felt particularly strong about the issue. This may have been because agencies and corporate advertising managers realized that there was no better system for ratings measurement than Nielsen. Consequently, because of Nielsen's monopoly on cash, distribution, and development, Nielsen staved off multiple attempts by emerging ratings measurement companies, and it remained the lone system for television ratings measurement. Recently, however, Rentrak Corporation has emerged as a notable competitor to Nielsen and has made inroads on the latter's monopoly of broadcast television station clients. Offering services for motion picture, television, and social media engagement measurement, Rentrak is used in all 210 markets nationwide across all four major network affiliate groups (Thomas, 2013).

Today's audience measurement technologies, developed by both Nielsen and other companies, provide more comprehensive data than ever, including digital set-top boxes that provide up-to-the-second ratings to information as well as methods of measuring DVR, online, and out-of-home use. Unfortunately, Nielsen's more recent efforts to advance measurement technologies to match the change in consumer viewing habits continue to be met with skepticism from advertisers and broadcasters. As more consumers began time-shifting their viewing habits with DVR technology, the traditional method of limiting ratings to original broadcasts was called into question, particularly by broadcasters who imagined an important segment of their audience was not being measured. A 2005 push by Nielsen to measure commercial ratings plus three days of DVR viewing was met with stiff resistance, this time from advertisers who pointed out Nielsen's inconsistencies in data amounted to buying on a currency with no intrinsic value (Lafayette, 2005). In spite of this resistance, Nielsen has not only continued to track DVR viewership, but has also rolled out new systems of measuring both streaming and mobile consumption; the company's recent association with Twitter is part of these new efforts.

With the seismic shift in the current media consumption landscape and the need for technological advances in how these audiences are measured, there also arose a call in academic circles for a broader definition of ratings analysis that includes new methodologies connected to new media consumption. Napoli (2012) notes traditional measurement services are adjusting their methods of capturing data in relation to changes in media usage, and other media companies and agencies are exploring new methods altogether to measure and monetize audience engagement. Ultimately, Napoli recommends new models for audience measurement that include a broader, multidimensional approach to media consumption; one that focuses less on audience behaviors, and more on the various methods in which an audience consumes media.

Social Media's Effect on Business

For businesses, the value of reaching mass audiences through social media, particularly Twitter and Facebook, is hard to ignore. As of this writing, 77 percent of Fortune 500 companies actively use Twitter, 70 percent use Facebook, and 69 percent use YouTube (Kerr, 2013). The rapid emergence of social media and other web-based technologies had caused dramatic shifts in traditional marketing and advertising. Adamson

(2008) has argued that these shifts, by and large, are not temporary, and companies need to develop long-term social media strategies.

As early as 2009, the extent of knowledge about social media, even an agreed upon definition of social media, was elusive. Given the growing focus that business executives place on the value of social media, Kaplan and Haenlein (2010) aimed to better define the concept, as well as differentiate the term's use among similar concepts such as "Web 2.0" and "user generated content." They categorized sub-genres of social media based on high versus low levels of personal disclosure along with a high, medium, and low amount of "richness" or social presence within the medium. They saw the use of the internet and online communication taking on a more conversational, interactive mode of discourse. Kaplan and Haenlein (2010) also offer suggestions to professionals with regard to the use of social media within their organizations' marketing strategies. Included in their recommendations are those geared toward how to use social media within a broader marketing scope, and others about navigating the nuances of social media communication. The article concludes with several insights on what to expect from social media in the immediate future, including the emergence of a "Mobile" Web 2.0.

For professional social media marketers, Kaplan and Haenlein (2010) provided a good outline of different social media platforms and their uses. For scholars, this is an adequate primer on the basics of social media, but it lacks a broader recognition or a deeper analysis of the effect of all social media applications available at the time. This is evidenced by the almost complete omission of Twitter, reinforcing once more the need for continued academic research relating to Twitter's influence on business marketing.

Beyond being merely communication tools or forms of collective wisdom, social media are also considered entertainment. Ferguson and Perse (2000) drew comparisons between web surfing and television. Written at a time when internet use was rapidly increasing, the article ultimately queried if the web could displace television as a vehicle for information and entertainment. Through a uses and gratification study detailing the media use of 250 college undergraduate students, data were collected to gauge the participants' motivation for general web use, the kinds of television-related web activities in which they participate, and finally the extent of their "web repertoire." The authors concluded that the web and television competed when it came to free time and entertainment. However, where television ranks high on the scale of being a relaxing activity, computer use did not. The research of Ferguson and Perse serves as an early glimpse into perceptions and activities of web consumers at a time when internet speeds were much slower than they are today. A similar study of web use today, especially with the arrival of streaming services such as Netflix and Hulu, would likely bring different results; in part because streaming services and online downloading have been more readily deployed by the entertainment sector.

As noted above, social media have created a fundamental shift in the paradigm of media consumption. For example, Wiederhold (2012) observed that, in their infancy, social media served the purpose of a way for companies to "listen in" on consumer feedback. Today, however, Wiederhold observes a growing but fundamental shift within the context of social media influence, whereupon consumer opinion means far more than it used to. This is backed up with recent data on second-screen use, online viewing of advertising, and references to recent research in Germany and Japan, where the social and traditional media have a much more synergistic relationship. The article concludes with a warning that advertisers that fail to recognize this shift in power back to the hands of the consumer will do so at their own peril (Wiederhold, 2012).

In some ways, businesses have heeded this warning. Fischer and Reuber (2011) measured how the use of social media, particularly Twitter, benefitted and shaped the decision making of business entrepreneurs. The authors sampled multiple business entrepreneurs who have adopted Twitter in the previous two years, but who use a wide variety of tactics with the medium. The authors interviewed each participant and documented their Twitter use for a predetermined period of time before and after the interview. The authors concluded that Twitter, along with other social media channels, is valuable and offers entrepreneurs opportunities to advance their businesses goals. They go on to caution that businesses need to consider social media as more than a medium with which to communicate marketing messages, and need to expand and experiment within the medium. Finally, although the research was relatively recent, it is notable that the authors address the lack of scholarly research with regard to social media beyond that of being a marketing tool.

Aside from business entrepreneurs, Mangold and Faulds (2009) argue that social media, also referred to as consumer-generated media, need to be added to the list of traditional marketing techniques utilized by current integrated marketing communications (IMC) strategists. The authors supported this argument by citing several examples of notable recent social media efforts by big businesses across several social media platforms. The authors go on to contrast traditional media as a "one-way" versus social media's "multiple-avenue model," which affords a marketer many more ways to communicate. They note, however, that the unpredictability of social media is often a barrier for entry by many traditionally minded IMC strategists.

At this point it is important to ask that, if businesses and their marketing and advertising efforts are shifting toward the use of social media, are the consumers listening to their messages? Logan et al. (2012) gauged audience perception on the value of advertising messages on social media sites compared to similar advertising messages on television. The authors used a slight variant from Ducoffe's Ad Value model for predicting a consumer's attitudes toward advertising, namely entertainment, informativeness, and irritation. An analysis of a 51-question poll sent to 500 social media and television consumers noted that entertainment was a key factor in assessing advertising value within social media. This is in contrast to television, where informativeness was a key factor. Although there were some limitations to the study, including a relatively narrow and small sample, it was interesting to note a difference in perception between persuasive messaging within the two mediums. The authors go on to suggest that media professionals should consider changing the tonality and content of messaging.

Amid the rapid emergence of social media and their effect on legacy media's long-standing advertising and marketing models, Collins and Brown (2012) outline how, within the new media landscape, traditional media outlets (specifically television stations and newspapers) have been slow to adapt to the new ways consumers seek and experience media. In their study, the authors compared the use of multimedia content in the daily operations of television stations and newspapers. Online and mail-in surveys were delivered to 1,000 newspapers and news-producing television stations nationwide. Results of the study reinforced the hypothesis that, regardless of market size, the legacy "attitudes" at local operations prevent traditional news media from actively changing workflow operations to bring their news content into new media applications. What makes this study noteworthy is that it reinforces legacy media's general reluctance to adapt and grow amid the expansion of social media and their growing influence on consumer behavior. Yet that reluctance appears to be dissipating where one legacy medium (television) and one social medium (Twitter) are concerned.

The Twitter and Television Relationship

Twitter is rapidly emerging as the social medium of choice for television media companies. In February 2013, Twitter spent $90 million to purchase startup company Bluefin Labs, which combines television viewer data with Twitter user behavior metrics (Isaac, 2013). This, for many reasons, is very valuable information for advertisers, television programmers, and even Nielsen Media Research. Not surprisingly, eight months later, Nielsen and Twitter jointly announced the launch of *Twitter TV Ratings*, a measurement of total activity and reach of television-related conversations on Twitter (Nielsen Holdings, 2013b).

Recently, Twitter also made efforts to partner with television media companies directly. In the summer of 2013, Twitter introduced *Twitter Amplify*, a new advertising product for media and consumer brands, which allows streamed video links within tweets (Indvik, 2013). Another innovation, *See It*, is a joint effort between Twitter and Comcast that allows for greater interconnectivity embedded in Twitter posts published by Comcast-owned channels. For Twitter, the feature is another opportunity to promote itself as a destination for television conversation and as a partner to the networks (Stelter, 2013).

An undeniable draw for television companies toward Twitter lies in their immense number of users, and the potential to reach these users with engaging messages. As of July 2014, Twitter boasted over 250 million users (Weise, 2014), and the company offers access by which developers can define resources to identify and target these users. The Twitter application programming interface (API) allows code-savvy users the freedom to extract a myriad of valuable information from the "big data" gathered by a global Twitter user base. The amount of data can be overwhelming, but in the right hands can unlock a treasure trove of data for analysts relating to tweet popularity and user demographics.

Burgess and Bruns (2012) explored big data in the areas where social media and television overlap. While they did not address how mined data on Twitter can be incorporated into parallel analyses with traditional television audience measurement systems, the authors did begin to explore how current approaches to collecting social media data were beginning to be undertaken by more than just computer scientists. Burgess and Bruns (2012) coin the phrase "big social data" as a means by which to categorize the rapid growth of quantitative data associated with social media. The authors argued that this brave new world of social data mining was creating new modes of scholarship in media, communication, and cultural studies. Although Burgess and Bruns felt big data analysis was inherently a technical process, they called for a greater level of code literacy among those occupying roles in non-science fields. They suggest incorporating broad computer science coursework for students in media and communications studies to truly overcome the barriers for using Twitter data in media scholarship (Burgess & Bruns, 2012).

The ability to parse and analyze data at the scope that Twitter can offer brings huge opportunities to companies willing to make the investment in the process. As noted, there is vast potential in partnerships between Twitter and corporations eager to tap into the mountain of information from which to strategically communicate to their respective consumer base. In spite of the rapidly developing business partnerships between Twitter and television corporations, the actual study of the symbiotic relationship between television and Twitter use is scant. One study by Wohn and Eun-Kyung, however, discussed common perceptions regarding Twitter use while watching television programming. Of note, tweets were not part of a "conversation" per se, but more of a running commentary. Other findings include the fact that tweets tend to occur almost immediately following a dramatic moment in the program, as opposed to a delay. Additionally, tweets tend to appear during commercial breaks, are indicative of personal engagement with the program, and generally include additional hashtags, retweets, and links. Another interesting finding includes the fact that 30 percent of the tweets came from mobile devices (Wohn & Eun-Kyung, 2011).

While their study notes that the dialogue relating to television among Twitter users is not technically a traditional call and response "conversation," television corporations are still eager to inject their product messaging into the commentary. Lin and Peña (2011) draw from existing scholarly works and recent conference notes to expand the current knowledge of television networks' brand messaging via Twitter. They then proceed to develop and outline resulting implications for brand managers. The authors categorized the tweets of nine television programs across multiple genres on the basis of being task-oriented or socio-emotional. The study also examined which tweets were retweeted more frequently as a measure of which kind of tweets are more influential. Lin and Peña conclude that, while television networks use Twitter for instructional messages, such as programming promotion, there is greater pass along value and overall influence with messages that are more social, such as opinions, jokes, and salutations. Not all television outlets have been adept at utilizing this medium, however. For example, Greer and Ferguson (2011) found that local television stations underutilize Twitter as a promotional vehicle for station programming, and they conclude that most non-public broadcasting stations use Twitter as news feed and seldom promote regular newscasts.

Beyond promotion, Harrington et al. (2012) further noted ways in which Twitter is reshaping television, from the ways audiences watch to the ways broadcasters produce programming with Twitter followers in mind. The authors also touched upon potential ways advertisers are benefitting from the synchronization of Twitter participation with live programming. In acknowledging the complexities of the relationship between television and social media, the authors attempt to identify and explore ways that television intersects with Twitter as a communication platform within the media sphere. The article concluded with a call for further dialogue regarding the symbiotic relationship between Twitter, television programmers, and the collective audiences they reach.

Additional Research/Additional Questions

The singular element that binds legacy and new media, particularly Twitter, is the battle for ad revenue. According to ratings historian Hugh Beville, effective mass communication requires a viable feedback system to report on how the media are being received, and the second is a strong financial structure, through subscribers, advertisers, or both (Beville, 1996).

Media, advertising, and audience measurement have always been closely linked, regardless of the fact that technologies and consumption of traditional media are changing. The $502 billion global ad spend market (Lunden, 2013) is shifting away from television and toward internet, and Twitter appears to be leading the strategic effort to leverage its data and consumer reach, through partnerships with Nielsen Media Research and big media companies such as Comcast.

Unfortunately, there is a noticeable gap in scholarly literature regarding the relationship between Twitter and television. A cursory online glance reveals an excess of television industry trade and consumer press relating to Twitter and its effect on consumer behavior, including television viewership, but most of it coincides with joint Twitter and Nielsen Media Research press announcements. Nielsen's causation study (Nielsen Holdings, 2013a) purports a direct correlation between Twitter use and TV ratings, yet there is no independent study, professional or scholarly, that supports or refutes this. The scholarly literature that does exist relating to new media's effect on television viewing is very limited. Most research in this area is isolated to either very broad topics, such as the internet's growing presence as an entertainment alternative (Liebowitz & Zenter, 2012), or is targeted to particular social media subsets, demographics, and/or programming (Logan et al., 2012). And although Ruth Deller's (2011) study shows some promise, her examples are often anecdotal and the scope of the study is limited.

Some of the reasons why there is a lack of independent, academic research on Twitter's influence on television ratings may also lie in the very nature of social media platforms. Beginning in 1997 with what is considered the first social networking site (SNS), sixdegrees.com, there were no fewer than 30 SNSs that launched before Twitter launched in 2006 (Ellison, 2007). This seems to be too small of a window to recognize the emergence of a dominant social media player, let alone conduct thorough research on a particular social media platform. To illustrate this further, current social media leader Facebook, with over three times the unique monthly visitors of Twitter, is currently seeing its popularity shrink among teens and young adults (Rodriguez, 2013). With the rapid rise and fall of SNSs, scholars may be asking if research on Twitter's relationship with television is long term. In addition, many of the developments that have integrated Twitter with Nielson and Comcast have happened within the last year. Given the lag-time of academic research and peer review publication, and the complex workflow of some academic journals and presses, it may be a while before the scholarly research on Twitter and television begins appearing in press. As this research emerges, we believe that there are some important issues scholars should consider.

First, we need independent and disciplined research to verify and test the claims that Nielsen makes in its 2013 causation study, with particular attention to the conclusions regarding Twitter activity and television ratings. This independent verification is needed because both Nielsen and Twitter have a vested interest in these favorable findings. Nielsen is trying to answer the complaints of advertisers and broadcasters who believe the company is behind the curve where social media is concerned. Although it had a successful IPO (initial public offering), Twitter had been performing poorly with the exception of a profitable second quarter in 2014. Indeed, it could be argued that the Nielsen study, and buzz surrounding Twitter prior to the spring upfronts, may have contributed to this new success by placing the platform in a enviable position by tying social media to the revenue stream of traditional television advertising (Weise, 2014).

Second, do tweets signify active viewer engagement? One of the perennial complaints about traditional Nielsen ratings is that they seldom distinguish actual viewing from the use of television as background for other household activities. Tweets about specific programming content would seem to indicate a viewer who is actually watching the programming, but is this the type of engagement that benefits advertisers? For example, Pynta et al. (2014) conducted a study measuring brain activity of subjects who used social media (Twitter and Fango) while watching television. They conclude that their findings are in line with Nielsen's own regarding Twitter usage and viewer engagement, and suggest that "higher levels of program engagement also bode well for advertisers, with advertising spots also likely to receive boosts in performance" (p. 78). If, however, as Wohn and Eun-Kyung (2011) suggest, most of the tweets that signify personal engagement happen during commercial breaks, then more research is needed to determine if advertising messages actually benefit from Twitter. Indeed, it is possible that the personal engagement that Twitter inspires may be at cross-purposes with the commercial advertiser. In other words, these tweets indicating program engagement may also index commercial disengagement. Therefore, more research is needed before we can determine if Twitter is an advantage or disadvantage to advertisers.

Third, if tweets become the new ratings currency, then what type of programming motivates tweets? In their study of Twitter feeds used during the 2012 Eurovision Song Contest, Highfield et al. (2013) verified that special events programs, especially programming with a strong fan base, could allow broadcasters to use Twitter hashtags "in assembling, interacting with, and potentially also in tracking and analyzing live audiences around their programming . . . promoting live viewing and thus maximizing audience ratings and advertising returns" (p. 334). Buschow et al. (2014) have also observed that certain genres of television, specifically reality shows, stimulate more social media discussions. Therefore, it would seem that advantages of Twitter may be reserved for certain types of television programs, and those parameters need to be explored, identified, and demarcated.

For example, if, as Greer and Ferguson (2011) observe, opinions and jokes are more likely to be retweeted and thereby drive Twitter traffic and trending, then there is little wonder why *Sharknado* trended so well. In fact, many of the tweets on the program were disparaging comments and jokes, similar to those found on an older SyFy network program: *Mystery Science Theater 3000*. In other words, *Sharknado*, as a television program goes, was a big joke, and that is our point. If bad programming motivates more tweeting, and tweets become the currency, then how well does that bode for the future of television programming? More recently, the joke got even bigger with *Sharknado 2*, which not only set a new ratings record for the SyFy channel, but also "generated one billion (yes, with a 'b') Twitter impressions—about three times as many as its predecessor—making it television's most social movie ever" (Wood, 2014, para. 1).

Conclusion

Since its inception, the internet has been the catalyst for new and innovative ways to communicate, gather information, and seek entertainment. An inherent competitor to traditional media, online entertainment has resulted in a steady decrease in traditional, live television viewership. Concurrently, Twitter has emerged as one of the top social media tools worldwide, bringing together millions of users and providing them a way to network, communicate, and share ideas. It has essentially changed the public discourse in society, setting trends and influencing behavior. Instead of considering it an internet-created threat, however, big media companies are embracing Twitter and are now exploring a relationship that is mutually beneficial.

Although there is ample research available examining social media's effect on consumer behavior and select research on the overall effect of internet use on television viewing, there is a significant absence of independent research noting Twitter's ability to directly affect television viewing. The financial value of thoroughly understanding this information is immense. The data are crucial to the multi-billion dollar media marketplace and vital to the activities of broadcasting management, sales representatives, program producers, advertisers, and their agencies.

Obviously, a great deal of additional work is needed if we are to be in a position to recreate and confirm current television audience measurement methodologies, and synthesize that with research relating to an ever-changing new media platform such as Twitter. We have offered some tentative suggestions of how that research might proceed, and these suggestions also raise some concerns. Some have claimed that television has entered a new golden age and, in spite of all the "Real Housewives," there are characters such as Walter White, Patty Hewes, Don Draper, and Selena Meyer, all of whom would not have appeared on our sets ten or twenty years ago. Let us hope that the quality of character-driven television can gain the same Twitter traction of the joke that was *Sharknado* and *Sharknado 2*.

References

Adamson, A. (2008). *Brand digital: Simple ways top brands succeed in the digital world*. New York: Palgrave Macmillan.

Asaravala, A. (2004). Nielsen "People Meters" draw fire. *Wired*, April 16. Online at www.wired.com/techbiz/media/news/2004/04/63080 (retrieved August 13, 2005).

Beville, H. M. (1985). *Audience ratings: Radio, television, and cable*. Hillsdale, NJ: Lawrence Erlbaum Associates.

Beville, H. M. (1996). Fashioning audience ratings—from radio to cable. In Dennis, E. E., & Wartella, E. (Eds.), *American communication research: The remembered history* (pp. 95–116). Mahwah, NJ: Psychology Press.

Burgess, J., & Bruns, A. (2012). Twitter archives and the challenges of "big social data" for media and communication research. *M/C Journal, 15*(5), 1–7.

Buschow, C., Schneider, B., & Ueberheide, S. (2014). Tweeting television: Exploring communication activities on Twitter while watching TV. *Communications 39*(2), 129–149. Doi: 10.1515/commun-2014-0009.

Buzzard, K. S. (2002). The peoplemeter wars: A case study of technological innovation and diffusion in the ratings industry. *The Journal of Media Economics, 15*(4), 273–291.

Carter, Bill. (2012). Prime-time ratings bring speculation of a shift in habits. *The New York Times*, April 22. Online at www.nytimes.com/2012/04/23/business/media/tv-viewers-are-missing-in-action.html?_r=0 (retrieved May 19, 2012).

Collins, S. J., & Brown, T. (2012). Convergence or business as usual?: Comparing new media use at television stations and newspapers. *Atlantic Journal of Communication, 20*(4), 248–260.

Deller, R. (2011). Twittering on: Audience research and participation using Twitter. *Participations, 8*(1), 216–245.

Ellison, N. B. (2007). Social network sites: Definition, history, and scholarship. *Journal of Computer-Mediated Communication, 13*(1), 210–230.

Ferguson, D. A., & Perse, E. M. (2000). The World Wide Web as a functional alternative to television. *Journal of Broadcasting & Electronic Media, 44*(2), 155–174.

Finn, B. (2013). *Nielsen releases study on two-way causal influence between Twitter and TV viewership*. Web log comment, August 7. Online at https://blog.twitter.com/2013/nielsen-releases-study-on-two-way-causal-influence-between-twitter-activity-and-tv-viewership (retrieved August 21, 2013).

Fischer, E., & Reuber, A. R. (2011). Social interaction via new social media: (How) can interactions on Twitter affect effectual thinking and behavior? *Journal of Business Venturing, 26*(1), 1–18.

Greer, C. F., & Ferguson, D. A. (2011). Using Twitter for promotion and branding: A content analysis of local television Twitter sites. *Journal of Broadcasting & Electronic Media, 55*(2), 198–214. doi:10.1080/08838151.2011.570824.

Harrington, S., Highfield, T., & Bruns, A. (2012). More than a backchannel: Twitter and television. *Participations: Journal of Audience & Reception Studies, 10*(1), 405–409.

Highfield, T., Harrington, S., & Bruns, A. (2013). Twitter as a technology for audiencing and fandom. *Information, Communication & Society, 16*(3), 315–339. doi: 10.1080/1369118X.2012.756053.

Indvik, L. (2013). Twitter amplify will bring sponsored video clips to your feed. *Mashable*, May 23. Online at www.mashable.com/201/05/23/twitter-amplify/ (retrieved May 25, 2014).

Isaac, M. (2013). Why Twitter dropped close to $90 million on Bluefin labs. *All Things*, February 12. Online at http://allthingsd.com/20130212/why-twitter-dropped-close-to-90-million-on-bluefin-labs/ (retrieved March 15, 2013).

Kaplan, A. M., & Haenlein, M. (2010). Users of the world, unite! The challenges and opportunities of social media. *Business Horizons, 53*(1), 59–68.

Kerr, D. (2013). Fortune 500 companies give social media the thumbs up. *C/Net*, July 24. Online at http://news.cnet.com/8301-1023_3-57595401-93/fortune-500-companies-give-social-media-a-thumbs-up (retrieved August 9, 2013).

Lafayette, J. (2005). Skeptical buyers await DVR stats. *Television Week, 24*(47), 3–21.

Liebowitz, S. J., & Zentner, A. (2012). Clash of the titans: Does internet use reduce television viewing? *Review of Economics and Statistics, 94*(1), 234–245.

Lin, J. S., & Peña, J. (2011). Are you following me? A content analysis of TV networks' brand communication on Twitter. *Journal of Interactive Advertising, 12*(1), 17–29.

Logan, K., Bright, L. F., & Gangadharbatla, H. (2012). Facebook versus television: Advertising value perceptions among females. *Journal of Research in Interactive Marketing, 6*(3), 164–179.

Lunden, I. (2013). Digital ads will be 22% of all U.S. ad spend in 2013, mobile ads 3.7%; total global ad spend in 2013 $503B. *TechCrunch.com*, September 30. Online at http://techcrunch.com/2013/09/30/digital-ads-will-be-22-of-all-u-s-ad-spend-in-2013-mobile-ads-3-7-total-gobal-ad-spend-in-2013-503b-says-zenithoptimedia/ (retrieved October 10, 2013).

Mangold, W. G., & Faulds, D. J. (2009). Social media: The new hybrid element of the promotion mix. *Business Horizons, 52*(4), 357–365.

Marszalek, D. (2013). CRE: Nielsen diaries worse than you thought. *TVNewsCheck*, October 8. Online at www.tvnewscheck.com/article/71023/cre-nielsen-diaries-worse-than-you-thought (retrieved November 10, 2013).

Moreland, T. J. (1995). Advertising professionals' uses and perceptions of AC Nielsen syndicated television ratings. Unpublished doctoral dissertation, University of Southern Mississippi, Hattiesburg.

Napoli, P. M. (2012). Audience evolution and the future of audience research. *JMM: The International Journal on Media Management, 14*(2), 79–97. doi:10.1080/14241277.2012.675753.

Nielsen Holdings. (2013a). New study confirms correlation between Twitter and TV ratings. *Press Room*, March 20. Online at www.nielsen.com/us/en/press-room/2013/new-study-confirms-correlation-between-twitter-and-tv-ratings.html (retrieved April 9, 2013).

Nielsen Holdings. (2013b). Nielsen launches "Nielsen Twitter TV Ratings." *Press Room*, October 7. Online at www.nielsen.com/us/en/press-room/2013/nielsen-launches-nielsen-twitter-tv-ratings.html (retrieved April 9, 2013).

Pisharody, A. (2013). The future of television: Will broadcast and cable television networks survive the emergence of online streaming? Unpublished doctoral dissertation, New York University, New York City.

Poggi, J. (2014a). How data will play a role in TV upfronts. *Advertising Age, 85*(8), 30.

Poggi, J. (2014b). Networks shine spotlight on social reach in TV upfronts. *Advertising Age, 85*(8), 12.

Pynta, P, Seixas, S., Nield, G., Hier, J., Millward, E., & Silberstein, R. (2014). The power of social television: Can social media build viewer engagement? A new approach to brain imaging of view immersion. *Journal of Advertising Research, 54*(1), 71–80. doi:10.2501/JAR-54-1-071-080.

Rodriguez, S. (2013). Tumblr more popular than Facebook among young people, survey says. *Los Angeles Times,* January 11. Online at http://articles.latimes.com/2013/jan/11/business/la-fi-tn-tumblr-facebook-teens-survey-survata-20130111 (retrieved January 20, 2013).

Rosen, C. (2013). Mia Farrow's "Sharknado" tweet with photo of Philip Roth was a joke. *The Huffington Post,* July 12. Online at www.huffingtonpost.com/2013/07/12/mia-farrow-Sharknado-tweet_n_3585444.html (retrieved July 20, 2013).

Stelter, B. (2013). Comcast hopes to promote TV shows in Twitter deal. *The New York Times,* October 9. Online at www.nytimes.com/2013/10/10/business/media/through-twitter-partnership-comcast-hopes-to-encourage-tv-viewing.html (retrieved October 21, 2013).

Sullivan, D. (2013). Syfy's #Sharknado racks up impressive tweets per minute. *Marketing Land,* July 11. Online at http://marketingland.com/Sharknado-takes-over-twitter-51480 (retrieved July 30, 2013).

Thomas, L. (2013). Nielsen vs. Rentrak: How to use the data in your local media campaign. *Local Media Methods,* March 20. Online at www.localmediamethods.com/nielsen-vs-rentrak-how-to-use-the-data-in-your-local-media-campaign/ (retrieved April 4, 2013).

THR Staff. (2013). "Sharknado": What Hollywood is saying about Syfy's movie. *The Hollywood Reporter,* July 11. Online at www.hollywoodreporter.com/news/Sharknado-what-hollywood-is-saying-584052 (retrieved August 2, 2013).

Vinga, P. (2013). "Sharknado" and the tricky business advertising on Twitter. *The Wall Street Journal: Money Beat,* November 22. Online at http://blogs.wsj.com/moneybeat/2013/11/22/twitter-and-the-Sharknado/ (retrieved December 3, 2013).

Webster, J. G. (2005). Beneath the veneer of fragmentation: Television audience polarization in a multichannel world. *Journal of Communication, 55*(2), 366–382.

Weise, E. (2014). Twitter stock surges on strong Q2 results. *USA Today,* July 30. Online at www.usatoday.com/story/tech/2014/07/29/twitter-earnings-beat-wallstreet/13291645/ (retrieved August 10, 2014).

Wiederhold, B. K. (2012). Social media is shifting power from advertisers to consumers. *Cyberpsychology, Behavior & Social Networking, 15*(11), 577–578. doi:10.1089/cyber.2012.1560.

Wohn, D., & Eun-Kyung, N. (2011). Tweeting about TV: Sharing television viewing experiences via social media message streams. *First Monday, 16*(3). Online at http://firstmonday.org/ojs/index.php/fm/article/view/3368/2779 (retrieved April 10, 2013).

Wood, J. (2014). Three secrets that made Sharknado 2 the biggest TV movie ever. *Wired,* August 4. Online at www.wired.com/2014/08/sharknado-2-marketing/ (retrieved August 9, 2014).

Part II

RESEARCH ISSUES AND ADVANCES IN GLOBAL BROADCASTING

4

BROADCAST AND NEW MEDIA USE IN CHINA

Findings from a National Survey

Fei Shen, Zhi'an Zhang, and Mike Z. Yao

China has gone through a period of historic growth in recent decades. Rapid developments in China's social, political, and economic systems have not only brought power and prosperity, but have also led to dramatic shifts in Chinese people's media consumption patterns. At the same time, the diffusion of various new media technologies enabled by the internet has also changed the ways in which people communicate and access information. These new technologies offer a segment of the population an unprecedented ability and opportunity to circumvent or bypass strict official censorship on traditional media. Together, the unique social changes that took place in China and the broad technological revolution in media and communication systems worldwide create a great opportunity for researchers to explore and examine the role of the media in shaping Chinese people's beliefs, attitudes, and behavior.

Changes in a social system are likely to be caused by both socio-structural forces and individual actors (Giddens, 1984). Although a great deal of intellectual focus has been placed on media texts and media effects in China (Shen & Guo, 2013; Shen et al., 2011; Wang et al., 2011), few studies have closely examined individual Chinese people's media usage and interests. Such a void has left many interesting questions unanswered. For example, what are Chinese people watching and/or listening to today? Through which channels? From what sources? How frequently are Chinese people exposed to different types of media content? Are there regional differences? With these questions in mind, this study aims to provide a snapshot of people's media use habits and interests.

The discussions and analyses are organized in four sections. The first section discusses the development of the media system in China after 1979 and paints an overall picture of the contemporary media scene. The second section introduces a nationally representative survey that covers all provinces, autonomous regions, and municipalities directly under the central government in Mainland China. The third section draws upon some preliminary findings of the survey to provide a detailed description of Chinese residents' media device ownership, media use, and interests. The final section sums up the findings and discusses the social implications.

A Landscape of China's Media Ecosystem

Since the Chinese Communist Party (CCP) took power in 1949, the Chinese mass media system has primarily functioned as a mouthpiece and a propaganda machine. The production and distribution of media products were highly centralized and controlled. However, the unprecedented economic growth resulting from the transition from a centrally planned economy to a market-driven economy since 1979 has created an enormous thirst for popular culture and media products. While the national state-run media outlets such as Xinhua, CCTV, and *People's Daily* continue to control a large share of China's media market, the provincial and local media industries, particularly in less politically sensitive domains such as sports, finance, and entertainment, have experienced exponential growth and have become increasingly commercialized. For example, the number of television channels has grown from 12 in 1965 to now more than 700 broadcast channels and over 3,000 cable channels nationwide. CCTV, which operates 21 public channels and 19 pay channels as of early 2012, remains the most powerful television network in China; but regional media giants such as Shanghai Media Group (SMG) and Hunan Broadcasting System are quickly catching up.

In addition to the dramatic growth of the domestic media industry, foreign media companies also heavily influence the Chinese media market. China began to selectively import popular culture products from non-communist countries in early 1980s. Between 1980 and 1990, the percentage of imported programs shown on Chinese TV grew from 10 percent to 30 percent. In the same period, the number of imported programs increased by more than 800 percent, from 21 programs from 11 countries to 174 programs from 23 countries (Wang & Chang, 1996). Into the 2000s, the proliferation of new television channels, DVD players, and internet-based video sharing services allowed imported programs to penetrate the Chinese media market more deeply. In addition to the omnipresent music and entertainment programs from Hong Kong, Taiwan, and the US, media entertainment in China also arguably came from a wider range of sources, with the growing popularity of Korean and Japanese popular culture in China.

The expansion of non-domestic cultural and media products in China did not occur without meeting any resistance. For the Chinese government, the task of modernizing and marketizing its media system is an intricate balancing act between allowing foreign media products to help ease the monstrous demands from its domestic market and maintaining a tight control over its media industries and market. Culturally, there is a fear of cultural imperialism—the idea that the one-way flow of Western media products would bring in undesirable foreign values and erode indigenous cultures (Boyd-Barrett, 1977; Lee, 1980; Schiller, 1976, 1989, 1991; Tunstall, 1977). Politically, the state-owned mass media in China have historically been used as mouthpieces for the Communist Party's agenda and policies. Although this function of the mass media has become less obvious in recent years in a market-oriented economy, the Chinese government is still concerned about losing its grip on citizens' ideological "purity" and the role of Western media in fostering democratic movements (Zhao, 1998, 2000, 2003). Economically, the government wants to protect the interest and profitability of China's domestic companies against the much more powerful and well-developed global media conglomerates.

To maintain control, the Chinese government implemented various protective measures. Prior to joining the World Trade Organization (WTO) in 2001, there was a tremendous concern that multinational media conglomerates would come in to gobble up China's domestic media outlets or to terminate the latter's monopolistic advantages; thus, domestic media outlets were organized by official decree into ever-larger "media groups," presumably to meet potential foreign competition (Lee, 2004). After joining the WTO, China was able to protect its media groups from foreign threat by excluding cultural fares from the organization's "open market access" rules. As a result, multinational media conglomerates have made very limited inroads directly into the Chinese market, especially in terms of owning news production companies. The influence of foreign media companies is largely limited to the forms of capital injections, joint ventures, partnerships, and special licensing. For example, the Chinese government granted limited TV broadcasting rights to Viacom, News Corp, and AOL Time Warner in the Guangdong Province and the Pearl River Delta Economic Zone in southern China. Viacom started a joint-venture TV deal to produce children's programming in Mandarin with SMG, and Warner Brothers started the first foreign joint venture to produce films in China in 2004. Direct access to foreign TV channels, such as HBO and CNN, is only permitted in hotels and apartment compounds where foreigners live. Meanwhile, China's domestic media groups, despite their cultural rhetoric to the contrary, have concentrated their efforts on maximizing profits without offending the authorities (Lee et al., 2006, 2007).

In addition to protecting the traditional media outlets, the Chinese government also conducts strict censorship. More than 60 internet regulations have been enacted, and censorship technologies are vigorously implemented by state-owned internet service providers (ISPs), business companies, and organizations (OpenNet, 2005). Some of the most popular websites in the world, such as Youtube.com and Facebook.com, are blocked in China. Google was forced out of the Chinese market in 2010 because of the company's unwillingness to comply with China's strict web censorship. Users of Wikipedia maintain a comprehensive list of banned foreign websites in China. Ironically, the popular online encyclopedia itself was among the victims of such government censorship.

In the broadcasting scene, the State Administration of Radio, Film and Television (SARFT), the government department in charge of regulating the broadcasting media in China, may also put forward specific measures from time to time limiting the use of imported programs by Chinese television stations. In 2012, SARFT banned all imported programs during prime time. The new rules also requested all stations to limit imported programs to no more than a quarter of a channel's programming each day. In 2014, Chinese authorities ordered two of the largest video-streaming websites to stop showing several legally licensed popular American TV shows.

Despite a plethora of control mechanisms, however, Chinese people continue to have access to foreign media content through various channels. Legally imported programs are widely available to Chinese viewers on their local TV channels. Carefully screened, censored, and dubbed by domestic production companies and broadcasters, these programs can be widely viewed by average Chinese people regardless of their income, education, and foreign language proficiency. In addition to this "koshered" foreign content, some Chinese people can directly view a number of pre-selected but uncensored foreign television channels in high-end hotels, or if they live in luxury residential compounds with foreign residents.

Millions of Chinese families have installed satellite dishes with direct access to hundreds of non-domestic TV channels, even though the government does not permit Chinese citizens to install satellite dishes and receivers at their homes. This is because the restriction on satellite dishes is difficult for local authorities to enforce when it only applies to Chinese citizens but not foreigners living in China and the returning overseas Chinese. Moreover, many "illegal" satellite dishes are manufactured by subsidiary companies operated by the Chinese government, such as the Ministry of Electronics, the Army, and the Ministry of Radio, Film and Television. Banning these dishes would mean a loss in profit for these state-run businesses (Severin, 1994). As such, use of satellite dishes is only "illegal" in the most superficial sense, and yet no one would want to lift the thin veil to reveal the real picture.

Finally, despite the introduction of copyright laws, media piracy is so common in China that pirated foreign TV programs and movies can be bought at nearly every street corner. Widespread access to broadband internet and online video sharing would also allow savvy computer users to download, view, and circulate foreign TV shows through new technologies such as file-sharing software and IPTV (Internet Protocol television). Although no reliable statistics are available, most observers would agree that pirated foreign movies and TV shows are now a part of many Chinese people's regular media diet.

Unlike 30 years ago, when Chinese audiences had only a few choices other than CCTV and the *People's Daily*, the new media era overwhelms audiences with a large pool of diverse choices. It is important to know audiences' choices and preferences. The following analysis can be considered as an attempt to fill this void in current research. Overall, we intend to answer four main research questions:

RQ1: To what extent people are connected to different types of broadcasting media and new media, including the internet and mobile phone?

RQ2: How frequently do Chinese people use broadcasting media and the internet?

RQ3: What are the most popular services among Chinese people when they are using television, radio, the internet, and mobile phones?

RQ4: How are demographic variables related to media use frequency?

Method

Data

The data of the study came from a national survey project titled *Social Change and Mass Media in Contemporary China* (Li et al., 2010), housed at Fudan University in Shanghai. A total of 37,279 nationally representative samples were interviewed via door-to-door interviews. The survey followed a multi-stage stratified random sampling design. Within each of the 31 provinces in Mainland China, samples were chosen from municipalities/ provincial capital city districts, prefecture-level cities/city districts, and counties or county-level cities (see the Appendix of this chapter for the detailed sample distribution). The survey was fielded between July 15 and October 23, 2010. The execution was contracted out to CSM Media Research, a leading television and radio audience research company. On average, a respondent took about an hour to finish the questionnaire interview. The response rates were 62 percent for provincial capital cities and 69 percent for other localities. Post-stratification weights were calculated based on age and gender to make the data more representative of the population.

Measures

Device Ownership

Device ownership was operationalized as to whether the respondent's household or the respondent possessed a particular type of media or communication device. Televisions, LCD televisions, set-top boxes, and dish satellite receivers were measured at the household level. Radio receivers, mobile phones, and internet connection devices were measured at the individual level. A dichotomous variable was created for each type of device.

Media Use

Media use was operationalized by three sets of questions that examined the frequency and duration of use. The first set of questions asked the respondents to indicate the number of days on a weekly basis they used television, radio, or the internet. The second set of questions asked the respondents to estimate the number of minutes on a typical day they used television, radio, or the internet. The third set of measurement items examined the detailed services or content each media or communication platform provided. For television and radio use, respondents were asked to provide the levels of attention they paid to local news, national news, international news, entertainment programs, lifestyle, commentary, and financial information. For the internet, respondents were asked to rate the frequency of use for 12 online activities, including news, search engines, video and music, gaming, browsing discussion forums/blogs, instant messengers, email, social media, creating content in discussion forums or on blogs, online shopping, banking, and circumvention tools. Finally, for mobile phone use, seven items were used: receiving and placing phone calls, short message services (SMSs), mobile phone apps, entertainment, mobile internet, radio via phone, and television via phone.

Demographics

Demographic variables included gender, age, education, income, and residential area (rural vs. urban). Gender was a dichotomous variable with female coded as larger. Age was a continuous variable. Education was an ordinal variable containing seven categories ranging from "no formal education" to "post-graduate degree." Personal income contained 48 categories—from "no income" to "100,000 RMB and above."

Findings

Our first research question examines the extent to which people are connected to different media technologies in China. Table 4.1 shows the penetration rates of different media devices. First of all, television's penetration rate is close to 100 percent and the difference between urban and rural areas is negligible. But LCD television is not yet widespread: only about 10 percent of the households in China possess LCD television sets and the percentage in urban areas is higher. Similarly, a large percentage of urban households own television set-top boxes and fewer than 10 percent of rural households do so. In contrast, almost a third of rural households have dish satellite receivers while very few urban household possess these. Only 8.2 percent of Chinese people possess a radio receiver and 72.5 percent use mobile phones. In terms of access to the internet, about 30 percent of the Chinese people are online. Obviously, the rural–urban gap of internet connection was huge—more than half of the urban residents are connected, compared to fewer than 20 percent of urban residents.

Our second research question concerns the frequency and duration of media use. According to Table 4.2, television is the most frequently used medium in China. More than six out of seven days in a week Chinese people watch television. On average, they spend more than 3 hours watching television every day. Radio is the least used broadcasting medium. For those who listen to the radio, they roughly spend an hour doing so. The urban–rural divide in terms of television use is relatively small. But there is a considerable gap between urban and rural residents in terms of their internet use.

Table 4.1 Broadcast Media Reception and Internet Penetration

	Urban (%)	Rural (%)	All (%)
Television (household)	98.6	97.9	98.1
LCD television (household)	17.5	6.8	9.8
Set-top box (household)	46.4	7.4	18.2
Dish satellite receiver (household)	4.0	32.0	24.3
Radio receiver	12.9	6.4	8.2
Mobile phone	85.0	67.7	72.5
Internet connection	50.2	18.2	27.0

Table 4.2 Broadcast Media and New Media Use Frequency

	Urban	Rural	All
Television (days per week)	6.28	6.30	6.29
Television (minutes per day, users only)	208.3	189.1	194.3
Radio (days per week)	1.26	0.58	0.77
Radio (minutes per day, users only)	72.5	80.3	76.9
Internet (days per week)	2.95	0.92	1.48
Internet (minutes per day, users only)	198.6	150.7	175.1

Our third research question concerns the popularity of different content and services offered by television, radio, the internet, and mobile phones. Table 4.3 shows the levels of attention people paid to different types of television content. Results show that local news, entertainment programs, and national news are the most popular television content. Commentary and finance were not given too much attention. A similar pattern was observed for radio content (see Table 4.4). The most frequently used internet services are instant messengers, news, search engines, and video/audio services (Table 4.5). The least frequently used services were online banking and circumvention tools. For mobile phone services, making and receiving phone calls and SMS were the dominant function whereas mobile phone's other functions were not widely used (see Table 4.6). Rural and urban residents were not very different in terms of the services

The last research question concerns the demographic predictors of media use, which are summarized in Table 4.7. Overall, demographic variables only explain a tiny portion of variance for television and radio use. In other words, how frequently one uses television or radio has little to do with one's demographic background. However, demographic variables accounted for almost 40 percent of the variance in

Table 4.3 Television Content Attention

	Urban	*Rural*	*All*
Local news	3.78	3.45	3.54
Entertainment program	3.37	3.14	3.20
National news	3.39	3.03	3.13
Lifestyle	3.17	3.07	3.09
International news	3.36	2.97	3.07
Commentary	2.47	2.18	2.26
Finance	2.17	1.80	1.90

Table 4.4 Radio Content Attention

	Urban	*Rural*	*All*
Local news	3.55	3.40	3.47
Entertainment program	3.19	3.08	3.13
National news	3.02	2.73	2.86
Lifestyle	3.05	3.03	3.04
International news	2.98	2.73	2.84
Commentary	2.23	1.97	2.08
Finance	2.12	1.77	1.92

Table 4.5 Internet Activity Frequency

	Urban	Rural	All
Instant messengers	3.69	3.94	3.81
News	3.66	3.00	3.34
Search engines	3.43	2.92	3.18
Online video/audio services	3.22	3.11	3.17
Online gaming	2.87	2.84	2.86
Browsing—discussion forums or blogs	2.10	1.65	1.88
Email	2.27	1.44	1.87
Social media	1.65	1.23	1.44
Content production—discussion forums or blogs	1.45	1.13	1.29
Online shopping	1.44	0.80	1.13
Online banking	1.10	0.46	0.79
Circumvention tools	0.23	0.15	0.19

Table 4.6 Mobile Phone Activity Frequency

	Urban	Rural	All
Receiving and placing phone calls	4.67	4.58	4.61
Short message services	3.29	2.56	2.80
Mobile phone apps	2.13	1.75	1.78
Entertainment	1.87	1.65	1.72
Mobile internet	1.07	0.66	1.64
Radio	0.39	0.19	0.90
Television	0.17	0.09	0.57

Table 4.7 Demographic Predictors of Television, Radio, and Internet Use

	Television	Radio	Internet
Gender (female)	0.014**	−0.030***	−0.022***
Age	0.034***	0.056***	−0.337***
Education	0.058***	0.083***	0.249***
Income	0.019**	0.141***	0.116***
Urban	−0.031***	0.076***	0.195***
R^2	0.3%	5.5%	38.5%

Note: $**p < 0.01$, $***p < 0.001$.

internet use frequency. The frequency of internet use highly depends on one's gender, age, education, income, and geographical region. Female respondents used television more frequently than male respondents, but they used radio and the internet less frequently. Older respondents used television and radio more frequently than younger respondents, who are frequent internet users. Both education and income are positively related to television, radio, and internet use. Urban residents used radio and the internet more frequently, but rural residents used television more.

Conclusion and Discussion

The current study aimed to understand Chinese audiences' patterns of broadcast and new media use by drawing upon data from a national survey. Largely descriptive notwithstanding, our study does make an important contribution, insofar as almost all previous audience studies in China have focused on a certain part of China, mostly developed coastal areas and cities, while our study paints a general picture of Chinese audiences based on a nationally representative sample. Without overinterpreting the descriptive statistics, some interesting patterns emerged from our findings.

First, despite 30 years of economic reform, as a whole, China seems to fall well into the category of developing countries. Almost every household owns a television set, yet LCD televisions, set-top boxes, radio receivers, and internet connections are not widespread. A large percentage of people rely on television as their source of information and entertainment. The low percentages of LCD televisions and internet connection are primarily due to the low average income the nation has. However, the limited spread of radio receivers and set-top boxes is more or less an indicator of the amount of resources put into the industries by the government. Radio has been the major means of communication as the country established itself. Political mobilization was realized through radio broadcasting, but later the development of radio programs was given little attention as television started to thrive. Today, frequent radio users are the elderly and those who own a car.

Second, our findings suggest that the distribution of media resources between rural and urban areas is extremely unbalanced. If we only look at first-tier city residents, China seems to be highly similar to any Western developed nation. However, when rural residents are taken into consideration, it is surprising to find that the internet penetration in rural areas was only around 20 percent. There exists a considerable urban–rural gap in terms of new media use. Nevertheless, this is not to say that rural areas are inferior to urban areas in every aspect. Interestingly, the penetration rate of satellite dishes in rural areas is more than 30 percent and that number for city dwellers was only 5 percent. While the law prohibits individuals from installing satellite receivers, rural residents seem to ignore such regulations. More importantly, the vast space rural residents possess easily accommodates a satellite dish. In contrast, it would be relatively difficult to receive satellite signals given the limitations of urban living space. But this does not mean that rural residents will be exposed more frequently to foreign channels and content. Given their low levels of education and limited foreign language capability, they spend little time on consuming foreign cultural products.

Third, our findings also suggest that the primary motivations for Chinese audiences to use media are to obtain local news and to seek entertainment. For internet users, the most popular functions of the internet are interpersonal communication and news reading. The proportion of internet users who use circumvention tools is very small. It is well known that the Great Firewall prevents Chinese people from accessing foreign social media and news websites. Both lack of interest and capability could be a reason for this.

To conclude, despite the diversification of media products in China, audience choice is quite homogeneous. Television is the dominant channel for the whole nation to obtain news information and acquire entertainment. Although the internet offers a far larger range of content, the existing digital divide between rural and urban residents, and between people with high and low socio-economic status, prevents the underprivileged from accessing the new media.

References

Boyd-Barrett, J. O. (1977). Media imperialism: Towards an international framework for an analysis of media systems. In J. Curran, M. Gurevitch, & J. Woollacott (Eds.), *Mass communication and society* (pp. 116–135). London: Edward Arnold.

Giddens, A. (1984). *The constitution of society: Outline of the theory of structuration*. Cambridge: Polity.

Li, L., Pan, Z., Lu, Y., Zhou, B., & National Residents Lifestyle and Media Use Survey Group. (2010). *National Residents Lifestyle and Media Use Survey*. Shanghai: Fudan University.

Lee, C. C. (1980). *Media imperialism reconsidered*. Beverly Hills, CA: Sage.

Lee, C. C. (2004). *Beyond Western hegemony: Media and Chinese modernity*. Hong Kong: Oxford University Press.

Lee, C. C., He, Z., & Huang, Y. (2006). Chinese Party Publicity Inc. conglomerated: The case of the Shenzhen Press Group. *Media, Culture & Society, 28*(5), 581–602.

Lee, C. C., He, Z., & Huang, Y. (2007). Party-market corporatism, clientelism, and media in Shanghai. *Harvard International Journal of Press/Politics, 12*, 21–42.

OpenNet. (2005). *Country profile: China (including Hong Kong)*. Online at http://opennet.net/country/china (retrieved October 1, 2008).

Shen, F., & Guo, S. (2013). The last refuge of media persuasion: News use, national pride and political trust in China. *Asian Journal of Communication, 23*(2), 135–151.

Shen, F., Lu, Y., Guo, Z., & Zhou, B. (2011). News media use, perceived credibility, and efficacy: An analysis of media participation intention in China. *Chinese Journal of Communication, 4*(4), 475–495.

Schiller, H. I. (1976). *Communication and cultural domination.* New York: International Arts and Sciences Press.

Schiller, H. I. (1989). *Culture, Inc.: The corporate takeover of public expression.* New York: Oxford University Press.

Schiller, H. I. (1991). Not yet the post-imperialist era. *Critical Studies in Mass Communication, 8*(1), 13–28.

Severin, W. J. (1994). The new cultural revolution: The spread of satellite dishes in China. *International Journal of Public Opinion Research, 6*(1), 72–76.

Tunstall, J. (1977) *The media are American.* London: Constable.

Wang, J., & Chang, T. K. (1996). From class ideologue to state manager: TV programming and foreign imports in China, 1970–1990. *Journal of Broadcasting & Electronic Media, 40*(2), 196–207.

Wang, N., Guo, Z., & Shen, F. (2011). Message, perception, and the Beijing Olympics: Impact of differential media exposure on perceived opinion diversity. *Communication Research, 38,* 422–445.

Zhao, Y. Z. (1998). *Media, market, and democracy in China: Between the party line and the bottom line.* Urbana and Chicago: University of Illinois Press.

Zhao, Y. Z. (2000). From commercialization to conglomeration: The transformation of the Chinese press within the orbit of the party state. *Journal of Communication, 50*(2), 3–26.

Zhao, Y. Z. (2003). "Enter the world": Neoliberal globalization, the dream for a strong nation, and Chinese press discourses on the WTO. In C. C. Lee (Ed.), *Chinese media, global context* (pp. 32–56). London: Routledge.

Appendix

Table 4.A Sample Distribution

	Municipality/ Provincial Capital City District	Prefecture-level City/City District	County/ County-level City	All
Anhui	504	310	401	1215
Beijing	736	0	391	1127
Chongqing	736	0	447	1183
Fujian	507	310	399	1216
Gansu	504	326	417	1247
Guangdong	510	309	411	1230
Guangxi	504	316	408	1228
Guizhou	505	312	399	1216
Hainan	504	315	400	1219
Hebei	504	309	399	1212
Henan	504	306	399	1209
Heilongjiang	504	316	416	1236
Hubei	504	317	406	1227
Hunan	504	310	400	1214
Jilin	504	313	412	1229
Jiangsu	504	310	400	1214
Jiangxi	503	308	398	1209
Liaoning	504	322	408	1234
Inner Mongolia	505	338	381	1224
Ningxia	504	308	400	1212
Qinghai	504	339	393	1236
Shandong	504	310	401	1215
Shanxi	504	325	418	1247
Shaanxi	504	313	412	1229
Shanghai	736	0	401	1137
Sichuan	505	307	398	1210
Tianjin	734	0	401	1135
Tibet	505	0	402	907
Xinjiang	503	321	410	1234
Yunnan	503	310	401	1214
Zhejiang	504	314	396	1214
Total	16560	8194	12525	37279

5

SENSATIONAL PICTURES

An Analysis of Visual Structure on Five
Transnational Arab News Channels

Michael D. Bruce

In 2005, the Project for Excellence in Journalism reported that we are
in the midst of unprecedented upheaval of news media. Over the last
two decades, the rapid convergence of satellite, fiber-optic, video, computer, and phone technologies has allowed the synchronous transmission
and rebroadcast, as well as asynchronous sorting and retrieval, of audio,
video, communication, and data on a global scale.

Pan-Arab Television

Nowhere is the interaction of new digital communication technologies and
their impact on society currently more interesting than in the Arab world.
For more than a decade, events have rippled through the Arab world like
a "political tsunami" powered by information and communication technologies (ICTs) (Cottle, 2011, p. 649). Recent buzz concerning digital
communication has focused on the influence of internet- and cellphone-
based communication and social networking technologies. This may help
explain why some experts argued that the 2011 political crises in Tunisia, Bahrain, Egypt, and Libya were "Twitter revolutions" (Zuckerman,
2011, p. 1). At the same time, television is often relegated to "traditional"
or "old" media status suggesting limited influence in today's social mediated world (Hoffman, 2006). While there is strong evidence to support
the influence of ICTs and social networking technologies in these recent
political uprisings (see Beaumont, 2011), Cottle (2011) and Pintak (2011a,
2011b) argue that satellite television is still an important communication
technology in the region.

The rise of pan-Arab media began rather inauspiciously in the late 1990s, but they have become a driving force in the region because of the rapid growth of independent satellite networks. Satellite television viewership has increased in the region over the last decade due to Arabs' media habits, the availability of relatively inexpensive direct broadcast satellite dishes, and the lifting of restrictions on satellite dish ownership among many nations in the region. For example, the BBC's David Lomax discovered that more than 7 million satellite dishes were purchased in Iraq in less than a year, following the fall of the Baathist regime (2005). An Iraqi sociologist said, "I thought Iraqis were hungry for food, but they were hungry for television" (as cited in Lomax, 2005, p. 2).

Kenny (2009) goes further by arguing television is the technology that will have the most profound effect on the planet. He refers to television as the "kudzu of consumer durables," noting that it is rapidly approaching ubiquity (p. 2). In addition, surveys reveal television still ranks as the most common source for international news. Fifty-eight percent of respondents to the 2011 Annual Arab Public Opinion Survey (Telhami, 2011) identified television as their primary source for international news, compared to 20 percent for the internet. During the Egyptian uprising in the Spring of 2011, 86 percent of respondents to an Egyptian survey conducted by the Broadcasting Board of Governors (BBG, 2011) listed television as the most used source of information about the protests and political developments. Pintak (2011b) argues that Arab satellite television is at the "vanguard of articulating" new political developments "that have fueled a sense of common cause among Arabs across the region every bit as real as the 'imagined communities' that are at the core of the concept of nation" (p. 1).

A 2010 survey (al-Failakawi, 2010) found 371 satellite channels operating on the Arabsat and Nilesat satellites. Several channels (e.g., Al Arabiya, Al Manar, Abu Dhabi) operate as 24-hour pan-Arab news channels. In addition to the numerous pan-Arab satellite networks, a number of international broadcasters are also beaming content into the region (e.g., Germany's Deutsche Welle, France 24, Russia TV Today, China Central TV, Alhurra, and BBC Arabic). Alhurra and BBC Arabic have been two of the most talked about Arabic-language foreign news channels.

These new Arab-controlled and technology-enhanced transnational television channels are allowing information to transcend artificial obstacles of language, culture, geography, and government. Many experts believe the impact of digital communication technologies, including satellite television, has helped facilitate new transnational connections among Arabs, with references to a new regional "public sphere" (e.g., Lynch, 2006, 2007). The term has been used synonymously for new transnational media and their role in creating shared identity of common interests, values, situations, and interdependence through new arenas of public discourse, which bypass traditional news gates and the elites of society, help people learn about and debate the issues that impact them, and reveal potential responses to those issues (Feenberg, 2002; Lynch, 2006).

Despite the proliferation of pan-Arab media outlets and corresponding peak of interest by foreign policy experts and media scholars, there has been a general lack of systematic investigation of the pan-Arab satellite news channels (Ayish, 2008). The present study is an attempt to fill the void by providing a theoretical examination of typical news visuals, as well as visuals from crisis coverage (e.g., the Arab Spring), on Arab satellite news channels. Five of the most widely discussed transnational satellite channels—Al Jazeera, Al Arabiya, BBC Arabic, Alhurra, and Al Jazeera English—broadcasting to and/or emanating from the Arab world were chosen for this analysis. This comparative analysis was conducted at two levels: (1) the individual network; and (2) through a two-dimensional taxonomy—western (BBC Arabic, Alhurra, and Al Jazeera English) and liberal commercial (Al Jazeera, Al Arabiya)—of pan-Arab stations.

Television News Visuals

News visuals have not received the same level of systematic research attention that has been devoted to the verbal, or textual, news elements (Graber, 1989; Matthes, 2009). Graber argues that ignoring visual news elements is detrimental to a complete understanding of the audiovisual message because the analysis not only loses the meaning contained in the visuals, but also misses the verbal meanings that are modified by the interaction of the visual content. Thus, as Grabe and Bucy (2009) explain, much of the meaning of television news is disregarded.

Television researchers have noted the twofold nature—content and structure—of audio/visual messages (Lang, 2000; Tuchman, 1978). The message content carries the manifest story information. This has traditionally been the basis of most research on TV news (Lang), and sensational television (Grabe et al., 2003).

Structural Features of TV News

Structural features of TV messages include music, sound effects, cuts, edits, luminance levels, movement, time manipulation (fast or slow motion), animation, zooms, pans, motion graphics, and field of view selections (Grabe et al., 2000; Lang et al., 1993; Tuchman, 1978). Scholars examining the structural features of images have struggled to find a theoretical home for their analysis. This is illustrated by the variety of theories—"videostyle" (Kaid & Davidson, 1986); cultivation (Newhagen & Lewenstein, 1992); vividness (Nisbett & Ross, 1980); and the limited capacity model (Grabe et al., 2003)—that have been applied to the examination of image content and sensational structural features. More recent examinations of structural news features have abandoned the traditional "bias" label for more descriptive labels of presentation elements, and their influence on audiences. For example, tabloid, or sensational, news packaging, which has traditionally been considered a form of bias resulting from content selections, has instead been operationalized as a structural feature (e.g., Grabe et al., 2000, 2001, 2003; Lang, 1995; Lang et al., 1996, 1999; Vettehen et al., 2005; Zhou, 2005).

Examinations of this sort are theoretically important due to the impact sensational content and structure can have on message comprehension and retention. For example, Grabe et al. (2003) found that the structural features of TV news influence how news content is processed. They suggest that sensational features cause audiences to perceive stories as less objective and less believable. Klijn (2003) notes that sensationalism boosts attention but reduces comprehension. Vettehen et al. (2005) applied the concepts of vividness theory and the limited capacity model to a content analysis of sensational production techniques in Dutch television newscasts. Results revealed a general trend of increased sensational production techniques on Dutch TV networks between 1995 and 2001. Silcock (2007) used field observations, interviews, and questionnaires to investigate cross-cultural differences in editing routines. His findings also suggest that news editors operate using cultural routines that result in stories that are visually structured for their specific cultural audience.

Hypotheses

In addition to cultural pressures, increased competition may affect the use of sensational production techniques in TV newscasts. Epstein (1973) stated that the primary purpose of TV news was not to inform, but to keep the audience interested enough to stay tuned in. Even though the majority of these networks are government funded, their continued operation is dependent upon the ability to attract and hold an audience. In some cases, news managers resort to sensationalism, which can be accomplished through the application of sensational production techniques. Therefore, it is expected that:

H1: News visuals on the liberal commercial networks will contain higher levels of sensational production techniques than on western networks.

Sensational journalism is designed to appeal to emotion and attract attention, and is driven by market pressures (Grabe et al., 2001; Graber, 2001). Vettehen et al. (2005) note that increased competition may put pressure on broadcasters to increase the attractiveness of their newscasts by utilizing technological innovation and journalistic routines. From its beginning, Al Arabiya has embraced technological innovation for the purpose of covering breaking news and creating newscasts which utilize cutting-edge production techniques. In addition, Al Arabiya—a for-profit network which relies on advertising revenue—was one of the first networks to consistently challenge Al Jazeera's audience share (BBG, 2011; Telhami, 2011). Due to the network's reliance on advertising, embrace of technological innovation, and competitive status in the marketplace, it is expected that:

H2: News visuals on Al Arabiya will contain higher levels of sensational production techniques than shots on the other networks.

The original intent of this project was to examine the visuals of "normal" or "routine" news coverage in transnational, pan-Arab television. While it was expected that there would be several major international news stories during the sample frame, it was impossible to predict in advance that a single issue—the Arab Spring—would have such an important impact on the news agenda for more than half of the sampling period.

The term Arab Spring refers to the political unrest that occurred throughout a wide swath of the MENA (Middle East and North Africa) region in late 2010 and early 2011. The first uprisings were centered in Tunisia in mid-December, 2010. The civil unrest quickly spread, as did the media coverage of these events. Because the coverage of the Arab Spring was so prevalent during the sample period, and because international crises provide unique opportunities to spotlight differences in visual news coverage (Fahmy, 2010), it seemed prudent to include some comparison of visuals from the Arab Spring coverage to the current study.

Coverage of political crises has often provided news organizations with opportunities to distinguish their programming from competitors (e.g., Al Jazeera's coverage of the 1998 Desert Fox Campaign). In a highly competitive media environment, efforts to attract and maintain an audience often include being the first to report breaking developments, providing visuals that give the audience "a sense of presence" (Cho et al., 2003, p. 312), and creating sophisticated packaging techniques to identify the story. As events drag on for weeks and sometimes months, sophisticated packaging techniques (identifying graphics, animation, music, and other production enhancements) are often employed to define the coverage. Based on the status of Al Jazeera and Al Arabiya as commercial stations in a highly competitive media environment, it is expected that:

H3: News visuals from the coverage of the Arab Spring on the liberal commercial networks will be more likely to contain elements of sensational structural features than in coverage on western-style networks.

From its inception Al Jazeera has shown a preference for emphasizing viewership over political and religious programming considerations. While similar trends are occasionally evident on transnational Saudi media, these outlets are simultaneously constrained by a strong state influence (Kraidy, 2012). Due to the hyper-competitive forces of Arab Spring coverage, and contravening political sensitivities of most of the networks, it is predicted that:

> H4: News visuals in Al Jazeera's coverage of the Arab Spring will be more likely to contain elements of sensational structural features than coverage on Al Arabiya, Alhurra, Al Jazeera English and BBC Arabic.

Method

A quantitative content analysis was conducted at two levels: (1) the individual network; and (2) through a two-dimensional taxonomy—western and liberal commercial—of pan-Arab stations. The five networks were chosen because they represent some of the most widely discussed examples of pan-Arab satellite news networks.

Network Taxonomy

The main characteristic used to determine the taxonomy[1] of each network was commercial status. The author borrowed the term liberal commercial from Ayish (2002) and used it to classify Al Jazeera and Al Arabiya since they were both originally conceived as commercial networks. The commercial undertones and resulting competitiveness of these networks tend to contribute directly to other characteristics found in the liberal model. Alhurra, BBC Arabic, and Al Jazeera English (AJE) are considered non-commercial international broadcast networks and therefore represent the western style. The term western was originally chosen to classify the western-based Alhurra and BBC Arabic networks. Considering the network's stated mission, it could be argued that AJE more appropriately fits into an entirely different dimension. However, AJE is considered western in this context due to the network's non-commercial status, intense effort to reach an international audience including the United States, and its attempts to distance itself in subtle ways from its Arabic-language sister station.

Sampling

The sample frame consists of more than ten months of news programming from August 1, 2010, to June 15, 2011. A one-hour late evening newscast was recorded live via satellite from Al Jazeera, Al Arabiya, AJE, and BBC Arabic on each weekday, and many weekends, for the duration of the sample period. Alhurra's[2] broadcasts are not available via satellite in the

United States. They were recorded from daily archives available on the Alhurra website. The goal was to create a sample that represents longitudinal "normal" or "routine" news coverage, and minimizes the impact of a single major news event on the sample.

A non-probability sample of three broadcasts was drawn from the entire sample frame using a random date generator to construct the sample of routine news coverage. The selected dates were Wednesday, December 29, 2010, Thursday, January 27, 2011, and Tuesday, June 14, 2011. The programming from all five networks was analyzed for each selected day in the sample resulting in 15 hours of content.

Measurement

Each story from the sample (n = 438) was also coded for Arab Spring coverage. Stories were coded Arab Spring if they contained coverage of the uprisings in Algeria, Bahrain, Egypt, Jordan, Libya, Syria, Tunisia, or Yemen. This coding resulted in an Arab Spring sample of 89 stories (22.6 percent) comprising 1,951 shots (29.6 percent).

Each story was coded into one of 17 possible story types that have been outlined in previous studies (e. g. Groshek, 2008). The 17 story types were collapsed into the following four dummy coded variables: (1) politics/crime (politics, political unrest/war/terrorism, military/national defense, crime/criminal justice/law); (2) business/technology (business/economics, technology, education, agriculture, accidents/natural disasters); (3) humanitarian (humanitarian/social problems, health care, race/religion/culture, ecology/environment); and (4) entertainment/other (oddities, sports, tease, undecided). These categories were included as control variables in the analysis with politics/crime as the reference category. This is a conservative assessment, which results in more confidence that the control variables are not interfering with the focus variables under investigation.

The unit of analysis for the hypotheses was the individual image or shot (n = 6,595). Using guidelines set forth by Keith et al. (2009), a shot was counted "each time the shot (subject) changed by video editing or, in the case of a pan, each time the subject changed" (p. 7). The breakdown of shots by network was Al Jazeera (n = 1,445); Al Jazeera English (n = 1,457); Alhurra (n = 1,431); BBC Arabic (n = 840)[3]; and Al Arabiya (n = 1,422).

Acquisition and Presentation Features

Structural features of newscast visuals were explored for all shots. Two scales of sensational structural features were developed, based on previous work by Grabe et al. (2001) and Vettehen et al. (2005), to consolidate findings from a number of individual indicators. Rather than relying on a multiplicity of elaborate scales, or the separate analysis of each individual variable, these indicators were divided into two groups: (1) acquisition features—zoom movements; eyewitness camera; extreme close-ups; dramatic sounds; high-angle shots; and low-angle shots—and (2) presentation features—decorative transitions; slow motion; visual enhancements; audio manipulations; graphics; animations; split screen or boxes; and monitor or video wall backgrounds. The indicators are dichotomous and were recorded as either present or absent in each shot.

Acquisition features refer to specific image characteristics that are established during the recording, or acquisition phase, of television news. These characteristics are generally the result of camera operation decisions. Zoom movements were coded present if either a zoom-in or zoom-out movement occurred in the shot. The eyewitness camera perspective, also referred to as subjective camera, occurs when a photographer takes the camera off the tripod and moves with the camera. The presence of eyewitness camera was coded if shaky video, or a movement of the camera with the action, was identified. Field of view refers to how close or far an object appears to be from the viewer. Presence of the extreme close-up (ECU) field of view was coded if a shot of a human face occupied more than one-third of the screen. High- and low-angle shots were included as separate indicators because each of these shots implies different meanings to the audience. Presence of a high-angle shot was coded if a subject was shot from above. Presence of a low-angle shot was coded if a subject was shot from below. Although technically not a visual element, dramatic sounds were also included as elements of sensational packaging. Dramatic sounds were coded as present if any of these sounds—exploding ammunition; gunshots; sirens; military vehicles; aircraft; people screaming, crying, yelling, or applauding—could be heard in the shot.

Presentation features refer to elements that are added to news items after acquisition, generally through editing (post-production), or as the visuals are presented on a newscast. The standard transition between shots in television news is the cut. Use of other types of transitions, including the dissolve, fade-in, fade-out, wipe, and flash, are less common and considered more sensational. Decorative transitions were coded present if one or more of these transitions were used between shots. Slow motion was coded present if the effect occurred in a shot. Visual enhancements refer to post-production techniques that are designed to draw attention to, or away from, particular elements in an image. These include the freeze frame, highlight, and mosaic. The presence of any one of these techniques in the shot was coded as a visual enhancement. "Audio manipulations" (Grabe et al., 2001, p. 288) refer to sound effects and music added to news items. Sound effects are sounds that have not been recorded during the acquisition phase, but are instead added during the post-production process. Audio manipulations were coded as present if either of these was added to a shot. A graphic was coded present if a full-screen image containing video, text, or photo-based images was shown. Animation was coded present if 2D or 3D images in motion were shown. Finally, split screen/boxes and monitor/video walls were included as sensational presentation features. Split screen/boxes are used to divide the audience's video screen into multiple display areas, with separate subjects in each area. The monitor/video wall effect refers to graphics or other visual elements that are presented on a video wall behind, or monitor next to, an anchor or interview subject. Monitor/video wall was coded present if compelling visual images appeared on the video wall or monitor. Generic background images, network logos, and cityscapes displayed on a monitor/video wall were not considered compelling and were therefore coded not present.

Coding and Reliability

Before coding could begin, the author, aided by a research assistant, determined the parameters of each news story and also the in and out (beginning and end) points for each shot. A codebook was developed as a reference for the coders to use to operationalize choices. After successfully completing training and pre-testing, the coding was conducted by the author and a second coder. For reliability purposes, 10 percent of the sample was double coded, to determine reliability scores. Agreement, using Krippendorff's alpha, was 0.97 for determination of Arab Spring content, 0.90 for story type, and 0.77 for both sensational presentation features and acquisition features.

Data Analysis

Multilevel linear regression was needed for analyzing the data since this sample was based on nested sources of variability. The unit of analysis, the shot, is nested within stories giving the data a multilevel, or hierarchical, structure. To ignore the structure of these data and collapse the data across the shots or to analyze the data without consideration for the multilevel structure could lead to an increase in either alpha (false positive) or beta (false negative) errors (Hox, 2002). Multi-level linear regression models—with controls for story type—were used to separately examine acquisition and presentation features for all four hypotheses. The Bayesian method, Markov chain Monte Carlo (MCMC), was used for fitting all multilevel models. Only the significant results are reported for each hypothesis.

Results

According to H1, shots on the liberal commercial networks would be more likely to contain sensational features than on the western networks. The multi-level linear regression model utilized a dummy coded taxonomy featuring western networks as the reference category. Statistically significant differences in the application of acquisition features between western and liberal networks were not found. In looking at sensational presentation features for H1 (see Table 5.1), entertainment/ other ($B = 0.64$, $SE = 0.08$, $p < 0.001$) was the only story type control variable found to vary significantly with the dependent variable. The implication is sensational presentation features were more likely in shots from entertainment/other stories than from politics/crime stories (reference category). In analyzing the hypothesis, sensational presentation features were found to differ significantly by network taxonomy. Use of sensational presentation features was more likely on the liberal networks ($B = 0.47$, $SE = 0.07$, $p < 0.001$) than on the western networks. Partial support for H1 is found for presentation features only.

H2 predicted visuals on Al Arabiya would be more likely to contain sensational elements than visuals on Al Jazeera, Al Jazeera English, Alhurra, and BBC Arabic. The five networks were dummy coded with Al Arabiya as the reference category in the regression model. Results from the model for acquisition features reveal no statistically significant differences. Once again, the presence of sensational presentation features (see Table 5.2) was more likely in shots from the entertainment/other story control group ($B = 0.67$, $SE = 0.08$, $p < 0.001$) than from the reference category (politics/crime). In terms of the hypothesized relationships, a significant difference was found between networks for sensational presentation features. The prediction Al Arabiya ($B = 1.60$, $SE = 0.08$, $p < 0.001$) would utilize more sensational presentation features than BBC Arabic ($B = -0.55$, $SE = 0.13$, $p < 0.001$), Al Jazeera ($B = -0.59$, $SE = 0.11$, $p < 0.001$), Al Jazeera English ($B = -0.67$, $SE = 0.10$, $p < 0.001$), and Alhurra ($B = -0.80$, $SE = 0.10$, $p < 0.001$) was confirmed. H2 is partially supported for presentation features, but not acquisition features.

H3 stated news visuals from coverage of the Arab Spring on liberal networks would more likely contain sensational features than visuals from western networks. The regression model featured a dummy coded taxonomy with western-styled networks as the reference category.

Table 5.1 Sensational Presentation Features by Network Taxonomy

Variable	B	SE	T	p
Constant	1.40	0.07	19.11	<0.001
Liberal commercial	0.47	0.07	−6.73	<0.001
Story type—Business/Technology	0.10	0.10	1.00	0.317
Story type—Humanitarian	−0.05	0.15	−0.30	0.764
Story type—Entertainment/Other	0.64	0.08	8.19	<0.001

Note: Shots ($n = 6,595$). Stories ($n = 438$). Iterations = 40,000. Burn-in = 2,000. The variance of the constant across stories is 0.48 ($\chi^2 = 153.42$, $df = 1$, $p < 0.001$).

Table 5.2 Sensational Presentation Features by Network

Variable	B	SE	T	p
Constant	1.60	0.08	19.75	<0.001
Al Jazeera	−0.59	0.11	−5.38	<0.001
Al Jazeera English	−0.67	0.10	−6.91	<0.001
Alhurra	−0.80	0.10	−8.18	<0.001
BBC Arabic	−0.55	0.13	−4.35	<0.001
Story type—Business/ Technology	0.11	0.10	1.10	0.273
Story type—Humanitarian	−0.00	0.14	0.02	0.983
Story type—Entertainment/ Other	0.67	0.08	8.74	<0.001

Note: Shots (n = 6,595). Stories (n = 438). Iterations = 75,000, Burn-in = 5,000. The variance of the constant across stories is 0.44 (χ^2 = 148.71, df = 1, p < 0.001).

Results from the model for acquisition features reveal no statistically significant differences. The examination of sensational presentation features for H3 reveals a significant relationship for only one control variable (see Table 5.3). As the presence of the entertainment/other story type (B = 1.39, SE = 0.24, p < 0.001) increased, the use of sensational presentation features also increased. In other words, sensational presentation features were more likely in entertainment/other type stories when compared to the reference category. As for the hypothesized relationship, significant differences were found in the use of sensational presentation features, providing partial support for H3. As predicted, the use of sensational presentation features was determined to be significantly more likely on liberal networks (B = 0.70, SE = 0.16, p < 0.001) than on western networks.

According to H4, Arab Spring visuals on Al Jazeera would be more likely to contain sensational structural features than Al Jazeera English,

Table 5.3 Presentation Features in Arab Spring Coverage by Network Taxonomy

Variable	B	SE	T	p
Constant	0.85	0.11	8.13	<0.001
Liberal commercial	0.70	0.16	4.45	<0.001
Story type—Business/Technology	−0.32	0.31	1.03	0.304
Story type—Humanitarian	−0.07	0.71	0.10	0.920
Story type—Entertainment/Other	1.39	0.24	5.87	<0.001

Note: Shots (n = 1,951). Stories (n = 89). Iterations = 95,000. Burn-in = 5,000. The variance of the constant across stories is 0.51 (χ^2 = 34.43, df = 1, p < 0.001).

Alhurra, BBC Arabic, or Al Arabiya. The five networks—dummy coded with Al Jazeera as the reference category—were analyzed for the presence of both sensational acquisition features and presentation features. The sensational acquisition features of Al Jazeera were found to differ significantly for only one network (see Table 5.4), BBC Arabic ($B = -0.42$, $SE = 0.15$, $p < 0.004$). The use of sensational acquisition features was determined to be significantly more likely on Al Jazeera than on BBC Arabic. In terms of presentation features, only limited support was found for the hypothesized prediction (see Table 5.5). First, an examination of the control variables reveals the entertainment/other control variable was more likely ($B = 1.40$, $SE = 0.24$, $p < 0.001$) to contain sensational presentation features when compared to the reference category. When evaluating the results of the hypothesis for sensational presentation features, only partial support for the predicted results was found. In this case, Al Jazeera was

Table 5.4 Acquisition Features in Arab Spring Coverage Between Networks

Variable	B	SE	T	p
Constant	0.89	0.11	8.06	<0.001
Al Jazeera English	0.19	0.17	1.16	0.248
Alhurra	−0.11	0.14	0.77	0.441
BBC Arabic	−0.42	0.15	2.86	0.004
Al Arabiya	−0.13	0.13	−1.00	0.317
Story type—Business/Technology	−0.32	0.18	1.80	0.072
Story type—Humanitarian	0.13	0.41	0.31	0.760
Story type—Entertainment/Other	0.09	0.16	0.56	0.574

Note: Shots ($n = 1,951$). Stories ($n = 89$). Iterations = 200,000. Burn-in = 5,000. The variance of the constant across stories is 0.13 ($\chi^2 = 19.42$, $df = 1$, $p < 0.001$).

Table 5.5 Presentation Features in Arab Spring Coverage Between Networks

Variable	B	SE	T	p
Constant	1.15	0.18	6.26	<0.001
Al Jazeera English	−0.21	0.28	0.76	0.445
Alhurra	−0.47	0.23	2.03	0.042
BBC Arabic	−0.18	0.25	0.71	0.478
Al Arabiya	0.68	0.22	3.13	0.002
Story type—Business/Technology	−0.20	0.30	0.66	0.510
Story type—Humanitarian	0.10	0.71	0.14	0.886
Story type—Entertainment/Other	1.40	0.24	5.89	<0.001

Note: Shots ($n = 1,951$). Stories ($n = 89$). Iterations = 200,000. Burn-in = 5,000. The variance of the constant across stories is 0.45 ($\chi^2 = 31.88$, $df = 1$, $p < 0.001$).

MICHAEL D. BRUCE

significantly more likely to air shots containing sensational presentation features than Alhurra ($B = -0.47$, $SE = 0.23$, $p < 0.042$), but significantly less likely to air shots containing sensational presentation features than Al Arabiya ($B = 0.68$, $SE = 0.22$, $p < 0.002$).

Discussion and Conclusions

Significant differences were not found in the sensational acquisition features—specific image characteristics that are established during the recording phase—used between western and liberal networks in routine or Arab Spring coverage, or between the individual networks in routine news. In Arab Spring coverage at the network level, significant differences were only found between Al Jazeera and BBC Arabic. BBC Arabic's Arab Spring coverage was found to be less likely to use sensational acquisition features than Al Jazeera. Differences in BBC Arabic's newscast formatting could account for some of these differences.

The lack of statistically significant differences in the use of sensational acquisition features was somewhat surprising. The author expected to see greater differences across the board in the application of these features because western—specifically American—TV news visuals generally conform to a standard set of codes (Tuchman, 1978). The eyewitness camera technique provides a good illustration of these codes. The frequent use of eyewitness camera has traditionally been discouraged in American TV newscasts because it violates what Tuchman (1978) referred to as visual neutrality. Therefore, it was expected that shots from the western networks would reflect this proclivity. However, eyewitness camera was heavily utilized in shots from all the networks in the sample. In summary, the visual structure of acquired content is not that different among these five transnational networks.

There are several possible explanations for the overall lack of difference in the use of acquisition features, particularly when it comes to conflict or breaking news coverage. First, the rather shaky, eyewitness camera appearance of some of the conflict footage may be the result of journalists getting so close to the action that it is impractical to achieve more stable and objective shots. Second, in some cases, this footage may have originated from laypersons using cellphones or amateur recording devices to capture the events rather than from professionally trained journalists. Third, the availability of news footage from breaking news events is often limited to a small number of sources. A network may not always have a news crew in an area where breaking news occurs. In such instances, a network may air footage acquired from another network, or a news agency. Finally, the cultural sensitivities and professional standards of media professionals at the various networks may not be as diverse as expected. Scholars have documented the significant numbers of both western-trained (BBC) and professional Lebanese journalists (Kraidy, 2012) spread throughout Arab media outlets. These factors have likely contributed to similar journalistic routines and codes for the acquisition of visuals at each of the transnational Arab networks.

Conversely, significant differences in the use of sensational presentation features were universally found. Presentation features are the "bells and whistles" of news production that are applied after shots are acquired and before they are delivered to the audience for viewing (Grabe et al., 2001). The results from the analysis of the hypotheses show liberal networks were more likely than western networks to apply sensational presentation techniques in both normal coverage and Arab Spring coverage. The analysis of presentation features reveals a distinct separation between western and liberal networks. Visuals on the liberal networks emphasized a more provocative production style reflected in attention-grabbing visual treatments, sound enhancements, and a quicker shot pace.

When comparing the individual networks, shots on Al Arabiya were more likely to emphasize sensational presentation features. These distinctions were also found to a lesser extent in Al Arabiya's Arab Spring coverage. The author had predicted that the competitive forces inherent in the coverage of the Arab Spring conflict and breaking news by competition-driven media outlets would lead to increased reliance on sensational presentation features by Al Jazeera. Contrary to expectations, this prediction was only partially supported. Instead, Al Arabiya's coverage utilized more sensational presentation features in Arab Spring coverage as well.

In retrospect, these findings should not be surprising in light of statements by Al Arabiya's management that their news product would emphasize technological innovation and "flashy graphics." A segment of story detailing an insurgent attack on a government compound in Baquba, Iraq, illustrates the network's commitment to technologically sophisticated news visuals. The story starts with full-screen video footage from the aftermath of the attack and then transitions to shots of the anchor standing in front of a large video wall in the studio. The anchor describes the attack while a montage of still images scrolls across the screen behind him. This transitions to a minute and a half-long visual re-enactment of the attack. The animated re-enactment illustrates the location of the attack and how the attack was carried out. The animation is complete with burning vehicles, exploding suicide bombers, and muzzle flashes from the weapons of insurgents and Iraqi military engaged in a firefight.

These sophisticated visual techniques are beyond the level of "flashy graphics." Instead this material "amuses, titillates, and entertains" (p. 637), which Grabe et al. (2001) define as sensationalism. The term sensational can be problematic due to the negative connotations associated with it. It is important to note that none of the individual variables making up these scales should necessarily always be considered sensational production elements on their own. Instead, these independent elements likely have a cumulative effect on sensationalism, which Klijn refers to as a "super-fluity of attention-getting devices" (2003, p. 127). Klijn suggests having multiple production features applied to a shot is more indicative of a sensational production style. Future research may benefit from the adoption of a term—such as visual prominence (Entman, 1993)—which carries less of a stigma.

Several caveats in relation to both the content and size of the sample should also be addressed. The design of this study called for examining every single shot from each newscast in the sample. This approach was undertaken to capitalize on the cumulative impact of images that may be repeated multiple times throughout a single newscast, or series of newscasts. While this holistic visual approach provides opportunity to include repetitive symbols in news coverage, it introduces other limitations. One limitation is that all visuals, regardless of type (e.g., graphics, animations, studio shots, field shots), were treated the same. Future research could make nuanced distinctions based on the type of visual using a visual prominence score similar to those utilized by Doyle (1982). The relatively small sample size introduces additional limitations. The purposive sample consisting of only three days was designed to make the project manageable. While the resulting 15 hours of programming provided thousands of images for the analysis, the three days are not a representative sample of visuals on pan-Arab TV news channels. Furthermore, two of the three randomly chosen dates were within a month of each other. Taken together, these limitations increase the likelihood that the presence of non-routine news events severely impacted the data.

Final Thoughts

One purpose of this volume was to examine the nature of broadcast programming and its delivery at home and abroad. This chapter reveals how the five pan-Arab TV networks have embraced the increased capabilities of digital acquisition and production technologies. However, the bulk of the differences in visual structure were primarily accentuated through the presentation process rather than through acquisition processes.

This research provides the beginning of an important area of inquiry into Arab news culture. The findings, while somewhat descriptive, provide important benefits over the anecdotal evidence often presented concerning pan-Arab media. Insights gained here can serve as building blocks for the future development of more sophisticated models of Arab broadcasting, which should be the ultimate goal. Thus, future attempts at building macro-theoretical frameworks of pan-Arab television must more fully account for the cultural, political, historical, technological, and competitive factors that shape each network.

Notes

1 The author recognizes the proposed categorization—liberal commercial and western-styled—may include contested terms. For example, neither Al Jazeera nor Al Arabiya is by definition a liberal media outlet. However, the liberal commercial label seemed appropriate within the context of the Arab media sphere and previous research. These terms were chosen simply to provide obvious distinction within the taxonomy. Nuanced taxonomy development like that undertaken by Rugh (2004) and Hallin and Mancini (2004) was beyond the scope of this project.

2 Alhurra revamped its daily news show *The Global* with a new look during the sample period. Alhurra newscasts in the sample include the old (two shows) and new (one show) visual styles. The new style featured new graphics, decorative enhancements, and other production features. An analysis based only on newscasts featuring the new look could lead to different results from those presented here.

3 BBC Arabic's reliance on in-studio interviews and analysis resulted in coverage of fewer stories and fewer shots than the other networks.

References

al-Failakawi, Y. (2010). Media changes in the Middle East: The first decade of the 21st century. Paper presented at the meeting of the Broadcast Education Association, Las Vegas, NV, April 15.

Ayish, M. I. (2002). Political communication on Arab world television: Evolving patterns. *Political Communication, 19*, 137–154.

Ayish, M. I. (2008). Arab world media content studies: A meta-analysis of a changing research agenda. In K. Hafez (Ed.), *Arab media: Power and weakness* (pp. 105–124). New York: Continuum.

Beaumont, P. (2011). The truth about Twitter, Facebook and the uprisings in the Arab world. *The Guardian*, February 25. Online at www.guardian.co.uk/world/2011/feb/25/twitter-facebook-uprisings-arab-libya (retrieved March 14, 2011).

Broadcasting Board of Governors. (2011). *Media consumption during the uprising in Egypt*. Washington, DC: Author.

Cho, J., Boyle, M. P., Keum, H., Shevy, M. D., McLeod, D. M., Shah, D. V., & Pan, Z. (2003). Media, terrorism, and emotionality: Emotional differences in media content and public reactions to the September 11th terrorist attacks. *Journal of Broadcasting & Electronic Media, 47*, 309–327.

Cottle, S. (2011). Media and the Arab uprisings of 2011: Research notes. *Journalism, 12*, 647–659.

Doyle, P. K. (1982). A descriptive study of bad–good news content in television newscasts. Unpublished master's thesis, University of Tennessee, Knoxville.

Entman, R. M. (1993). Framing: Toward clarification of a fractured paradigm. *Journal of Communication, 43*(4), 51–58.

Epstein, E. J. (1973). *News from nowhere*. New York: Random House.

Fahmy, S. (2010). Contrasting visual frames of our times: A framing analysis of English- and Arabic-language press coverage of war and terrorism. *The International Communication Gazette, 72*, 695–717.

Feenberg, A. (2002). *Transforming technology: A critical theory revisited*. New York: Oxford University Press.

Grabe, M. E., & Bucy, E. P. (2009). *Image bite politics: News and the visual framing of elections*. New York: Oxford University Press.

Grabe, M. E., Lang, A., & Zhao, X. (2003). News content and form: Implications for memory and audience evaluations. *Communication Research, 30,* 387–413.

Grabe, M. E., Zhou, S., & Barnett, B. (2001). Explicating sensationalism in television news: Content and the bells and whistles of form. *Journal of Broadcasting & Electronic Media, 45,* 635–655.

Grabe, M. E., Zhou, S., Lang, A., & Bolls, P. D. (2000). Packaging television news: The effects of tabloid on information processing and evaluative responses. *Journal of Broadcasting and Electronic Media, 44,* 581–598.

Graber, D. A. (1989). Content and meaning. What's it all about? *American Behavioral Scientist, 33,* 142–155.

Graber, D. A. (2001). *Processing politics: Learning from television in the Internet age*. Chicago: The University of Chicago Press.

Groshek, J. (2008). Homogenous agendas, disparate frames: CNN and CNN International coverage online. *Journal of Broadcasting & Electronic Media, 52,* 52–68.

Hallin, D. C., & Mancini, P. (2004). *Comparing media systems: Three models of media and politics*. New York: Cambridge University Press.

Hoffman, B. (2006). *Inside terrorism*. New York: Columbia University Press.

Hox, J. (2002). *Multilevel analysis: Techniques and applications*. Mahwah, NJ: Lawrence Erlbaum Associates.

Kaid, L. L., & Davidson, J. (1986). Elements of videostyle: Candidate presentation through television advertising. In L. L. Kaid, D. Nimmo, & K. R. Sanders (Eds.), *New perspectives on political advertising* (pp. 184–209). Carbondale, IL: Southern Illinois University Press.

Keith, S., Schwalbe, C. B., & Silcock, B. W. (2009). Visualizing cross-media coverage: Picturing war across platforms during the U.S.-led Invasion of Iraq. *Atlantic Journal of Communication, 17,* 1–18.

Kenny, C. (2009). Revolution in a box. *Foreign Policy*, November/December. Online at www.foreignpolicy.com/articles/2009/10/19/revolution_in_a_box (retrieved January 10, 2010).

Klijn, M. E. (2003). Attention-getting and comprehension-raising attributes in visuals in Dutch and American, public and private television news about violence. *Journal of Broadcasting & Electronic Media, 47,* 124–144.

Kraidy, M. M. (2012). The rise of transnational media systems: Implications of pan-Arab media for comparative research. In D. C. Hallin & P. Mancini (Eds.), *Comparing media systems beyond the Western world* (pp. 177–200). New York: Cambridge University Press.

Lang, A. (1995). Defining audio/video redundancy from a limited-capacity processing perspective. *Communication Research, 22,* 86–115.

Lang, A. (2000). The limited capacity model of mediated message processing. *Journal of Communication, 50,* 46–70.

Lang, A., Bolls, P. D., Potter, R. F., & Kawahara, K. (1999). The effects of production pacing and arousing content on the information processing of television messages. *Journal of Broadcasting & Electronic Media, 43,* 451–475.

Lang, A., Geiger, S., Strickwerda, M., & Sumner, J. (1993). The effects of related and unrelated cuts on television viewers' attention, processing capacity, and memory. *Communication Research, 20*(1), 4–29.

Lang, A., Newhagen, J., & Reeves, B. (1996). Negative video as structure: Emotion, attention, capacity and memory. *Journal of Broadcasting & Electronic Media, 40*, 460–477.

Lomax, D. (2005). Iraq's television revolution. *Newsnight,* February 25. London: British Broadcasting Company. Online at http://news.bbc.co.uk/1/hi/programmes/newsnight/4298455.stm (retrieved March 13, 2013).

Lynch, M. (2006). *Voices of the new Arab public: Iraq, Al-Jazeera, and Middle East politics today.* New York: Columbia University Press.

Lynch, M. (2007). Arab arguments: Talk shows and the new Arab public sphere. In P. Seib (Ed.), *New media and the new Middle East* (pp. 101–118). Basingstoke, UK: Palgrave Macmillan.

Matthes, J. (2009). What's in a frame? A content analysis of media framing studies in the world's leading journals. *Journalism & Mass Communication Quarterly, 86*(2), 349–367.

Newhagen, J. E., & Lewenstein, M. (1992). Cultivation and exposure to television following the 1989 Loma Prieta earthquake. *Mass Communication Review, 19*(1–2), 49–56.

Nisbett, R., & Ross, L. (1980). *Human inference: Strategies and shortcomings of social judgment.* Englewood Cliffs, NJ: Prentice-Hall.

Pintak, L. (2011a). Arab media revolution spreading change. *CNN,* January 31. Online at http://edition.cnn.com/2011/OPINION/01/29/pintak.arab.media/?hpt=Sbin (retrieved February 15, 2011).

Pintak, L. (2011b). The Al Jazeera revolution. *Foreign Policy,* February 2. Online at www.foreignpolicy.com/articles/2011/02/02/the_al_jazeera_revolution (retrieved March 5, 2011).

Project for Excellence in Journalism. (2005). Overview—Intro. *The State of the News Media.* Online at http://stateofthemedia.org/2005/overview/ (retrieved January 14, 2014).

Rugh, W. A. (2004). *Arab mass media: Newspapers, radio, and television in Arab politics.* Westport, CT: Praeger.

Silcock, B. W. (2007). Every edit tells a story sound and the visual frame: A comparative analysis of videotape editor routines in global newsrooms. *Visual Communication Quarterly, 14*(1), 3–15.

Telhami, S. (2011). 2011 Arab Public Opinion Poll. *Brookings Institution,* November 21. Online at www.brookings.edu/research/reports/2011/11/21-arab-public-opinion-telhami (retrieved January 21, 2012).

Tuchman, G. (1978). *Making news: A study in the construction of reality.* New York: The Free Press.

Vettehen, P. H., Nuijten, K., & Beentjes, J. (2005). News in an age of competition: The case of sensationalism in Dutch television news, 1995–2001. *Journal of Broadcasting & Electronic Media, 49*, 282–295.

Zhou, S. (2005). Effects of arousing visuals and redundancy on cognitive assessment of television news. *Journal of Broadcasting & Electronic Media, 49*(1), 23–42.

Zuckerman, E. (2011). The first Twitter revolution? *Foreign Policy,* January 15. Online at www.foreignpolicy.com/articles/2011/01/14/the_first_twitter_revolution (retrieved February 21, 2012).

6

TELEPRESENCE AND IMMERSION WITH ULTRA-HIGH-DEFINITION DIGITAL DISPLAYS

Background and Future Directions
for Research

Peter B. Seel

Introduction

Television and video displays have evolved over the past 80 years from crude circular cathode-ray tubes in the 1930s to very large 60- to 70-inch LCD models which are now ubiquitous. In a related development, most motion picture theaters in the United States (with screens that range in width from 30 to 90 feet) now feature digital video projection systems, so even "movies" are now digital. A recent television development has been the creation of "4K" Ultra-High-Definition Television (UHDTV) displays that feature more than 4,000 pixels in screen width. Not to be outdone, the Japan Broadcasting Company (NHK) demonstrated in 2013 a Super High-Vision (SHV) "8K" camera and a linked 8K LCD display at the National Association of Broadcasters (NAB) trade show that featured spectacular projected footage of the 2012 Olympics in London captured with the new SHV camera (Seel, 2013). On the other end of the digital display size scale, a new head-mounted display (HMD) technology developed by Oculus Rift features an ultra-wide 110-degree (diagonal) angle of view.

What these widely diverse display technologies have in common is the *potential* for creating a greater sense of viewer immersion in program content. They achieve this phenomenon by physically filling the viewer's peripheral frame of view by either getting them to sit closer to a high-resolution display or placing it right in front of the viewer's eyes, as the

Oculus Rift 3D HMD does. This chapter will review the evolution of wide-screen images for film and television technologies, analyze the recent development of wide-angle HMD and "ultra" 4K and "super" 8K high-definition display systems, assess the implications for greater viewer immersion in digital video and television content, and suggest possible focal areas for future telepresence research.

Telepresence and Immersion Defined

Presence is defined by *Merriam-Webster* as "the fact of being in a particular place: the state of being present" (2013). Electronic telecommunication and video games have made it possible to be "present" in environments that are distant for television audiences—or virtual in the case of game players.

Research into presence (Biocca & Delany, 1995; Held & Durlach, 1992; Kim & Biocca, 1997; Lombard & Ditton, 1997) can be summarized by Kim & Biocca's (1997) definition that a key determinant of telepresence in a "mediated environment is the user's sensory immersion into the mediated information." Telepresence has also been defined as a sense of being present in a mediated virtual environment (Held & Durlach, 1992; Kim & Biocca, 1997; Steuer, 1992).

Other researchers have found that larger screen sizes and closer viewing distances are also factors that influence the viewer's sense of telepresence. Higher resolution displays (at 1,920; 3,840; and 7,680 pixels in screen width) facilitate closer viewing distances. Interlace display artifacts that were apparent with low-resolution NTSC video (such as dot-crawl) are not visible with progressively scanned high-resolution screens. Closer viewing distances yield a wider angle of view and wide-screen 16:9 HDTV displays create an aspect ratio that is better suited for side-by-side binocular human vision. Figure 6.1 illustrates that wide-screen high-resolution HDTV displays allow viewers to sit as close as three screen heights away with a 30-degree angle of view compared with a low-resolution 4:3 NTSC display with a recommended viewing distance of seven screen heights (Seel & Dupagne, 2004).

Digital 3D displays further enhance a sense of immersion by adding depth to televised images that are essentially flat in two dimensions. Human binocular vision inherently provides a sense of depth that was essential for our survival as a species as both hunters and as potential prey for larger carnivores (Seel, 2010). Our peripheral vision is sensitive to motion at the margins, whether that might be a tiger leaping toward us out of the darkness or a tossed ball approaching our head. One might make the case that 3D imagery is natural for humans to view as it mimics our binocular view of the world, while 2-D images are an artificial construct where producers have to work to create Zettl's Z-axis for implied image depth on a flat screen (Zettl, 2013). Humans enjoy seeing images in three dimensions, as anyone who recalls using a childhood View-Master™ toy will attest. Almost all animated theatrical films produced at present are being delivered in 3D, as audiences have come to expect the immersion that 3D motion images provide to audiences in theaters and those at home with 3D televisions. Sales of 3D television displays since 2010 have been a disappointment to manufacturers (Seel, 2012), but it is only a matter of time until all larger (42-inch or greater in diagonal screen size) digital TV sets include 3D display capability built-in, with an on-off switch for a 3D picture included in the remote control.

Television Before the Advent of HDTV

The first cathode-ray tube television displays were essentially the bottom of a glass beaker coated with phosphors and scanned by a beam of electrons from the closed neck of the tube. Some of the first console televisions were a circular display housed in large wooden cabinets that contained the electronic equipment needed to present one or two local television channels and their sound signals (Fisher & Fisher, 1996).

In 1929, Vladimir Zworykin, a Russian-born engineer working for RCA, developed and patented a round "Kinescope" television display tube that was revolutionary at the time (Figure 6.2). At the same time in a small San Francisco laboratory, Philo Farnsworth had perfected a working all-electronic television camera and Oscillite display (Fisher & Fisher, 1996). Both systems were remarkably crude and low-resolution when compared with the analog NTSC (National Television System Committee) television standard, but they worked and a 60 year-long race was on to improve the resolution and screen size of television displays.

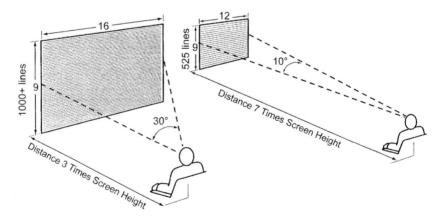

Figure 6.1 A wider angle of view is facilitated by a wide-screen 16:9 aspect ratio and sitting closer to the display.

The point is that television was originally designed to be looked *at* across a room as a piece of home furniture and, until the recent development of very large flat-screen HDTV displays and digital projectors, television viewing was not an immersive experience. However, as flat-screen and projection technologies enable ever-larger displays with 4K and even 8K image resolution, the potential to mimic the immersive capability of theatrical motion picture presentations will increase. Motion picture producers and game developers have noted the immersive potential of these large displays and are creating program and game content that will capitalize on these ultra-high-definition technologies.

The Development of Cinerama, CinemaScope, and Other Wide-Screen Motion Picture Technologies

It is ironic that television manufacturers are today attempting to replicate steps taken by the motion picture industry in the 1950s to compete with the threat posed by television in siphoning away movie audiences. To differentiate their images, film studios began to experiment with technologies that might enable the production and projection of wide-screen images in

Figure 6.2 Vladimir Zworykin demonstrates an early cathode-ray tube display in 1934. The tube in this model was mounted face up so that its reflection in a mirror mounted under the lid could be viewed by more than one person at a time.

Source: The Smithsonian Institution.

97

both 35mm and 70mm formats. Examples of such innovative technologies include wide-screen CinemaScope (in 1953) and VistaVision (in 1954) in both formats, and the 70mm Todd-AO format used by producer Michael Todd to shoot and project the film *Around the World in 80 Days* in 1956. Cinerama film technology was first commercially displayed in 1952 in New York City and used three 35mm projectors aimed at a massive rectangular screen (100 feet wide and 35 feet high) using a 2.65:1 aspect ratio for the combined three images (Seel, 2013). The first film produced using the new technology, *This is Cinerama*, featured a filmed roller-coaster ride that had audience members groaning at the visceral telepresence sensation it induced. As *New York Times* critic Bosley Crowther noted in his October, 1952 review of the film:

> Somewhat the same sensations that the audience in Koster and Bial's Music Hall must have felt on that night, years ago, when motion pictures were first publicly flashed on a large screen were probably felt by the people who witnessed the first public showing of Cinerama the other night. The shrill screams of the ladies and the pop-eyed amazement of the men when the huge screen was opened to its full size and a thrillingly realistic ride on a roller-coaster was pictured upon it, attested to the shock of the surprise. People sat back in spellbound wonder as the scenic program flowed across the screen. It was really as though most of them were seeing motion pictures for the first time . . . the effect of Cinerama in this its initial display is frankly and exclusively "sensational," in the literal sense of that word.

Crowther noted that much of the impact of the wide-screen display was due to the fact that the image filled much of the viewer's peripheral vision. This was most viscerally experienced in rapid motion sequences where the Cinerama camera was mounted in the front of a roller-coaster (see Figure 6.3) or in an airplane flying over the edge of Niagara Falls. The point-of-view camera put the audience members in the front seat of the roller-coaster as it sped over the track and created a visceral sensation similar to an actual ride. Such dramatic visceral effects later became a staple of ultra-wide-screen technologies such as 70mm IMAX films, which filled the viewer's peripheral vision with a relatively close massive square screen.

The Wide-Screen IMAX Phenomenon

Much like Cinerama, the IMAX motion picture system (a portmanteau of Image MAXimum) was designed to provide an immersive viewing experience. Using innovative motion picture technology developed in Canada,

Figure 6.3 The point-of-view camera position on a roller-coaster in the film *This Is Cinerama*. This still image does not convey the immersive aspect of the enormous 100-foot-wide curved screen which filled a viewer's peripheral vision.

the first IMAX film was shown at Expo 70 in Osaka, Japan. IMAX inventor Graeme Ferguson stated that the purpose of the large image was to fill the field of view of the audience (Disse, 2013). The IMAX 70mm film frame is ten times larger than that of 35mm film and has an almost square

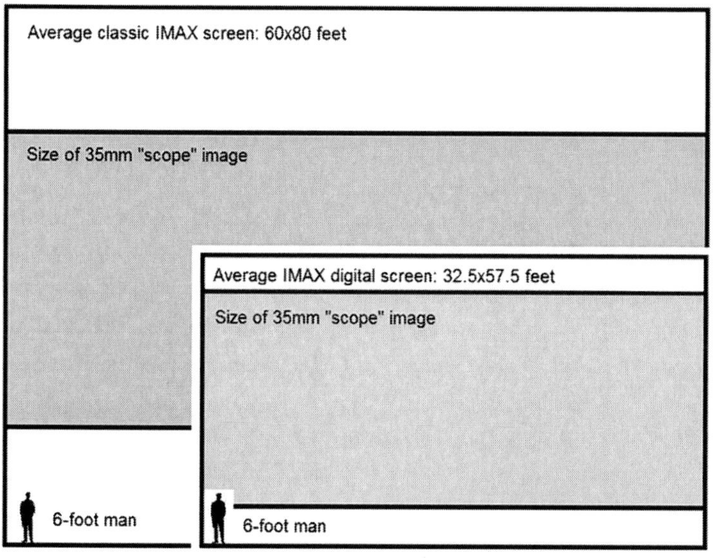

Average classic IMAX screen: 60x80 feet

Size of 35mm "scope" image

Average IMAX digital screen: 32.5x57.5 feet

Size of 35mm "scope" image

6-foot man

6-foot man

Figure 6.4 "Classic" analog IMAX screen size compared with digital IMAX and 35mm screens. Diagram from the *LF Examiner*. © 2012 Energetics LLC.

aspect ratio (*Film Format Facts*, 2013) (Figure 6.4). However, it wasn't until the 1976 creation of a huge IMAX screen 86 feet wide and 66 feet high in the then-new National Air and Space Museum in Washington, DC that some viewers first experienced visceral motion sickness while watching the IMAX film *To Fly!* The use of the larger screen filled the viewer's peripheral vision horizontally and vertically with aerial motion sequences such as flying over the edge of the Grand Canyon, which produced a dramatic sense of telepresence that made some motion-sensitive viewers ill. For most viewers, however, the massive wide-screen aerial images produced a vivid sensation of flying virtually over multiple US landmarks. *To Fly!* is the longest running film in the history of the Air and Space Museum and for many visitors it was their first memorable viewing of an IMAX film.

The Development of Large UHDTV Displays

One of the most easily visible hallmarks of high-definition television technology was its 16:9 (or 1.78:1 in film parlance) wide-screen aspect ratio. It was chosen by the NHK, the developers of HDTV technology, as a compromise between the 1.85:1 aspect ratio of modern motion picture formats and the 1.33:1 aspect ratio of older SECAM, PAL, and NTSC analog television standards (Seel & Dupagne, 2010).

Over the past 15 years, HDTV displays have steadily grown in size as LCD technologies have gradually supplanted that of plasma displays and manufacturing costs have dropped for larger screen sizes. At present, the largest LCD set sold in the world is a 90-inch (diagonal) LCD-LED model manufactured by Sharp Electronics and introduced at the 2013 Consumer Electronics Show in Las Vegas, Nevada (Figures 6.5 and 6.6). Sharp also makes a 60-inch 4K LCD model that displays 3,840 pixels in screen width by 2,160 pixels in height (for 8,294,400 total pixels) in the ultra-high-definition display (Ulanoff, 2013). As these large UHDTV

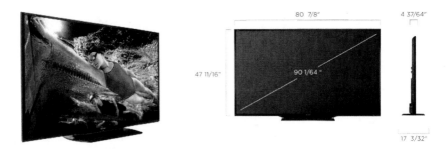

Figures 6.5 and 6.6 Sharp's 90-inch Aquos LCD-LED television with dimensions at right—the 2014 price is $9,200.

100

models become available to researchers, one possible area for investigation is to study the viewer's sense of presence at varied distances from the screen and with diverse types of content (action vs. static, televised vs. filmed). One might hypothesize that reduced viewing distances used with very large UHDTV displays might yield a greater sense of telepresence in viewers by filling their peripheral vision, similar to that experienced by IMAX 70mm film viewers compared with conventionally projected 35mm films on smaller motion picture screens.

OLED Technology and Cisco's "Fresco" Proof-of-Concept

The next step in the expansion of screen size to enhance telepresence in viewers may be to "tile" displays in a video wall configuration. This is not a new concept, but has been used for the past two decades to create very large multi-screen displays for expansive public areas. At the 2013 NAB show, Cisco displayed their innovative "Fresco" technology, which tiled 50-inch LCD monitors in a wall-sized array five screens wide by two screens high (Figure 6.7). Cisco predicts that emerging organic light-emitting diode (OLED) display technology will allow multiple screens to be "tiled" together, eliminating the visible bezel between the displays. OLED screens can be produced as thin films that would lend themselves to be being mounted on a glass substrate without gaps

Figure 6.7 Simon Parnall demonstrates Cisco's multi-screen "Fresco" display technology to a group of telecommunication executives at the 2013 NAB Show. Note that the weather forecaster in the multi-screen image is almost life-size compared with Parnall. Photo by the author.

101

between the displays. In theory, if tiling OLED screens proves to be practical, video displays could be created in very large sizes, perhaps approaching the size of the massive LED screens at the AT&T Stadium in Dallas, Texas.

One unique factor in the Fresco demonstration suite at the NAB Show in 2013 was the relative proximity of the seating area to the multi-screen array. A large couch (identical to one that might be commonly found in a home television room) was placed barely 6 feet in front of the monitors to enhance the telepresence of the program content for a small number of viewers—typically less than six at a time in the small Fresco demonstration "living room" (Seel, 2013). Placing the viewer 6 feet from an extremely wide display had the desired effect of enhancing a sense of presence and immersion even though the program content was conventional television fare: a weather forecast, a cooking show, and the NBA All-Star Game. The action inherent in fast-paced sports such as basketball, soccer, tennis, and American football means they might lend themselves to more immersive viewing by increasing screen sizes and moving the viewer closer to a higher-definition screen. Again, the key—as with an IMAX film—is to fill the viewer's peripheral vision to enhance the sense of presence in the scene being shown.

Figure 6.8 In his Fresco demonstration, Simon Parnall points to a list of ingredients for a recipe being prepared on the television program *MasterChef*. The ingredients and the Twitter feed are displayed on the wall-sized screen as "connected" or over-the-top (OTT) digital content distributed via internet broadband and linked to the primary broadcast program. Photo by the author.

It was a proof-of-concept exhibit designed to demonstrate how over-the-air broadcast programs could be displayed simultaneously with over-the-top (OTT) content accessed from the internet (Figure 6.8). In this example, the cooking show *MasterChef* was synchronized with recipe ingredients and a Twitter feedback loop, both accessed from the internet. The demonstration did not take full advantage of the large multi-screen display in an effort to enhance immersion or telepresence, but rather to show how the large screen could be divided in combining a large broadcast image with supplemental OTT content, or even very low definition black-and-white video from a baby monitor camera in a nursery in the same home. However, the wide-screen "real estate" of the ganged five-by-two monitors would lend itself to creating a home or business version of an IMAX theater in terms of powerful telepresence and viewer immersion in the images shown on it. Imagine the widescreen view, from a front-row seat on the twelfth green on the Augusta National Golf Course for the annual Masters Tournament, that would take in all of the Amen Corners' holes 11, 12, and 13 in one frame.

Small Immersive Digital Displays—the Oculus Rift HMD

At the far opposite end of the digital display spectrum is the new Oculus Rift head-mounted display (HMD) designed for immersive video game play. Set to go on sale in 2016 at a cost of around $300, it is revolutionary in terms of its ultra-wide 110-degree field of view compared with other HMDs (Figures 6.9 and 6.10). Video games are designed to be immersive

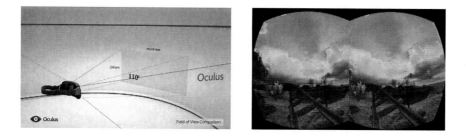

Figures 6.9 and 6.10 The Oculus Rift head-mounted display yields a 110-degree equivalent field of view that fills the peripheral vision of the game player wearing it. Note that the Oculus Rift-compatible game imagery displayed at right is almost square in its aspect ratio, much like the original 70mm IMAX format. The presence-inducing scene is of a roller-coaster-like ride that invokes similar stomach-churning scenes in *This Is Cinerama* and one of the first IMAX films, *To Fly!*

environments and the Oculus Rift was developed to enhance that sense of presence in these virtual worlds. Video game and communication technology reviewers have been enthusiastic in their coverage of the development of the new technology, from its birth as a Kickstarter-funded prototype developed by Palmer Luckey at the University of Southern California to demonstrations of the first consumer models at game developer conferences in 2014 (Rubin, 2014).

If immersion in finely detailed virtual worlds is the sine qua non of successful video games, the development of a low-cost, high-resolution (1,080p in the latest model) HMD has the global game community waiting impatiently for the Oculus Rift to finally go on sale for consumers. For telepresence and immersion researchers, the new technology will provide a low-cost means of studying a key demographic of young consumers deeply immersed in game play. The technology may also have applications for the treatment of phobias by safely simulating the feared stimulus and gradually desensitizing the patient. However, game reviewers who have used the Oculus Rift HMD in technology convention settings have commented on the fact that games with frightening elements may be too intense for some players due to its immersive nature. Experienced game players had to take their HMDs off at especially scary points in the games being played (Klepek, 2013). It appears that the level of immersion may be too intense for some content. The social media site Facebook made a significant $2 billion investment in Oculus Rift's HMD technology by purchasing the start-up company in July 2014 (Dredge, 2014).

Summary

As television and video displays grow in screen size and sharpness with improved 4K and 8K resolution, future research needs to be conducted on the effects of telepresence and immersion at closer viewing distances. Certain types of television and cable/satellite programming may lend themselves to more immersive viewing. Sports, travel, action films, adventure, and reality series are types of programs where viewers could viscerally experience being part of the action by sitting close to a UHDTV screen that fills their peripheral vision. Three dimensional displays will likely accentuate the sense of immersion. The effects may mimic that previously experienced in a large-screen IMAX theater or with a head-mounted display such as that produced using the wide-angle Oculus Rift technology. As these display technologies decline in price, their adoption for research purposes becomes more practical. The barrier to their use as research tools will likely not be one of cost, but rather the imagination and creativity of researchers in designing projects that shed new light on the visceral effects of telepresence and immersion for televised and projected content.

References

Biocca, F., & Delaney, B. (1995). Immersive virtual reality technology. In F. Biocca & M. R. Levy (Eds.), *Communication in the age of virtual reality* (pp. 57–124). Hillsdale, NJ: Lawrence Erlbaum Associates.

Crowther, B. (1952). New movie projection shown here: Giant wide angle screen utilized: Novel technique in films unveiled. *The New York Times Review*, October 1. Online at www.nytimes.com/movie/review?res=9E0DE6DF1E3CE 23BBC4953DFB6678389649EDE (retrieved August 21, 2014).

Disse, D. (2013). *The birth of IMAX*. IEEE Canada. Online at http://ieee.ca/millennium/ imax/imax_birth.html (retrieved February 11, 2014).

Dredge, S. (2014). Facebook closes its $2bn Oculus Rift acquisition. *The Guardian*, July 22. Online at www.theguardian.com/technology/2014/jul/22/facebook-oculus-rift-acquisition-virtual-reality (retrieved September 7, 2014).

Film Format Facts. (2013). McGillivray Freeman Films. Online at www.macgillivray freemanfilms.com (retrieved October 1, 2013).

Fisher, D. E., & Fisher, M. J. (1996). *Tube: The invention of television*. New York: Counterpoint.

Held, R., & Durlach, N. (1992). Telepresence. *Presence: Teleoperators and Virtual Environments, 1*(1), 21–26.

Kim, T., & Biocca, F. (1997). Telepresence via television: Two dimensions of tele-presence may have different connections to memory and persuasion. *Journal of Computer-Mediated Communication, 3*(2). Online at http://onlinelibrary. wiley.com/doi/10.1111/j.1083-6101.1997.tb00073.x/full (retrieved August 21, 2006).

Klepek, P. (2013). Horror and the Oculus Rift are no joke. *Giant Bomb*, October 2. Online at www.giantbomb.com/articles/horror-and-the-oculus-rift-are-no-joke/1100-4757/ (retrieved November 21, 2013).

Lombard, M., & Ditton, T. (1997). At the heart of it all: The concept of presence. *Journal of Computer Mediated-Communication, 3* (2). Online at www.ascusc. org/jcmc/vol3/issue2/lombard.html (retrieved June 2, 2011).

Merriam-Webster Dictionary. (2013). Presence. Online at www.merriam-webster. com/dictionary/presence (retrieved December 20, 2014).

Rubin, P. (2014). The inside story of Oculus Rift and how virtual reality became real-ity. *Wired, 22*(06), May 20. Online at www.wired.com/2014/05/oculus-rift-4/ (retrieved June 3, 2014).

Seel, P. B. (2010). Visualizing the world in 3-D. *Television Quarterly, 39*(1), 9–12.

Seel, P. B. (2012). Digital television and video. In A. E. Grant & J. H. Meadows (Eds.), *Communication technology update and fundamentals* (13th ed.). Boston: Focal Press.

Seel, P. B. (2013). The 2013 NAB Show: The evolution of digital television and video. *International Journal of Digital Television, 4*(3), 345–351. Online at www. intellectbooks.co.uk/journals/view-Article,id=16332/ (retrieved July 17, 2014).

Seel, P. B., & Dupagne, M. (2004). Digital television. In A. E. Grant & J. H. Meadows (Eds.), *Communication technology update* (9th ed.). Boston: Focal Press.

Seel, P. B., & Dupagne, M. (2010). Digital television and video. In A. E. Grant & J. H. Meadows (Eds.), *Communication technology update and fundamentals* (12th ed.). Boston: Focal Press.

Steuer, J. (1992). Defining virtual realities: Dimensions determining telepresence. *Journal of Communication, 42*(4), 73–93.

Ulanoff, L. (2013). Sharp intros world's largest LED. *Mashable.com*. Online at http://mashable.com/2013/01/07/sharp-intros-worlds-largest-led-hdtv (retrieved November 2, 2013).

Zettl, H. (2013). *Sight, sound, motion: Applied media aesthetics* (7th ed.). Boston: Wadsworth.

Part III

INTERNATIONAL PERSPECTIVES ON BROADCASTING IN THE DIGITAL AGE

7

THE FUTURE OF TELEVISION

An Arab Perspective

Joe F. Khalil

The future of television carries many useful yet also contradictory meanings. As a description of an impending experience that is interconnected more than ever before through technology across time and space, this chapter certainly makes sense: it aims to describe the state of contemporary economic, political, and cultural structures and their impact on television technologies in the Arab world. Throughout this chapter, I will emphasize three overlapping areas for examining a rapidly changing media landscape: the history of Arab broadcasting, the structure of Arab television, and the existing distribution technologies.

Arab television is ubiquitous. This is not only because of the significant increase of volume and diversity of channels and the technologies designed to increase and expand communication processes, but also because more and more individuals and groups are finding in audiovisual content a platform for "self-expression." From North Africa to the Arabian Gulf, audiovisual content is being produced and distributed using wide-ranging converging technologies. These include, but are not restricted to, more than 1,000 channels (terrestrial, satellite, pay-TV, etc.) and hundreds of YouTube channels, all offering trans-media content on TV screens, laptops, and mobile phones.

In the face of the exponential qualitative and quantitative growth of Arab television, the scholarship of this particular medium has moved out of the scholarly margins and taken its place in the mainstream of global media studies. For the past 20 years, academic interest has been broadly focused on the rise, role, and impact of Arab television within politics and culture. The few projects that engaged with media institutions paid little or no attention to the technological infrastructures that became indispensable adjuncts of this "information revolution" (Emirates Center for Strategic

Study and Research, 1998). Technology was invoked from a regulatory and political perspective in the context of the nation-state (Boyd, 1993; Kamalipour & Mowlana, 1994; Rugh, 2004); from a political economy perspective (Ayish, 2010; Sakr, 2007); as part of the necessary tools for media institutions' growth, reach, and perceived impact (Kraidy & Khalil, 2010); and as globally integrated television production and programming practices (Khalil, 2014).

Discussions on technologies as enabling environments for media development and distributions are often limited to trade press such as *Arab Ad*, *TV Studio Middle East*, *Communicate Middle East*, and others. Also, insights on technologies can be found in professional publications from think tanks and corporate research groups. The apparent rift between industry and academic undertakings on the role of technologies in Arab media is nourished by perceptions of techno-determinism, conventions of academic research, and the absence of reliable and transparent sources. This chapter is a preliminary attempt to bridge the gap and offer academic and professional insights into the future of television in the Arab world.

Following a brief consideration of what can be called the television market in the Arab world, the chapter is divided into three parts. In the first part, the structure of Arab television is considered. It includes regulation, ownership, and economics of television channels and distributors. The chapter's second part provides a breakdown of the evolving technologies used in Arab television distribution and suggests some of their political, economic, and cultural implications. In the third and final section, I attempt to draw the contours of the future of Arab television as being closely linked to global and local threats and opportunities.

None of the above is peculiar to the Arab world, and most of these tendencies have been experienced in broadcasting systems worldwide (as noted elsewhere in this volume). Each region has had to deal with these in its own way, and the similarities and variations are particularly instructive in providing a more generalized view of the future of broadcasting from a global perspective. From the research and data summarized in this chapter, these factors provide a set of messy, ambivalent, but essentially convincing frames of evidence to support the theory that the future of broadcasting in the region can be placed on a spectrum of globally integrated industries and locally anchored trans-media activities, both of which are facilitated by economic, political, and technological capabilities.

The Arab World and Its Television Market

The concept of an Arab world's television market suggests two related visions. First, the term implies all of the various configurations of state-owned and privately held commercial channels that are regulated, funded, and viewed within the boundaries of Arab states and/or Arabic-speaking communities. A discussion about a television market should include a recognition that the Arab world is comprised of 22 sovereign states spanning four distinct regions: the Arabian Gulf, the Levant or the Near Eastern Mediterranean, the Nile River area (Egypt and Sudan), and North Africa. Because these countries are spatially dispersed but held together by historical, religious, linguistic, and cultural affinities, they could be considered what Straubhaar (2007) calls a geo-linguistic or geo-cultural area. Thus, any discussion of an Arab television market would be concerned with Egyptian, Lebanese, Syrian, Saudi, and Moroccan television, among others. It would also be concerned with US and European-based television stations broadcasting in Arabic to the region.

A second meaning of an Arab world television market refers to an "imagined community" largely formed out of mediated interactions around political ideologies, economic interests, cultural practices, and post-colonial legacies (Anderson, 1991). This community was largely formed around mass media platforms such as radio, film, television, the internet, and—most recently—social media. Unlike other platforms, television remains the most popular medium due to its technology, ownership, program distribution, and audiences (Dennis et al., 2014). With the use of technologies such as direct-broadcast satellite (DBS), Internet Protocol television (IPTV), and others, Arab television is reaching across the boundaries of nation-states into homes inside and outside the geographic region of the Arab world.

As a construct, the Arab world is rarely recognized as a unified geographic entity for statistical data. For example, audience ratings are provided on a country-by-country basis. Attempts to provide unified audience ratings across the 22 countries are limited by different reporting methods, contentious results, and inability to collect data in certain countries (Kraidy & Khalil, 2010). Other indices are available by country, by a regional grouping of countries such as the Gulf Cooperation Council (GCC), or by international organizational groupings based on geographies, such as the Economic and Social Commission of Western Asia (ESCWA). Even organizations under the banner of the League of Arab States, such as the Arab States Broadcasting Union (ASBU) and the Arab Satellite Communications Organization (Arabsat), have different reporting standards and practices. These differences challenge the ability to provide comparable statistical data and limit the discussions to various case studies.

In this chapter, the data are provided for the Arab world, defined as all or the majority of the 22 Arab countries. Other data are provided under the caveat that they include the broader MENA regions. Where possible, up-to-date statistics and figures are used to illustrate the patterns involved. However, this is a field notoriously subject to rapid changes, and undoubtedly some figures will have changed by the time of publication. Nevertheless, one would expect the broad patterns of transformation to hold true regardless of modifications to specific details.

Historical Milestones in Arab Television

To understand how the future can be formed, this section examines milestones from the past. The intention is to illustrate the introduction, development, and expansion of Arab television as interrelated cultural, political, and economic cycles in which technology is one of many factors.

With the appearance of modern Arab states after World War II, broadcasting became an all-pervasive political force. Newly independent states sought broadcasting as a way to consolidate their independence, foment a national identity, and promote their political ideology beyond their immediate borders. In his seminal work on Arab broadcasting, Boyd (1993) highlighted the importance of radio in pioneering the missions, structures, and regulation of broadcasting in the region. In addition, radio could be credited with developing a vision of what it means to be an Arab, to be educated, entertained, and informed (or misinformed). With radio, the Arab world was also subject to international broadcasts from the British Broadcasting Corporation (BBC), Deutsche Welle (DW), Voice of America, and others, and in a later era from Voice of the Arabs (Egypt) or Radio Orient (Lebanon) (Wood, 1992). Similarly, today's Arabs are subject to international satellite television broadcasts from the BBC, DW, US-sponsored al-Hurra Television, and about a dozen other international state-sponsored broadcast channels. Interestingly, though, the current television ecology, if there is one, is more complex than that of radio, partly because television is the most popular medium, the most economically profitable, and the most politically influential.

With the advent of terrestrial television in the early 1960s, one could argue, mass media emerged as a set of technologies capable of promoting discourses across the Arab world. Programs were produced in one Arab country and distributed across the region. Production hubs started to emerge, building on specific cities' educational, cultural, technological, economic, and political capital (Khalil, 2013a). For example, Beirut emerged as a hub for entertainment television production capitalizing on literary expertise, liberal attitudes, economic laissez-faire, political stability, and enterprising individuals. At the same time, Cairo ascended to become another major center for television production and distribution supported by government initiatives, a history of filmmaking, skilled labor, and the largest audience in the region. Technologies of production, duplication, and transmission were crucial in these cities' ability to reach beyond their country's borders.

While terrestrial broadcasting initiated the era of mass media, it took the introduction of satellite television to usher in an era of broadcasting mass information and entertainment from the very few to very many people. Introduced in 1991 from London, the Middle East Broadcasting Center (MBC) put together a multinational team to develop programs for Arabic speakers across the region and beyond. With private commercial satellite television broadcasting first provided by MBC, Arabs could watch and listen to the variations in cultures, economics, and politics of other Arabs. Satellite television also allowed for diverse and complex television economies with private commercial and pay-television configurations gaining a sizeable portion of the market. For the past two decades, satellite television has managed to accommodate economic, political, and cultural challenges and restrictions.

Benefiting from private and public investments and political democratization, these "offshore" channels based in Europe relocated to the Arab world. Ushering in another era in Arab television, the introduction of economic free zones for media production, better known as "media cities," lowered economic, regulatory, and technological barriers to entry (Khalil, 2013a). For example, in Dubai Media City, individuals and corporations can set up television stations in record times, benefiting from access to skilled labor, ready-to-broadcast infrastructure, tax incentives, and a promise of the "Freedom to Create." From radio to terrestrial and now satellite television, politically or economically motivated broadcasting has adopted and adapted to changing technologies.

The Structure of Arab Television

Between 2004 and 2014, the number of television stations grew from 100 to around 800 free-to-air channels available to a potential audience of over 300 million viewers. It is now commonplace in television-industry circles to describe the changes that have occurred in the broadcasting arena in the last decade (2004–2014) in terms of the development and consolidation of a television "ecosystem." The aim of this section is to offer a more nuanced examination of the structure of Arab television that goes beyond the biological shortcomings of an "ecosystem." This section considers how changes in ownership, regulations, and technologies are interacting to facilitate the emergence of specific patterns of production, distribution, and consumption.

Ownership

With the exceptions of Lebanon, the first 40 years of Arab television were marked by the state as the main owner, operator, financier, and controller of broadcasting. Since the 1990s, private investors, both local and international, such as US-based News Corp, started owning television stations in the region. Today's ownership patterns include radical groups such as Hamas or Hezbollah, political parties for example in Iraq and Libya, and religious groups (Sunnis, Shias, or Christians), which independently own television stations. For example, Egypt currently has about 100 private channels and 26 channels that are owned by the government; the United Arab Emirates (UAE) has 68 private or mixed channels and 21 government-owned channels. The numbers change if you look at Libya (26 mixed and three government-owned channels) and at Lebanon (28 mixed and one government-owned channel) (Haddad & Qweider, 2013).

Decisions about channel headquarters are closely associated with ownership patterns. In fact, Arabic channels are headquartered in the Arab world and beyond. For instance, of 14 private channels currently broadcasting from the UK, only one (BBC Arabic) is government sponsored. The five Arab countries with the most television-station headquarters are Egypt (126), UAE (91), Saudi Arabia (81), Iraq (74), and Jordan (29) (Haddad & Qweider, 2013). There are specific reasons why channels are concentrated in specific countries. For example, in the case of Egypt, UAE, and Jordan, the development of media cities since the late 1990s has provided a regulatory framework that allows 100 percent ownership of television stations. As a result, Arab individuals and businesses interested in media production and distribution are establishing their headquarters in media cities. The ownership of television stations is increasingly multi-Arab and operating transnationally across the Arab world.

Regulation

Broadly defined as influences on media operations and media content, regulation of Arab television may come from government-related regulatory bodies that have a legal basis for their authority over national media operations, or from non-governmental bodies such as political groups, advertisers, audiences, and the television channels themselves. As Arab television is increasingly globally integrated, transnational, and commercially oriented, the traditionally forceful role of governments in regulating media operations and content is being replaced by television channels themselves and civil society groups.

In the 1950s and 1960s, the initial regulatory frameworks for television were established when over-the-air broadcasting was the only means of transferring signals from the broadcaster to the television set. As newly independent states, regulation was inspired by, if not directly plagiarized from, the departing colonial power, but had a keen interest in developing national identity and sovereignty (Rugh, 2004). These media-regulatory philosophies have been challenged by the transnational political economy of commercial television. In the 1990s, offshore television stations benefited from the deregulation of European telecommunications industries and the post-Soviet political situation (Khalil, 2014). In the 2000s, the establishment of free zones for media production and processes of democratization helped nurture a growing satellite television industry. One index, perhaps, of the repercussions of the so-called Arab Spring is a "new order" in television regulation that is yet to fully emerge. In Tunisia and Egypt, the "old order" was marked by the subordination of the private sector to the political establishment's goals set in the context of an opaque licensing process. While television had a regional outlook and was generally self-censored in principle, Arab television increasingly has a largely national character with free-speech yearnings.

Two technological developments challenge the principles that guide the regulation of transnational television content. In the 1990s, the introduction and instant growth of the commercial satellite television market has irreparably undermined the state's monopoly over broadcasting (with Lebanon as an exception), since this technology can only be controlled by limiting access to satellite receivers. Attempts to limit this access only made audiences more committed to accessing television signals, such as developing innovative ways of smuggling satellite receivers (Saudi Arabia), configuring "homemade" receivers (Lebanon), and sharing pirated signals (Egypt). Satellite television became a true regional medium requiring further attention to transnational and regional regulation.

In response, various regulatory attempts to control satellite signals relied on technological solutions, such as the use of cable to distribute broadcast content as well as control its content. Though most governments resorted to complex forms of monitoring and censoring content, regulating content has happened in a somewhat piecemeal fashion. Throughout the 1990s, cable television was introduced throughout the gulf in an attempt to control content and circumvent access to satellite signals (Sakr, 2007). Due to a combination of government mandates, high population densities, and investments in infrastructure, cable service providers in the Arabian Gulf are well established in comparison with those in other MENA countries struggling with economic and geographic constraints. Gulf cable service providers include: Kuwait Cable Vision (Kuwait), Invision (Saudi Arabia), QCV and Al Muftah Cable Vision (Qatar), and eLife and du TV+ (UAE). As technologies and infrastructures developed, these cable operators reinvented themselves to become providers of technologies such as broadband internet, telephone, digital quality signal, electronic program guides (EPGs), and digital video recorders (DVRs).

In most cases, television regulation is locally concentrated in ministries of information or regulatory bodies that tend to be slow in providing frameworks for digital terrestrial television broadcasting (DTTB). The very few regional bodies governing television regulation, such as the ASBU, are very limited in jurisdiction. More than 15 years after the introduction of private satellite broadcasts to the Arab world, a non-binding charter, "Principles for Organizing Satellite TV in the Arab World," was adopted by all member states of the Arab League with the exception of Lebanon and Qatar (Kraidy, 2011). The charter aimed to impose several restrictions on talk shows, news coverage, and criticism of political and religious figures. More importantly,

115

the charter called on the member states to impose penalties on non-compliant television stations; these penalties ranged from temporary suspension to closure. Such attempts to provide regional regulatory structures or codes lacked the support of several Arab states and were consequently doomed to fail. Perhaps the most effective control on television channels comes from satellite operators and IPTV providers. By controlling distribution, they mandate that channels refrain from airing any (1) commercials for alcohol or cigarettes, (2) nude or obscene material, and (3) material that offends Islam and other religions (Kraidy & Khalil, 2010).

Television Economies

Neither statistics from industry sources nor any published documents about advertising expenditures can provide a reliable assessment of the economies of Arab television. It is expected that MENA satellite TV revenues will reach $3.74 billion in 2020, an increase of $1 billion since 2013 (Digital TV Research, 2014).While the figures are debatable even when available, there are two recognizable industry patterns that have emerged over the past 20 years: broadcast funding and content distribution are in transition.

The first pattern is that broadcasting funding is in an era of transition, and it is growing. Traditionally, Arab television stations were funded by government budgets, contributions from political parties, groups or private individuals, and advertising, or some combination of these. In today's ecologies, these funding structures are often combined, blurring the traditional barrier between private, commercial, and government-owned channels. Increasingly, government-owned channels with a secure financial stance are soliciting advertising revenues, while channels with demonstrated popularity are interested in revenues from value-added services (interactive SMS and MMS), sponsorship, and syndication. Others are developing ways to increase advertising and sponsorship revenues, developing synergies and cross-promotion practices.

Despite the financial collapse of 2008 and the ongoing uprisings, Arab television is still growing (Arab Media Outlook, 2011). Cheaper access to satellite technology and talents, commercial and political patronage, and local, regional, and global players are some of the reasons behind this growth. As early signs of the future of broadcasting, a pattern of mergers and IPOs is energizing business interests in Arab media. In 2009, Kuwaiti-owned Showtime Arabia merged with the Saudi-owned Orbit Group, creating the Orbit Showtime Network (OSN) and offering fully digital, multi-channel, and multi-lingual primarily Western programs. OSN is believed to be the most profitable pay-TV platform with self-declared annual revenues of $700 million. This is no surprise: over the last decade (2004 to 2013), the number of primary pay-TV subscribers nearly quadrupled from 1.33 million in 2004 to 4.35 million in 2013, growing at an annual average rate of 14.64 percent (Middle East Media Market Monitor, 2014). Audiovisual content distribution is also in transition. Radical and discontinuous environmental changes are reshaping it fundamentally, meaning that analysis is out of date almost before it is written, and certainly before it is published. In the strict sense, broadcasting is the distribution of content to a large audience. The introduction of new distribution technologies (from flash drives to online streaming) is fundamentally changing how producers and consumers relate to content (Khalil, 2013b). Particularly, the growing popularity of YouTube channels in Arabic reveals two characteristics of broadcasting: economies of scope and control of distribution. By assembling a "list" of potential "hits" with a distinct editorial identity, these YouTube channels are challenging the traditional role of Arab television networks. Saudi-based operations such as Telfaz 11 and U-Turn are demonstrating a viewership in the millions, which translates into significant advertising dollars. However, these YouTube channels are not able to provide a constant flow of novel products when compared with the quality and quantity of programs available on satellite TV.

The Technologies of Arab Television

After years of challenging political and cultural forms of control and censorship, both free-to-air (FTA) and pay TV are able to control the distribution of their products and ensure that advertising commitments are met. According to the *Digital TV Middle East & Africa Databook* (Digital TV Research, 2014), the MENA region will account for 60.3 million digital television households with satellite television contributing to the bulk of pay-TV revenues (estimated at around 4.4 billion dollars in 2014). At the same time, there is a growing belief that IPTV is growing fast and will surpass digital cable. In attracting the avid viewers of sports and movies, digital television may disrupt the traditional wisdom that Arab viewers favor the free content of FTA channels rather than content for which they have to pay. Technologically, television content is delivered terrestrially, via satellite, IPTV, and digital terrestrial.

Terrestrial Television

The golden period of terrestrial television stations was from the 1960s until the mid-1990s. Apart from governments, few broadcasters have invested in terrestrial broadcasting. This is partly because governments maintain a monopoly over terrestrial broadcasts, and partly because satellite technology offers a cheaper, more attractive and reliable delivery option. During the past 15 years, broadcasters in Egypt, Kuwait, and now Libya opted for satellite broadcasting precisely because of its low costs and high reach. In post-conflict transitional countries, the development of privately owned commercial television is often seen as part of the process of democratization and as a guarantee of freedom of expression. For example, the Iraqi Communication and Media Commission (CMC) has facilitated the licensing of Iraqi channels. As early as June 2004, there were 20 private terrestrial channels operating in various parts of Iraq (Al-Zeir, 2014).

In 2014, the total number of terrestrial channels in the Arab world is 115; most of these channels are also accessible on satellite. Iraq ranks first in the region, with 21 terrestrial channels, followed closely by Egypt's 20 channels (Al-Zeir, 2014). With the exception of Palestine, Iraq, Lebanon, and Tunisia, terrestrial television is still restricted to government-owned channels. In Morocco, the kingdom and the private sector jointly own the two terrestrial television stations.

Satellite Television

Satellite television in the Arab world is a complex web of technologies, institutions, and conglomerates operating in an equally complex environment. The main stakeholders are the satellite providers and television channels.

The story of satellite television in the Arab world can be generally traced to access to satellite providers. From Europe, privately owned pay-TV and FTA channels benefited from the highly competitive telecommunications market of the early 1990s. Interestingly, about 80 channels use the European satellite provider Eutelsat to broadcast interactive, religious, and political content. In doing so, they bypass Arab satellite providers' regulations against nudity and specific political speech.

Five satellite operators covering the MENA region compete for the distribution of FTA and pay-TV channels. Owned by a consortium of Arab States led by Saudi Arabia, the Arab Satellite Communications Organization (Arabsat) is headquartered in Riyadh (with a back-up facility in Tunisia) and carries more than 230 channels. Established in 1976 under the Arab League's jurisdiction, Arabsat is the oldest operator; it launched its first satellite in 1985. Born during the Arab boycott of Egypt after its peace treaty with Israel, the Egyptian Satellite Company, Nilesat, is the first Arab satellite owned by a joint stock public/private company. Based in Egypt Media Production City (EMPC), Nilesat benefits from a large, local, Egyptian customer base to carry more than 450 channels. Finally, Bahrain-based Noorsat carries more than 200 channels, while Qatar-based Es'hail has 51 channels, and UAE-based Yahlive has 50.

Satellite television channels are divided into FTA and subscription-based pay TV. It is beyond the scope of this chapter to discuss the diversity of more than 800 FTA channels (for an overview, see Haddad & Qweider (2013) and Kraidy & Khalil (2010)). Suffice to note that these channels include those that are government-owned and privately owned, are for profit and not-for-profit, have a regional or a local focus, offer general or niche programming, and so on. Some of these channels are conglomerates that follow the network business model and are globally integrated with co-ownership, co-production, and other forms of partnerships. Perhaps the most exciting aspect of Arab satellite channels is taking place in the pay-TV sector.

Four pay-TV satellite channels offer a combined total of 151 channels with investments in exclusive content and programming rights (Al-Zeir, 2014). Born out of the merger of the two oldest pay-TV networks, the Orbit Showtime Network (OSN) specializes in premium Western films and series. Formerly known as Al Jazeera Sports, BeIN Sports is a Qatar-based global network of 17 channels dedicated to local, regional, and global sporting events. Al Majd network has offered Islamic-sanctioned programming since 2003 through a pay-TV structure. Part of government-owned Abu Dhabi Media, Abu Dhabi Sports Channel complements two FTA sports channels with five HD pay-TV channels.

Despite various efforts to increase the number of subscribers, pay-TV networks are still lagging behind FTA TV in viewership. There are three possible reasons for this limitation. Although the cost of the satellite decoders has decreased dramatically, subscription costs range from US$20 to US$300 per month, depending on the type and number of channels in the package. Yet, viewers are still reluctant to pay for programs that they believe should be free, or are easily available on pirated platforms. With the exception of sports and recent American series and films, the pay-TV networks have not managed to create unique offerings. As a result, viewers opt to watch pirated DVD copies of the latest series and films, and the churn rates are usually high in the aftermath of major sporting events when subscribers decide to terminate their contracts. Finally, the pay-TV networks are still positioned as language-specific niche providers. Their over-reliance on English-speaking productions appeals to a narrow group of audiences. Despite pay-TV's efforts to present locally produced or dubbed Arab dramas, their offerings are also made available on FTA channels. Nevertheless, the projections for pay-TV are very positive, with an estimated total market revenue of US$2.5 billion between 2013 and 2015 (Al-Zeir, 2014).

IPTV

With an audience that is shifting from linear to tailored viewership, the TV viewing experience itself is changing rapidly. In various countries around the region, telecommunication operators are providing pay-TV services through IPTV, microwave links, or cable. The liberalization and privatization policies of the last 20 years forced these operators to develop the infrastructure and offer services including access to television content. With the increased adoption of broadband, 14 IPTV providers are operating in nine Arab countries. Given their advanced infrastructure and their need to control content, the countries in the Arabian Gulf have highly developed IPTV platforms with three providers in Bahrain, two in Saudi Arabia, and two in the UAE (Awwad, 2014). The reluctance to adopt IPTV across the region is related to widespread piracy, insufficient financial resources, absence of clear business models and regulatory frameworks, and limited exclusive content.

High Definition and Digital Terrestrial

A total of 134 unique high-definition (HD) channels are targeting the Arab world using four satellites: Arabsat (42), Nilesat (29), YahLive (27), and Noorsat (12)—channels available on special set-top boxes (24) (Al Asmar, 2014). Of these channels, 71 are provided free, making the HD offered in MENA higher than the total HD offered in Italy, Spain, and Russia combined. By February 2014, the total satellite HD channels constituted around 11 percent of the total satellite channels aired in the Arab World. HD TV channels have increased by 30 percent from 2013 to 2014. Unlike the US and UK operators, Arab pay-TV operators are not up-selling their HD content—except for sports channels. This recent interest in HD channels prompted a UAE-based company, My-HD, to offer 34 channels of which 19 are HD (Al Asmar, 2014). Saudi Arabia and the UAE together accounted for 75 percent of total My-HD subscriptions at the end of 2013—followed by Qatar (with 12 percent of total subscriptions), and Kuwait and Iraq (4 percent each) (Dataxis, 2014).

Although mandated by the International Telecommunication Union, digital terrestrial television broadcasting (DTTB) is only under development in 12 of the 22 Arab states (Al Asmar, 2014). This process is riddled with security, financial, legal, regulatory, and technological problems. As a result, it is unlikely that the countries will meet the digital transition goals. Only Morocco and Saudi Arabia have managed to set up Digital Video Broadcast Terrestrial (DVB-T) transmitters. Given the widespread adoption and popularity of direct-to-home (DTH) satellite, it might be some time before DTTB finds adopters in the private sector.

The Future of Arab Television

Regardless of the capabilities or limitations of television structures and technologies, ultimately it is what people (producers/audiences) do with these tools that determines how a television future can be formed. Four interrelated developments are setting forces in motion that may herald a new era.

First, there is a perceived growth in the technical possibilities of television resulting from increased "convergence." This has taken the media network model to television broadcasting, providing multi-platform trans-media. Networks such as MBC and Rotana target various audiences based on their geographic location, programming interests, or time shifts. As large media conglomerates, their network operations are usually complemented by other forms of online, print, and radio media. At the same time, these conglomerates are experimenting with various strategies of differentiation from video streaming to developing mobile applications.

Second, there is an emergent desire to exploit consumers' interest in technological capabilities (digital, HD, time shifting) for economic profitability both on the part of media conglomerates, notably transnational, and on the part of nation-states wishing to fuel economic growth via "the information society." Consequently, markets and states are actively engaged in the transfer, promotion, and adoption of these technologies. From format rights to channel licenses, regional media players are increasingly integrated fully or partially in global media industries. Wealthy Arab states such as Qatar and the UAE are investing in internet upgrades, infrastructure development, and satellite launches.

A third trend relates to Arab states' decisions to support spaces for media development. The success of free economic zones pioneered with the Egypt Media and Production City (1997), Dubai Media City (2001), and Jordan Media City (2001) has unleashed the appetite of states and groups to develop similar ventures. In return for an initial investment in infrastructure and other incentives, these governments and organizations hope to become part of a growing regional media business.

Lastly, there is an apparent consumer demand for more choice in television and a degree of dissatisfaction with the established order. Digital technology is not only challenging Arab television from within, resulting in a pull towards integration with global media practices, but it is also challenging the television business model from the outside as younger populations are acquiring the ability to produce and circulate their own content. While unbound by the rules of the television box, such content is still able to masquerade as television. Just consider that Saudis watch 90 million videos per day—an average of more than seven videos per person (Digibuzz, 2013).

By way of a conclusion, a leading consultant working for a leading global strategic management consulting firm suggested in a public discussion that the Arab world's television today is where the US was 20 years ago. Some may agree with her, and therein lies the danger: in setting up US practices as the industry benchmark, we fail to acknowledge the dynamic and often contradictory practices of a global television industry in which the US is definitely a player but does not set the rules. Looking at the future of television from the Arab world, the image is way more dynamic than what this consultant or another seems to think.

For additional information, see:
Arab States Broadcasting Union (ASBU) www.asbu.net
Arab Satellite Communications Association (Arabsat) www.arabsat.com/

References

Al Asmar, N. (2014). *High definition TV in the Arab world 2014*. Amman, Jordan: Arab Advisors Group (Media Strategic Research Service).

Al-Zeir, M. (2014). *Satellite pay TV in the Arab world: Kpis and projections*. Amman, Jordan: Arab Advisors Group (Media Strategic Research Service).

Anderson, B. (1991). *Imagined communities: Reflections on the origin and spread of nationalism* (Rev. ed.). New York: Verso.

Arab Media Outlook. (2011–2015). *Arab media: Vulnerability and transformation* (2011) (4th ed.). Dubai, UAE: Dubai Press Club.

Awwad, R. (2014). *IPTV in the Arab World 2014*. Amman, Jordan: Arab Advisors Group (Media Strategic Research Service).

Ayish, M. I. (2010). Arab state broadcasting systems in transition: The promise of the public service broadcasting model. *Middle East Journal of Culture & Communication, 3*(1), 9–25. doi: 10.1163/187398609X12584657078448.

Boyd, D. A. (1993). *Broadcasting in the Arab world: A survey of the electronic media in the Middle East* (2nd ed.). Ames: Iowa State University Press.

Dataxis. (2014). *Operator briefing: My-HD*. Online at http://dataxis.com/operator-briefing-my-hd/ (retrieved March 31, 2014).

Dennis, E., Martin, J., & Wood, R. (2014). *Arab media use study: An eight-country study by Northwestern University in Qatar*. Qatar: Northwestern University.

Digibuzz. (2013). Social media usage in Saudi Arabia [infographic]. Cairo: Digibuzz. Online at www.digibuzzme.com/social-ksa/ (retrieved January 5, 2014).

Digital TV Research. (2014). *Digital TV Middle East & Africa databook*. Online at www.digitalvresearch.com/ugc/DTV%20MEA%20Databook%202014%20 TOC_toc_97.pdf (retrieved September 11, 2014).

Emirates Center for Strategic Study and Research. (1998). *The information revolution and the Arab world: Its impact on state and society*. Abu Dhabi, UAE: Emirates Center for Strategic Studies and Research.

Haddad, D., & Qweider, H. (2013). *Satellite TV in the Arab world 2013*. Amman, Jordan: Arab Advisors Group (Media Strategic Research Service).

Kamalipour, Y. R., & Mowlana, H. (1994). *Mass media in the Middle East: A comprehensive handbook*. Westport, CT: Greenwood Press.

Khalil, J. F. (2013a). Towards a supranational analysis of Arab media: The role of cities. In T. Guaaybess (Ed.), *National broadcasting and state policy in Arab countries*. London: Palgrave Macmillan.

Khalil, J. F. (2013b). Youth-generated media: A case of blogging and Arab youth cultural politics. *Television & New Media, 14*(4), 338–350. doi: 10.1177/1527476412463449.

Khalil, J. F. (2014). Modalities of media governance in the Arab world. In N. Sakr, J. Skavgaard-Petersen, & D. Della Ratta (Eds.), *Arab media moguls*. New York: I. B. Tauris.

Kraidy, M. M. (2011). The emergent supranational Arab media policy sphere. In R. Mansell & M. Raboy (Eds.), *The handbook of global media and communication policy* (pp. 293–305). Chichester, UK: Wiley-Blackwell.

Kraidy, M. M., & Khalil, J. F. (2010). *Arab television industries.* New York: Palgrave Macmillan.

Middle East Media Market Monitor. (2014). Pay TV now reaches 4.35 million subscribers in MENA. DigitalTV.net, April 9. Online at www.digitaltveurope.net/169822/pay-tv-now-reaches-4-35-million-subscribers-in-mena/ (retrieved May 10, 2014).

Rugh, W. A. (2004). *Arab mass media: Newspapers, radio, and television in Arab politics.* Westport, CT: Praeger.

Sakr, N. (2007). *Arab media and political renewal: Community, legitimacy and public life.* New York: I. B. Tauris.

Straubhaar, J. D. (2007). *World television: From global to local.* Los Angeles: Sage.

Wood, J. (1992). *History of international broadcasting.* London: P. Peregrinus Ltd. in association with the Science Museum.

8

TOURISM AS A MEDIATED PRACTICE IN A GLOBAL MEDIA CONTEXT

The Gaze of Female Korean Tourists to
New York City and the Meaning of
Their Practices

EunKyung Lee

Introduction

New media and information technologies, including the internet and satellite TV, enable and further accelerate a flow of cultural discourse initiated from one area to all parts of the world. Audiences expand their cultural dimensions by both taking part in, and becoming part of, global media experiences. It is not only a discourse—images and products are also experienced through virtual worlds. In a certain sense, those experiences from the global media generate different kinds of desires toward tourism. Under these conditions, tourist practices interplay between a new kind of tourism and the media globalization process.

Considering that one of the definitions of globalization is "deterritorialization," which means the acceleration of the escape from a culture and a modality confined to one absolute territory (Appadurai, 1990), tourists' activity displays some ironic aspects of this. On the one hand, they become agents of globalization by having such a chance of escape. On the other hand, they still visit a certain territory in order to search the culture and modality belonging to that place. The contemporary globalization process has also influenced tourists' imaginations and the meaning of (modern) tourism itself. In addition, the contents and process of such deterritorialization become more complicated if the travel destination is New York City, a richly diverse city in the United States and, more importantly, the most frequently targeted city of mass media representations. The transformation in the practice of visiting New York City involves a number of historical conditions and cultural dimensions. Thus, it is interesting to look at how the global media experience intersects tourism with respect to the creation of tourist culture and the image of the city.

To assess the meaning of contemporary tourism in the age of globalization, this chapter examines Korean female tourists to New York City by asking the following questions:

1 What kinds of gazes are being directed at New York City when Korean women travel?
2 How are tourists' gazes constructed among Korean female tourists, especially in relation to their media experiences?
3 How are the traveling practices and experiences reconstructed in Korean female tourists' narratives and discourses?

Methods

This study adopted two major methods: in-depth interviews and analysis of travelogues posted on various web pages such as blogs and internet cafés. The in-depth interviews were conducted to explore what kinds of practices were performed during tourists' trips to New York City and their perception of the mediated nature of their experiences. The interviews also addressed what kinds of gazes have been usually carried with the tourists when they traveled.

The author conducted textual analysis of tourist narratives written both before and after the trip in order to examine the context and process in which the meaning of their practices is constructed. Internet cafés and personal blogs devoted to traveling to New York City were selected for analysis. The language used in all the narratives is Korean, and they were translated into English by the author. Some related media coverage, including news articles and columns, was examined as well.

Literature Review

Tourists and Audiences: Some Similarities

As parts of a cultural practice, there are some similarities between tourists and audiences. These similarities become a basis to see tourism in a contextual ground. Davin (2005) discusses the shared characteristics between tourists and viewers, and suggests them as converging points of the two practices. Both tourists and audiences pursue extended spectacles in addition to main-staged scenes. There is an increasing demand to include areas not previously considered as usual tourist spots. This expansion is described as "back stage spectacle" (Davin, 2005, p. 170), and it fosters a rising curiosity among media audiences about "invisible territories" within everyday mundane spaces (Davin, 2005, p. 171). The foregrounding of formerly hidden spaces—the kitchen area of a famous restaurant, news control room, or locker room in a stadium—has become a new spectacle for various reality programs on television and some thematic tours as well.

Another similarity pointed out by Davin (2005) comes from the shared institutional aspect of tourism and media. Due to the institutional roles of tourism and the media to usually support the status quo and dominant ideologies, viewers and tourists are both considered vulnerable to certain propaganda and to "fanciful narratives" (Davin, 2005, p. 172). Hence, they become the subjects of the tourism and television industries' pedagogic strategies.

The intrinsic aspect of the tourist-as-audience is mediated reality and how that reality relates to their expectations. As shown in various studies, audiences often take their mediated information or experiences as reference points. For example, the family on *The Cosby Show* was considered to be more representative of the middle class than middle-class families met by viewers in real life (Press, 1991). These types of experiences also apply when tourists take a trip. Rodaway (1995) points out that, rather than comparing Euro Disney's (now called Disneyland Paris) features to the original fairy tales, historical narratives, or real places on which they were based, visitors judge them in comparison to other, similar thematic representations at Disney World. Mediated reality has become so saturated in society that reality itself clashes with people's expectations, and they sometimes compete with one another. For instance, some tourist sites provide their guests with a mediated version of their attractions alongside the real ones (e.g., the Niagara Falls IMAX Theatre). This phenomenon produces a variety of responses among scholars: warnings for disappointed visitors (Rojek, 1997), fears for the omission of reality (Eco, 1986), and further accusations of escapism (Davin, 2005).

Mediated Reality and Space

Implications of this mediated reality for tourists as audiences (or audiences as tourists) lie in the ability to construct a mediated practice—and can be a consequence of this practice. Some scholars posit the "hyper-realism" rooted in mediated reality as one of the grounds for contemporary tourism (Jackson, 2005; Rojek, 1997; Urry, 2002). In this theory, a constant chain of construction and reconstruction of reality occurs in order to match tourists' expectations and, in turn, to fulfill media appeal. To meet tourists' expectations, reality should match its representations. To this end, many aspects of social practices have been re-created, modified, invented, or accommodated, as Davin (2005) describes:

[M]any artifacts large and small—from jewelry and clothing to boats and houses and even entire villages—have been redecorated, embellished, transformed, so that visitors can witness and "absorb the atmosphere" of the unique, "authentic" culture which they have come to consume, although they are clearly aware of these (re)construction processes.

(p. 174)

This is particularly true in urban spaces because the cityscape has more often been targeted in media representations and, thus, more salient icons and symbols are related to it. Benjamin (1969) examined cinema as a technology of visual pleasure that both shapes and reflects historical attitudes toward cities and city life. Sadler and Haskins (2005) extended this interpretive perspective to portrayals of cityscapes on television and suggested that a collection of different iconic fragments constructs a powerful narrative of the metropolis (particularly New York City in their study).

Furthermore, in other instances, reality itself becomes a media event that is gradually reorganized for maximum screen appeal (Eco, 1986). Images become hyper-real, for tourists as audiences begin to associate places and images with television shows instead of the city itself. In this mediated urban space, boundaries between viewers (audiences) and tourists become blurred, as expressed in Baudrillard's (1994) description of "implosion": it is the "dissolution of TV into life, of life into TV" (p. 54). The "real" and the "mediated," fact and fiction, document and spectacle, irreversibly mix and collide (Davin, 2005, p. 175).

In this way, the hyper-real representations of urban places become so reconfirmed that most viewers are content with seeing only fragments of the whole. Kirshenblatt-Gimblett (1998) argued that the "city becomes a museum in itself, for tourists travel to actual destinations to experience virtual places" (p. 9).

Converging Cultures, Converging Gazes

The tourist gaze and filmic gaze provide major frameworks for the analysis of converging cultures because those two gazes are intertwined in tourist practice. The tourist gaze, conceptualized by Urry (2002), is constructed "in relationship to its opposite" (p. 2) to explain how tourists understand the visited place and people as "the other." Drawing on Foucault's (1976) ideas of surveillance and power as shown in the medic/patient relationship, Urry incorporated notions of inquiry and surveillance into his theory. Thus, the tourist gaze, according to Urry (2002), scrutinizes from a position of power and imposes ideological understandings on the destination. Jackson (2005) argued that tourists exert knowledge brought from their own cultures and previous experiences, which gives them power over the destination, much as the medic's knowledge does. Yet the tourist gaze is not solely grounded in knowledge—it is also based on the imagination. The imagination, as Donald (1997) suggested, becomes one of the crucial parts of the tourist experience, for it is coupled with a physical visiting. It in fact makes up for something that is "missing" from the actual experience: "[T]o imagine is to make present to . . . one's mind's eye what is absent" (Donald, 1997, p. 183). Imagination implies the "incorporation of anticipation and curiosity" (Jackson, 2005, p. 191), framed by the expectations inherent in the tourist gaze. Also, it must be noted that much of the imagination is formulated by images in the media and audience experiences. In this way, the expectation of tourists is "constructed and sustained through a variety of non-tourist practices, such as film, TV, literature, magazines, records, and videos, which construct and reinforce that gaze" (Urry, 2002, p. 3). Therefore, the tourist gaze is constructed of signs underpinning their knowledge, ideology, and imagination. In this sense, Urry (2002) defined that "the tourist is a collector of signs" (p. 3). In other words, tourists compare the imagined experience with the actual, and with conventions of home, while the experience itself is framed by a succession of media (film/television) images about the destination.

Bringing the tourist and filmic gazes together helps contextualize the converging cultures of tourism and the media. The tourist gaze seeks the familiar, which relates in part to the filmic gaze. At the same time, both gazes maintain their own nature; while the tourist gaze keeps a critical distance as viewer, thus maintaining the power of surveillance, the filmic gaze is motivated by a desire to seek a closer relationship (Jackson, 2005). In this way, we can explain why people feel more comfortable when looking at the "virtual reality" of the tourist place than when actually occupying that space. As Urry (2002) argued, the converging gaze is "mediatized . . . direct[ing] our attention to famous spots while reactivating aspects of those media events that preceded our journeys" (p. 3). In sum, being a tourist and a film spectator/television viewer activates converging cultures in which the mediated imagination determines how people understand reality, space, and identity. Therefore, media experiences are transferred to the practice of tourism based on the similarities between the audience and tourist cultures, and tourism is transformed into a mediated practice within those converging cultures and gazes.

Cultural Globalization and Global Media

One of the issues underlying the debates surrounding the globalization process is cultural globalization. Most discussions about cultural globalization revolve around two opposing tendencies: cultural homogenization and cultural hybridization. According to the cultural homogenization thesis, because the icons of Western—especially American—popular culture are everywhere, it is inferred that eventually all cultural difference will be eroded and cultural sameness will be superimposed (Beck, 2000). Tomlinson (1991) termed this a "broad process of cultural convergence . . . in the cultures of the world" (p. 135). This fear of cultural homogenization or synchronization has been reflected in cultural imperialism, particularly media imperialism (Boyd-Barrett, 1977). Cultural imperialism focuses on the perceived threat of cultural domination posed by immensely powerful Western media corporations through their ownership and transmission of cultural goods (Mattelart et al., 1984; Schiller, 1985). These are the same goods that go toward constituting the tourist imagination.

Scholars agree that the merit of the media imperialism thesis lies in its recognition of global relationships and links between foreign policy interests, capitalist expansion, and media infrastructures and contents (Beynon & Dunkerley, 2000; Mohammadi, 1991; Morley & Robins, 1995). However, this model hardly avoids the criticism that it doesn't hold much relevance in the examinations of the deep and diverse cultural effects that global media could convey. Especially now, global media technologies are not limited to Western centers and many new media actors have begun to get involved since the 1990s. For instance, Mohammadi (1991) argued that the media imperialism model cannot explain reverse flow, such as Brazil's program in Portugal, or why Third World producers have become international exporters, as seen in the Latin American telenovelas that are shown in the United States (p. 607). Sinclair, Jack, and Cunningham (1996) pointed out the inadequacy of the media imperialism model to semi-peripheral settler societies such as Australia and Canada.

Particularly at the level of local reception and assimilation of global media, the media imperialism view is criticized for its vagueness about how media messages are actually received in specific cultural contexts. Critics suggest a more nuanced meaning-making process of the reception of global media and its creation of hybrid cultures, instead of such a simple assumption that watching American television means American values are adopted (Mohammadi, 1991; Sinclair et al., 1996). Furthermore, media imperialism has been criticized due to the fact that it is paradoxically more inclined to reinforce Western cultural influence by accepting, rather than challenging, its importance (Sinclair et al., 1996). Based on these criticisms, scholars have conducted numerous studies on cross-cultural textual analyses and global audience reception. This line of research adopts an optimistic voice regarding the diversity of media producers and local reception, and the many loops of cultural flows that have emerged (Liebes & Katz, 1990; Silj, 1988). It embraces the concepts of active audience reception and polysemy (e.g., Fiske, 1987) to suggest that diverse audiences bring their own interpretive frameworks and sets of meanings to media texts.

This leads to the cultural hybridization view, adopted to emphasize the dynamics of meaning-making processes between local and global actors. Drawing on the ambivalent nature of local reception, scholars claim that the indigenization of Western elements, the rate and magnitude of contemporary cultural change, and the complexity of the interaction between the global and the local must be taken into consideration (Appadurai, 1996; Cvetkovich & Kellner, 1997; Featherstone et al., 1995). It is through these lenses that subjects of this chapter (female tourists coming from a non-Western country) begin to confer cultural self-definition into their mediated experiences, transferring the nexus from the global to the local, and ultimately to oneself.

Findings and Discussions

Historical Background

Since the end of World War II, the United States of America has imposed tremendous cultural impacts, along with political and economic influences, on Korean society. The division and armistice of the Korean War have made South Korea maintain a peculiar relationship with the US. Ever since, the US has been a very complicated, multi-faced, and ambiguous country to South Korea and its people. There has been a steady presence of anti-American sentiment in South Korean society because of this complicated history and the fact that the US had supported the military dictators and their regimes' oppressive crackdowns of democratic movements throughout the 1980s. Yet, the gradual achievement of democratic reforms and establishment of civilian governments in the 1990s brought room for change in terms of cultural diversity and opening to foreign cultures.

As a result, more Korean people wished to visit the US. Yet, in terms of tourism, traveling abroad was not common due to governmental regulations and relatively high costs. Until 1987, Korean people who wanted to travel and were under 45 years old had to undergo an extra procedure beside the visa processing.[1] In 1989, nearly all of the regulations on traveling abroad were abolished in South Korea. Benefiting most from those deregulations were perhaps—besides the upper-middle class—college students. A new trend of the backpacking trip abroad appeared. First, Western European countries became the most frequently visited destinations. Gradually, the tourists' targets moved to Eastern Europe, Australia, India, the US, and China.[2] The reason why the US did not emerge as a popular destination immediately is that the US, unlike Western European countries, requires a visa for Korean tourists.

Thus, in the early days, traveling to the US was allowed only to those few highly educated people in the privileged class. As regulations have been eliminated and various cultural interactions (including tourism) have increased in Korean society, more people now participate and show high interest in tourist activity. Korean single women were one of the last groups who joined the fad, not only because of their socio-economic status, but also because of the fact that the American embassy maintained notoriously high visa denial rates toward unmarried and unemployed women.

Search for Authenticity

New York City is the destination for many tourists, since the city is often interpreted as the "epitome of American society" (Lagerkvist, 2004) and thus is chosen symbolically to represent the image of America. This view applies to Korean tourists as well. One interviewee (S1) stated the reason why she wanted to visit New York City:

Among the American cities, New York City is the most sought after one because I think the City shows the dynamic presence of America. I know the capital city of America is Washington DC, but I think New York is more accessible, unique, and fascinating. Well, I might be wrong, but I still believe it provides a vivid picture of America today.

In addition, it was found that New York City's image is easily romanticized among Korean women travelers due to numerous media representations of romantic movies that were filmed there. Due to constraints—including visa processes and budgeting—traveling to New York City appears to be an exceptionally special event as well. One of the bloggers wrote a post to describe what New York City meant to her:

For me, New York City is the place like a perfect guy who unrealistically approached to me to ask for a date and then left abruptly. It would become an unforgettable memory to me and I would think of it proudly during my entire life. Visiting the City is what I have been longing for so it gives me a lot of mixed feelings.

(Travelogue from the blog post by "dktadl1")[3]

The newly arrived Korean women tourists—mainly in their twenties or thirties, with a career—visit New York City to "make sense" of the America represented by the city. Also, they desire to perceive the city as what they have imagined. Their image of the city is a comprehensive product of their second-hand experiences related to it; it has been influenced by American media products such as films, TV shows, popular songs, books, and cartoons. Another interviewee (S2) pointed out this aspect and stated that cinema was the main source of her image of New York City:

Most of my image of New York City comes from the scenes of numerous movies. *Breakfast at Tiffany's, Taxi Driver, Autumn in New York, When Harry Met Sally, Spiderman* . . . etc. There are so many. TV programs such as documentaries and travel programs stimulate my curiosity too.

As such, the image of New York City is based on mediated experience from the media and other information channels, so the foremost gaze toward the city found in Korean women tourists is the one searching for authenticity—something that can endorse their imagination (Campbell, 2005). This gaze, in fact, becomes the aim of their tours in a broader sense—experiencing the originality of New York City. In the interviews, it is expressed using the concept of "aura" by the one of the interviewees (S3):

> At the moment I got out of Penn Station and stepped onto the street of Manhattan for the first time in my life, I felt like, "This is it!" I was able to feel the aura of what I've heard, seen, and imagined. That feeling made me realize I am seeing the genuine New York City. From the air of the streets and the force from the gaudy skylines I could sense the aura of the City.

In this context, aura implies that the interviewee tried to perceive the city as a whole. Benjamin (1969) explained this concept as "the originality of the work of art which withers in the age of mechanical reproduction" (p. 21). According to Benjamin (1969), mass reproduction of a unique existence reveals its social significance with new "visual and emotional enjoyment" (p. 29) and furthers contemporary mass movement. This is enabled by the destruction of aura and by the shattering of tradition, and it leads to changes in reaction of the masses toward art.

Yet, an ironic point related to the concept of aura is found here; people, at least Korean women tourists, are still searching for the aura of New York City, which is a symbolic center of the city of the mechanically reproduced arts such as film, popular arts, and music. Contemporary art and culture, often described as the spirit of New York City, are characterized by challenging traditions and alienating the aura. The city is the center of popular art in which Benjamin's (1969) conception of the "sense of the universal equality of things" (p. 29) is maximized. Incessant moves of media and tourism for breaking the aura produced a defined image of the city, and yet then impose another kind of aura to it. Moreover, the aura of the city that the tourists were hoping to find comes from the representation of the city. In other words, the source of the aura is given from the mechanical reproduction itself. Korean women tourists, thus, endeavor to fulfill their expectation of this expanded concept of aura. The gaze carried by Korean women tourists searching for this aura is expanded to the texts of urban imagery or visual atmosphere portraying New York City as well. The gaze necessitates confirmation of authenticity. Tourists often express an appreciation of the "real" New York City with a quite judgmental view based on the confirmation of what they already knew to be "true."

This first gaze is, to some extent, similar to what Said (1979) discussed as a "medial attitude" of the Western European viewer. According to

Said (1979), a medial attitude is a textual attitude, meaning that pre-conceived ideas of a place—constructed through prior textual and visual representations—are taken to express the unequivocal truth about the visited culture. Lagerkvist (2004) identified the medial attitude in six different viewing positions when analyzing Swedish travelogues about America in the mid-twentieth century. According to her framework, people begin with a simple "tourist" position in which they understand what they saw as a sight that was there for their eyes only (Lagerkvist, 2004). People in this position learn New York City through its typical sights and summarize the visited culture in an authoritative way (Urry, 2002). Yet, this leisurely approach gets complicated as the travel proceeds, due to accumulating other positions. For example, they can view with the position of "natural scientist" to observe and collect their impressions; they take the view of "colonialist" with more self-assertive and comprehensive gazes in command; sometimes, their gazes look beyond the skyscrapers with anxious "anti-hero" approaches; they contemplate social problems searching for the more truthful images in a "detective" attitude (Lagerkvist, 2004).

Similarly, this evolutionary process is found among Korean female tourists. They display different stages as the tour goes on:

> When I had a one-day "Big Apple" bus tour the first day of my trip, I visited most of the popular tourist spots; Empire State Building, Statue of Liberty, Wall Street, Central Park, etc. Some of them were exciting and some were not. Then, I decided to tour the upper west side, upper east side, Chelsea, east village . . . It's not easy to look around these areas as much as I want. Many places turned out different from what I expected. There are many areas I missed in my plan and those areas have a lot of spots to visit. So I felt I had to change my schedule and do it over and over.
>
> (Travelogue from the blog posting by 'may07110')[4]

Korean women tourists, who believed that they found the aura of New York City on the first day, now felt that they were losing confidence about it. They also saw the American fantasy contrasted with materialization. They found that New York City is easy to imagine and, at the same time, it's unknowable.

There is a notable difference between Largerkvist's (2004) travelers and this study's Korean women tourists. They are situated in different time periods: one is in twentieth-century America and the other is in the twenty-first century. In addition, the subject of the gaze comes from unequal historical and cultural backgrounds. Historically, Korean women have been the objects of the Western visitors' gaze rather than being subjects, meaning they were those who used to be portrayed by the Western perspective. As tourists, they now become the subject and try to behold "the other" who formerly was the subject:

It was quite exciting to watch the (Western) people passing by the window as I sit inside of the café in New York. I think about where they're heading, look at what they're wearing, and find how they're different and the same with people of the same generation in Korea.

(From the interview with S3)

This reversed position accompanies the struggling and learning process:

New York City is so cool, but at the same time is a cold (wicked) place as well. People in the City are all busy and fast . . . they ignore me unless I say something in a loud and aggressive voice. In this city, I had to be the same kind of person not to make myself invisible to them.

(Travelogue from the blog posting by 'irischu')[5]

As illustrated above, Korean women travelers observe New York City and learn from it. Yet, this process is not always a favorable one. Hence, they must decide how to react to it so as not to be frustrated in this city. In this sense, their gaze searching for authenticity gets complicated when they try to get involved with the city.

Korean female tourists' gazes were not particularly related to the colonialist's approach, which regards America as a "scene" in order to give him/her authority to make the final verdict about the place, as shown in Largerkvist's (2004) study on male Swedish tourists in the early twentieth century. In fact, they rather appreciate having a chance to see the "original" New York City than compromise their position as "knower." They do not take the opportunity of visiting the city for granted. However, they might compare the US to other Western countries or feel more superior to other Korean people who have never visited America. Yet, this attitude is more elitist than colonialist. Thus, Korean women tourists felt less deceived when they saw in authenticity, and compromised less their positions.

At this juncture, the origin of authenticity comes into question. Where does authenticity come from? Have tourists fulfilled their aim of searching for originality? If so, how was it done? These questions are enabled by the fact that their images of the authentic New York City are mixed with extremely mediatized gazes and commodified tourist culture. Various forms of media such as satellite TV, internet, and social media, which described or screened the city of New York, have created clear marks (e.g., Statue of Liberty, Times Square, the skylines, etc.) of the city of New York and these are embedded in the tourist's gaze. With their mediatized gaze to the destination culture, these women's travel moves forward a step to find the semantics of the images of the city. This practice seems to have a relation to another gaze they carry.

Visiting the City in the Postmodern Era

Regarding the formation of authentic images of New York City and the interaction process between hyper-real images and reality, a number of media theorists answer with concepts of "high modernity" (Giddens, 1990) and "post modernity" (Baudrillard, 1994). They have examined how media simulations and technologies have superimposed our everyday experiences, and how they deeply structure the perception of the world (Baudrillard, 1994; Giddens, 1991). Contemporary Korean female tourists are part of the generation that has begun to benefit from economic growth in Korea, and they are also in the center of a transitional process in which the South Korean modernism project has peaked and entered a different stage, such as postmodern or high modernity (Kim, 2005). Their gaze is entwined with the age of global media, causing their perception of New York City to develop into a postmodern meaning. Mass media, especially film and TV, have deeply influenced the building of their images and signs related to the image and life of New York City, and, further, "Americanness."

Hollywood blockbusters and other romantic dramas become a major source for Korean women to create images of both New York City and America. The represented images have been regarded as the authentic image of New York City. In addition, the representations in popular American TV shows such as *Friends*, *Seinfeld*, and *Sex and the City* from the late 1990s up to now suggest a collection of different iconic fragments that together construct a powerful narrative of this metropolis (Sadler & Haskins, 2005). This phenomenon reflects what was described as the "postcard effect" by Sadler and Haskins (2005). They argued that not only the tourist's perception but also the landscape of New York City itself is constructed through a fragmented collage of postcard-like shots that together constitute a dominant narrative of a tourist-friendly destination (Sadler & Haskins, 2005):

> During my trip to the City, I went to the brunch café shown in *Sex and the City*. As I was sitting and eating a bagel and coffee there, I watched a bus that looked similar to the one in the show's credit sequence. I felt compelled to take a cab and go shopping as the characters in that show do.
>
> (From the interview with S2)

Thus, when Korean women tour New York City, they fill their travelogues with some controlled icons and images they have seen in movies and TV. In fact, they are travelers, but, at the same time, they are a TV audience. Most of the popular travel guidebooks that they usually carry are organized focusing on the spots shown in media, along with the shopping and fashion items related to the media representations. Consider one guide book's suggestive statement: "you have to wear light colored sneakers to go to Battery Park on a gorgeous weekend as in a drama" (Kim, 2007). They confirm the icons and images with a norm of TV representations. Further, these images become hyper-real for television audiences, as they begin to associate these places and images with the television shows instead of the city itself. Hyper-real representations of New York City's sites reaffirm that most viewers would be content with seeing only fragments of the real city. In the end, tourist spots and places are chosen among Korean women visitors to be gazed upon because there is a prior anticipation, which is constructed and sustained through a variety of non-tourist practices, mainly media practices (Urry, 1995).

Yet, as both the information and culture rooted from mass media have flourished, images and signs about the city enter into a circle of relentless reproduction and form a self-cloning process. Those overabundant images and signs inundate and no longer have referential value, but instead interact solely with other signs. This marks the advent of "simulation" (Baudrillard, 1994). In this context, Baudrillard's (1994) notion of "simulacra" explicates this particular phenomenon. According to him, if there is no authentic, then the appearances themselves, by displacing the authentic, become the real (Baudrillard, 1994). Therefore, the mediatized, postcard-like images of New York City such as gaudy skyscrapers, thrilling yellow cabs, the romantic museum mile, and the spectacular view at the Empire State Building displace the reality of the city and then become hyper-real.

Through this process, the authentic image of New York City in the Korean women tourists' minds operates as a simulacrum. They encounter the scene in which their search for the originality of New York's images is trapped in the simulation of those images. The modern attitudes of those natural scientist, colonialist, and detective gazes are transformed to the postmodern hyper-real gaze. During their trip, Korean women tourists' practice becomes similar to that of TV audiences or moviegoers. They enter the virtual space to experience the very real New York City, which exists only as an imaginary city. Korean women who traveled in the millennial age have fewer problems with accepting the validity of their experience; rather, they do not care about the dichotomy of the imaginary versus the real. Instead, they have a tendency to embrace the conditions of their traveling, though not always willingly. As a matter of fact, some younger Korean tourists enjoy this inter-critiquing process between reality and simulacra, and the ambiguousness of their relationship:

> I enjoyed finding some familiarities when I was walking through the City. Familiar brands, familiar buildings, familiar scenes . . . with what I have seen in the movies, TV, photos, and somewhere else. It gave me a kind of feeling as like I am not here for the first time

and I'm not a stranger here. If I can't see the entire City, it would be okay to be a character in a movie or drama. By doing so, I can create my own memory. That's my image of the City.

(Travelogue from the blog posting by "may0710")[6]

In this way, they participate in the simulation process by rendering authenticity to the simulacra of New York City. This process is where New York City discourses of their own have started. Then, how does this story proceed? How can it be performed? How do they operate inside the hyper-real space of New York City? One of the answers to these questions is to be a *flâneuse*,[7] which can be described as the essential figure of the modern urban spectator with full possession of individuality (Benjamin, 1969).

To Be a Flâneuse

In watching American TV shows and movies that depict life in New York City, Korean women set the norms for it and start to incorporate it into their trip. Installing hyper-reality into their traveling begins with engaging in the various practices performed in the shows. It is completed when these women identify themselves as one of the lived characters of the global media products. Among those media products, participants in the interview identify *Sex and the City* as the most effective one. The TV series *Sex and the City* premiered on the American cable network HBO in 1998. It grew in popularity in the US and Korea as well, where young Korean women especially favor it:

> I pretty much enjoyed the show. I can sympathize myself to the characters in the show; I am 30 something, struggling in my working place, and desperate to know what love means to me. When I decided to go to New York, I wanted to walk the Manhattan as they do and chat with friends. Most of all, I used to talk to myself. I might meet someone in the corner of the avenue in the City.
>
> (Interview from the S2)

Thus, Korean women tourists arrive in New York City with a desire to behave like the characters on the show. Like the four main characters, most of the Korean women who travel to New York City maintain their careers while struggling with their lives, love, and/or work. They are willing to embrace the newly gained freedom from their socio-economic achievements. Often they are unmarried/single women, just like the characters of the show.

Korean women in this study want to emulate this as well. In some ways, they resemble the characters of the show. They are stylish, affluent young women and want to enjoy the freedom stemming from their career achievement and social acknowledgment. They similarly wander around with mixed feelings of bitterness and various romantic imaginations. How can a Korean woman tourist be an actress or a character in her own show? They do so as they connect their touring activity to the practice of the show. They desperately seek the meaning of the practice represented as the New Yorker's one, such as going to restaurants, visiting galleries/museums, or having parties. Probably the most available practice is walking the city streets. Thus, Korean women emulate the practice while trying to connect the visuality of the city to its concept. This activity is often described in the show of *Sex and the City*. In fact, scenes of walking in the city become major parts of the characters' practice and the series' *mise-en-scène*.

Just as Carrie becomes a flâneuse in a postmodern sense (Richards, 2003), Korean women tourists also try to see, walk, and observe as much as possible, even if they could not completely decode the life in the city and penetrate all the "thicks and thins" (de Certeau, 1984) of the city. A newspaper article reports that more female travelers try to make their trip beyond sightseeing; there is an increasing trend in women's traveling toward experiencing a new lifestyle.[8] Tourists tired of shifting from famous spot to spot move to their interest in catching up with the New Yorker's everyday life:

> I don't want to write my travelogue in such a tourist guider's manner; go there and see this and take pictures and move to another place . . . something like that. I want to meet a lived scene and a people's life there. Different colors, various jobs, and unique styles . . . are my guidebook for this trip to New York City. By observing their lives, I want to find another myself which is not confined to my past memories.
>
> (Travelogue from the blog posting by "may0710")[9]

Through their practices, they deconstruct the image that is usually regarded as the "essence" of New York City and its culture. They try to situate themselves to be free from conceptualizing, purifying, or generalizing the city. Their gazes only try to visually possess the city as the flâneuse practice gets deeper and takes in the city as it is. Then, they go further to interpret the city with their own words and images. Korean women tourists, in this sense, have the potential to be the flâneuses of the postmodern time and globalized space of New York City.

Conclusion

Creating a Hybridity?

When the trips end and the Korean women tourists return to their home country, they recreate images of New York City inside their own environments. The appreciation of the city by themselves gives them a position as providers of cultural experience. The experience of mediated hyper-reality renders them the reinforced simulacra of the city:

> I saw people who had visited New York become fans of the City. I didn't understand them. However, after I visited there, I was able to understand them. And I am the one of them. When I viewed the symbolic places such as Empire State Building, I couldn't fully realize that I loved the City clearly. But when I came back home and I remembered the trip, I could finally realize I really liked the City.
>
> (Posting in the message board of the Traveler's Café)[10]

Their visual memory, consolidated with a localized version of the touring practice, produces a pastiche culture and new trends. They disseminate their experience through various forms of cultural activities. For instance, the fad of having brunch in an American-style brunch café reflects one of those activities. Media critics in Korea agree with the fact that one of the reasons for, and backgrounds of, this fad is the appearance of brunch scenes in *Sex and the City*.[11] Young Korean women who have visited New York City along with other fans of the show together created this trend, making restaurants begin serving a brunch menu, which was not common before. The owner of one of the brunch cafés in Seoul, *Stove*, says that most of the previous customers had been foreigners living in Seoul when *Stove* opened five years ago, but nowadays young Korean women dominate, comprising about 90 percent of the guests.[12] This has coincided with the televising of *Sex and the City* on a cable TV channel[13] and the increase in trips to America, including New York City. While eating brunch and talking to friends about their lives as single women, they think they eat and enjoy life like New Yorkers. Thus, for them going to a brunch café is not just an eating habit; more than that, it is a cultural and/or tourist practice.

A variety of cultural trends can be counted as examples of cultural practice in Korea: popularity of the New York-style bagel, emergence of Broadway musical mania, and the appearance of other fashion icons and brands. This phenomenon can be read both as a transient fad and a long-term cultural adoption. In addition, it can be criticized as the result of commodification and blind emulation of other cultures. However, these activities have the potential for the development of hybridization of two different cultures.

The process of absorbing other cultural modalities as revealed in these activities shows how the virtuality of a city's image has reproduced in different places. The tourists create a virtual New York, New York style, or New York life that may not exactly be real or true. In this sense, their activity is a simulation. They endorse hyper-reality in their activity and cultural practice. On the one hand, they are influenced by various representations from global media such as satellite broadcasts. On the other hand, those media effects are reinforced and revitalized by traveling to New York City. They think they confirmed the life and style of New York during their travel, but those processes were also done in the context of the mediated and hyper-real gazes. Thus, it seems to form an incessant reproduction cycle.

As a result of this process, hybrid spaces are enabled: New York in Seoul and Korea town in Manhattan. They—the media audience and tourists alike—can develop their own intercultural space and practice of hybridizing the cities. Therefore, when Korean women tourists believe that they are authentic knowers of New York City and they have the authority to confirm authenticity of "New York-ness," they could be criticized for the essentialist view. When they travel, see, and appreciate New York City, they have to bear in mind that their gazes are mediated and searching simulacra. When they conceptualize the city and deconstruct it by their practice, they must remind themselves that the city is a living place and is still changing.

More and more women travel all over the world, either alone or together. Along this line, many Korean women are now traveling alone. Numerous responses were posted answering the question whether New York City would be safe for a woman to travel alone:

> Everybody dreams spending a week in the City . . . There are some places which are dangerous especially during late night. Yet, if you put a little caution on the information, it's not dangerous at all. The City is also the place people live . . . and there is danger, anger, and routine but it's always energetic and full of life.
> (Posting in the message board of the Traveler's Café)[14]

As traveling is one keyword of a quality life, women are emerging as the subject of travel. They come out to New York City despite some remaining danger in order to meet their new selves. Although their gazes begin with a mediated image of the city and mix with hyper-real experiences, they constantly try to learn the "thick and thin" life of the city. Their practices provide the inception of the hybridization of cultures, despite the caveat of the politics of hybridity between the cultures (Pieterse, 1994). Therefore, in the age of global media broadcasting and information technologies, touring practice can blur the boundaries of media experiences and expands the possibility of creating hybrid cultures.

Notes

1 *Yonhap Repere*, Korean tourists' newspaper (retrieved January 5, 2007).
2 Annual Report of Korea Tourism Organization, 2005 Survey.
3 http://blog.naver.com/dktladl1/ 20032979589 (retrieved February 4, 2007).
4 http://blog.naver.com/may07110 (retrieved January 20, 2007).
5 http://blog.naver.com/irischu (retrieved January 20, 2007).

6 http://blog.naver.com/may07110 (retrieved January 20, 2007).
7 The term comes from *flânerie*, which means strolling and idling, often connoting the idea of wasting time. However, the term has shaped ambiguous meanings: it contains curiosity as well as laziness; mindlessness as well as intelligence.
8 http://khan.co.kr (retrieved February 1, 2007).
9 http://blog.naver.com/may07110 (retrieved January 20, 2007).
10 http://bbs4.worln.media.daum.net (retrieved February 5, 2007).
11 *The Hankyoreh*. (2006). Like a young New Yorker, April 12. Online at www.hani.co.kr/arti/culture/travel/115226.html (retrieved April 28, 2007).
12 Ibid.
13 *Sex and the City* was first televised on 2002 on pay-per-view channel Catch On, but popular awareness rose when general cable channels such as OCN and OnStyle aired it in 2004 and 2005.
14 http://bbs4.worln.media.daum.net (retrieved February 5, 2007).

References

Appadurai, A. (1990). Disjuncture and difference in the global culture economy. In M. Featherstone (Ed.), *Global culture: Nationalism, globalization and modernity*. London: Sage.
Appadurai, A. (1996). *Modernity at large: Cultural dimensions of globalization*. Minneapolis: University of Minnesota Press.
Baudrillard, J. (1994). *Simulacra and simulation* (trans. S. F. Glaser). Ann Arbor: University of Michigan Press.
Beck, U. (2000). *What is globalization?* Cambridge: Polity Press.
Benjamin, W. (1969). *Illuminations* (ed. H. Arendt; trans. Harry Zohn). New York: Schocken Books.
Beynon, J., & Dunkerley, D. (2000). *Globalization: The reader*. New York: Routledge.
Boyd-Barrett, O. (1977). Media imperialism: Towards an international framework for the analysis of media systems. In J. Curran, M. Gurevich, & J. Woollacott (Eds.), *Mass communication and society*. London: Edward Arnold.
Campbell, N. (2005). Producing America: Redefining post-tourism in the global media age. In D. Crouch, R. Jackson, & F. Thompson (Eds.), *The media and the tourist imagination*. New York: Routledge.
Cvetkovich, A., & Kellner, D. (1997). *Articulating the global and the local: Globalization and cultural studies*. Boulder, CO: Westview.
Davin, S. (2005). Tourists and television viewers: Some similarities. In D. Crouch, R. Jackson, and F. Thompson (Eds.), *The media and the tourist imagination*. New York: Routledge.
de Certeau, M. (1984). *The practice of everyday life* (trans. S. Rendall, 2011). Berkeley: University of California Press.
Donald, J. (1997). This, here, now: Imagining the modern city. In S. Westwood & J. Williams (Eds.), *Imagining cities: Scripts, signs, memory*. London: Routledge.
Eco, U. (1986*). *Travels in hyperreality*. Orlando, FL: Harcourt Brace Jvanovich. [*English translation copyright.]
Featherstone, M., Lash, S., & Robertson, R. (1995). *Global modernities*. London: Sage.
Fiske, J. (1987). *Television culture*. London: Routledge.

Foucault, M. (1976). *The birth of the clinic*. London: Tavistock.

Giddens, A. (1990). *The consequences of modernity*. Cambridge, UK: Polity Press.

Giddens, A. (1991). *Modernity and self-identity: Self and society in the late modern age*. Cambridge, UK: Polity Press.

Jackson, R. (2005). Converging cultures; converging gazes; contextualizing perspectives. In D. Crouch, R. Jackson, and F. Thompson (Eds.), *The media & the tourist imagination: Converging cultures*. New York: Routledge.

Kim, S. (2007). *My stylish trip: Traveling to the city wearing a high heel*. Seoul: AhnGraphics.

Kim, Y. (2005). Experiencing globalization: Global TV, reflexivity and the lives of young Korean women. *International Journal of Cultural Studies, 8*(4), 445–463.

Kirshenblatt-Gimblett, B. (1998). *Destination culture: Tourism, museums, and heritage*. Berkeley: University of California Press.

Lagerkvist, A. (2004). "We see America": Mediatized and mobile gazes in Swedish post-war travelogues. *International Journal of Cultural Studies, 7*(3), 321–342.

Liebes, T., & Katz, E. (1990). *The export of meaning: Cross-cultural readings of "Dallas."* New York: Oxford University Press.

Mattelart, A., Delacourt, X., & Mattelart, M. (1984). *International image markets*. London: Comedia.

Mohammadi, A. S. (1991). The global and the local in international communications. In J. Curran & M. Gerevitch (Eds.), *Mass media and society*. London: Edward Arnold.

Morley, D., & Robins, K. (1995). *Spaces of identity: Global media, electronic landscapes and cultural boundaries*. London: Routledge.

Pieterse, J. (1994). Globalization as hybridization. In M. Durham & D. Keller (Eds.), *Media and cultural studies* (pp. 658–680). Oxford: Blackwell.

Press, A. L. (1991). *Women watching television*. Philadelphia: University of Pennsylvania Press.

Richards, H. (2003). Sex and the City: a visible flaneuse for the postmodern era? *Continuum: Journal of Media and Cultural Studies, 17*(2), 147–157.

Rodaway, P. (1995). Exploring the subject in hyper-reality. In S. Pile & N. Thrift (Eds.), *Mapping the subject*. London: Routledge.

Rojek, C. (1997). Indexing, dragging and the social construction of tourist sights. In C. Rojeck & J. Urry (Eds.), *Touring cultures*. London: Routledge.

Sadler, W., & Haskins, V. (2005). Metonymy and the metropolis: Television show settings and the image of New York City. *Journal of Communication Inquiry, 29*(3), 195–216.

Said, E. (1979). *Orientalism*. New York: Vintage.

Schiller, H. (1985). Electronic information flows as the new basis for global domination. In P. Drummond & R. Patterson (Eds.) *Television in transition*. London: BFI.

Silj, A. (1988). *East of Dallas: The European challenge to American television*. London: British Film Institute.

Sinclair, J., Jacka, E., & Cunningham, S. (Eds.). (1996). *New patterns in global television: Peripheral vision*. Oxford: Oxford University Press.

Tomlinson, J. (1991). *Cultural imperialism*. London: Pinter Publishers.

Urry, J. (1995). *Consuming places*. London: Sage.

Urry, J. (2002). *The tourist gaze* (2nd ed.). London: Sage.

9

ASSESSING THE ROLE AUDIENCE PLAYS IN DIGITAL BROADCASTING TODAY AND TOMORROW

Dwight DeWerth-Pallmeyer

In the early to mid-1990s, audience analysis was one of the hot topics in mass communication research. A number of books addressed the ways in which audience concerns were being factored into modern communication strategies: *The Future of the Mass Audience* (Neuman, 1991), *Desperately Seeking the Audience* (Ang, 1991), *Audiencemaking: How the Media Create the Audience* (Ettema & Whitney, 1994), my own *The Audience in the News* (DeWerth-Pallmeyer, 1997), and *The Mass Audience: Rediscovering the Dominant Model* (Webster & Phalen, 1997).

In that era, authors often pointed to the use of sophisticated audience research methods by media organizations, but many understood that audience imagery was typically fuzzy at best by those who wrote and created programming. I argued that both print and broadcast news producers operated with a tacit understanding of audience concerns that grew out of their day-to-day work with media products:

> Whether or not individual journalists have a clear understanding about the demographics or psychographics of their audience or whether they envision their audience as simply those with whom they come in contact during an individual week, those perceptions can and do have a potent effect on the news that is eventually produced. For example, direct contact with audience members, through letters and phone calls, has been shown to produce changes from even the highest levels of the newsrooms, albeit, typically stylistic changes.
>
> (DeWerth-Pallmeyer, 1997, p. 118)

Fast forward to the middle of the 2010s, and the differences between that era and today are vast indeed. Genuine audience interaction with all kinds of media is profound and an increasingly important part of the development of news, entertainment, and broadcasting efforts. Incidental observations of the audience by media producers are much less important in a world in which direct observation is seemingly readily available to media organizations that can effortlessly monitor the constant chatter and feedback via email, social media and social networking platforms.

The dramatic growth of the internet has catapulted the audience into the forefront of media production. By the end of 1995, less than half a percent of the world's population had internet access. Today, over 40 percent are accessing the internet, while North American internet penetration is nearly 85 percent (Miniwatts Marketing Group, 2014).

Of course, access is just one part of the initial equation. "Access" denotes a passive viewer or listener, akin to the relevant model of the broadcast audience in the mid 1990s. Today, audience members not only receive media messages, photos, sound, and video via the internet, they also immediately respond to those media creations online, and produce their own original programming. While those "first responders" may not be completely representative of the total audience, they do represent a more precise image of the audience for professional broadcast producers worldwide. They also represent a younger audience, the audience most coveted in the traditional advertising-supported programming model and the audience most relevant to those interested in what lies ahead for broadcasting.

Those "engaged" habits, learned and largely practiced by younger viewers and listeners, are the kinds of habits that stick around for a media consumer's lifetime. That is why one sees large discrepancies in media usage patterns between generations. Those who grew up watching TV in the traditional broadcast mode are much less comfortable accessing programming via cellphones and laptops than those who grew up taking for granted that kind of program transmission.

Evan Shapiro has served as President of IFC TV and Sundance TV. Today he is the president of "Participant TV." He characterizes the history of television as encompassing three different periods: the network era, characterized by "no choice," when viewers typically had only three network options to watch; the multi-channel era, when viewers had numerous cable channels from which to choose; and TV today, an era marked by niche programming in a time when viewers can choose what to watch, when they want to watch something, and wherever they want to watch something (Shapiro, 2012). "My entire thesis on television is that niche is new mass . . . So you have to cater your programming to a smaller, yet more passionate group of consumers. And that's because of technology" (Zammit, 2012).

Traditional broadcast television viewing patterns for older adults remain steady, while younger audiences are markedly turning away from traditional TV. A September 2014 analysis of three years of Nielsen viewing data concluded, "there's no denying a steady decline in traditional TV viewing by 18–24-year-olds; the weekly average has now dropped on a year-over-year basis for at least 10 consecutive quarters" (MarketingCharts Staff, 2014). Now, approximately half of those who watch network television are not among the coveted 25–54-year-old demographic. Traditional broadcast television viewing patterns for older adults remain steady, while younger audiences are markedly turning away from traditional TV (Crupi, 2013).

Traditional over-the-air radio is also seeing seismic changes due to changing listening patterns. Listenership is increasingly moving toward streaming services. In fact, from 2012 to 2013, streaming listening increased 32 percent (Hill, 2014). By early 2014, noticeable differences in listening patterns were emerging between the young and the old. Online radio use was much more popular for younger listeners: "75% of Americans ages 12–24 listen(ed) to online radio in the last month, compared to 50% of Americans ages 25–54 and 21% of Americans 55+" (Sass, 2014).

Additionally, the movement toward streaming listening is impacting the music industry as well. Industry analyst Paul Goldstein notes that sales of music and mp3s has been dwindling for some time and that future trends point to music supported from advertising-supported streaming services such as Pandora (Goldstein, 2014).

As this book attests, the broadcast landscape of today and tomorrow is dramatically different from the broadcast world of just a few years ago. One of the key factors in that change is the dramatically more engaged younger audience reacting to and self-producing the broadcast product. That means they are consuming programming on their own terms.

Key Players

Today it is often hard to distinguish between social media and broadcast entities and that will likely be all the more confusing in the future. The viewing models developing from the introduction of YouTube and Netflix, coupled with the peer-to-peer promotion of new, independent, and free programming services, pose as much a dramatic threat to traditional broadcast models as the advent of Napster and other peer-to-peer file-sharing programs altered the model of music sales and distribution in the late 1990s.

File sharing of music led to the loss of millions of dollars for record labels. Young consumers, who traditionally bought LPs and CDs, were now simply sharing digital data files of the music they acquired (Venturini et al., 2013). Without an easy way of policing the practice, music companies and recording artists were forced into new methods of procuring income for their efforts.

Prior to the Napsterization of music, recording artists and record companies largely toured and played live events in efforts to sell their records and CDs. Now that equation has largely been reversed. Many artists today virtually give away their music for free, hoping the music will help attract large audiences to their concert performances. That change came about due to the way audience members were interacting with each other and disrupting traditional distribution methods. Such dramatic change is going on within broadcasting today and will undoubtedly continue to do so in the future.

YouTube

The great success story behind YouTube lies in an active audience that not only embraced the new technology but also began producing the very material it consumed. One of the reasons for the quick, dramatic growth of YouTube was the way individuals could see themselves at the center of the media world they created for themselves. *The New Yorker* magazine media critic, Ken Auletta, writes, "In the world of YouTube, not only is every device a television but every viewer is a potential network and content provider." Auletta argues broadcast TV currently is seeing two major threats: challenges to the traditional advertising-supported programming model, and new competing streaming services that can deliver the programming outside traditional broadcast delivery systems (Auletta, 2014).

As part of his honors thesis at the Stern School of business at NYU, student Adity Pisharody boldly proclaimed, "YouTube is arguably the single most influential and revolutionary innovation of the 21st Century to date" (2013, p. 32). Pisharody credits YouTube's success to its simple formula, which allowed and enabled everyone who wanted to share video online the resources to do so. Broadcasters, have of course taken note. Producers now take the time to examine the content of YouTube in developing their own network ideas (Geere, 2013).

To say the YouTube model has been successful would be vastly understating the obvious. Google was able to see the value of the enterprise when it purchased YouTube for 1.65 billion dollars in 2006 (Marshall, 2006). By 2011, Google required those with YouTube accounts to acquire Google accounts, leading more and more users to engage with other Google products and develop strong ties with the Google infrastructure.

The YouTube phenomenon points to one of the most consequential shifts broadcasting has faced in recent years and will undoubtedly persist in the years to come—an audience so completely engaged with its own media consumption that it is forcefully taking charge of its overall viewing environment. The modern viewer, typically younger, is creating programming, deciding when to watch or listen to that programming, picking and choosing programming on an individual basis, and choosing what platforms and devices to use to both produce and consume the desired programming.

Netflix

The success story of YouTube is mirrored in the Netflix revolution. The growth of Netflix pointed to an audience seeking instant access to movies and prime TV programming for a very modest price. In its early days, Netflix was largely viewed as an inconsequential alternative to the video and DVD renting behemoth Blockbuster Video. It provided viewers with the chance to choose movies and order them in the mail, a seemingly novelty act.

But perhaps Netflix's real genius was in its decision to provide movies to its viewers online. No longer would media consumers need to make trips to video stores or wait for movies to be delivered by the mail. That instant delivery system paid off in dividends, drawing an audience that was already fading away from both video stores and DVD offerings.

In the early 2000s, Netflix was seeking to sell itself to Blockbuster Video for $50 million dollars, but Blockbuster refused to make the deal. By 2010, Blockbuster filed for bankruptcy protection and, by 2013, Netflix was valued at almost $20 billion dollars (Graser, 2013). The failure of Blockbuster to fully understand Netflix's potential and to appreciate the rapid change in its audience's viewing preferences doomed Blockbuster to future obscurity.

Netflix succeeded because it knew its technology, but perhaps, more importantly, knew its audience potential. That led to the company producing its first series, *House of Cards*. Netflix has successfully duplicated that approach with its two-season run of *Orange Is the New Black*, and has breathed new life into other series canceled by broadcast networks, such as *Arrested Development* and *The Killing* (Wikipedia, 2014b).

Developing its own series allowed Netflix the same posture afforded broadcast networks, the financial leverage inherent in both producing and distributing its own programming. It also allowed Netflix the chance to market its distribution service based on its own products, the same marquee strategy earlier demonstrated by pay movie channels, HBO and Showtime.

Netflix also took a leap of faith with its audience in making the decision to instantly stream entire seasons of its programming, allowing viewers to binge watch a show over the course of a couple of days (Auletta, 2014). Such a move allowed early bingers the chance to promote the shows to those who prefer to watch series over the course of days, weeks, or months. Netflix was using "word of mouth" advertising to generate its own hype.

The Netflix strategies have clearly worked with dramatic gains in streaming subscribers in the US and internationally too (Venturini et al. 2013).

One important impact the Netflix formula has had on digital broadcasting is in its incentivizing of a younger generation to cut the cord with cable (Venturini et al., 2013). Younger viewers, who never knew a time without having options for what to watch and when to watch, are now also choosing their own methods of acquiring distributed content. In late 2014, HBO announced plans to start delivering its programming to consumers who did not carry cable subscriptions.

Forrester analyst, James McQuivey, noted that while this might not change the TV industry overnight, it is another step that undermines the future of cable providers:

> While pay TV operators are certainly furious today, other cable programmers like Viacom and A&E are thrilled that HBO is shining a light down a path they may all have to contemplate in the future," McQuivey said. "None of them will have as easy a time as will HBO, but they all know they need an escape hatch for that moment when the current, bundled TV model begins to collapse.
>
> (Abbruzzese, 2014)

Once again, while this move clearly comes in efforts to further increase revenues for HBO, it also points to consumer demands. Of course, the audience wants to pay only for the TV it consumes, not for extra channels that it finds bloated and unnecessary. The growing end-games viewers have made to circumvent cable-bundling strategies demonstrate that distribution strategies will inevitably change, likely in the short term.

Amazon Prime

The model of a retail distributor streaming inexpensive video programming, and then developing its own programming, is now also practiced by Amazon Prime. As part of its marketing and audience research efforts, Amazon has begun streaming show pilots to its broad audience. Viewers are prompted to rate each show and leave comments.

While such a strategy indeed offers Amazon useful information, it also does something just as important—it engages its viewers. Those who take the time to rate a show will undoubtedly feel more invested in the show and in its future. In turn, these viewers will more likely purchase and renew their Amazon prime memberships, and shop for other products Amazon distributes. Just as astute retailers know how to place products in their stores in locations to entice shoppers to make unintended purchases, Amazon uses an online strategy to entice its Prime viewers to glance at its wares as well.

Social Media Interaction

Amazon's model is one that illustrates a direct feedback connection with its audience, but of course savvy broadcasters have developed many ways of assessing audience response and input in the past. Now they also have a wide net of social media sources they can monitor.

Smartphone Consumption

Clearly, another impetus for changes to the broadcasting picture is the fast adoption of the smartphone. By 2014, over 60 percent of Americans owned a smartphone, while 80 percent of those aged 18–34 owned one (T. Webster, 2014). Smartphones have given individuals the chance to listen to digital programming, view digital programming, and produce digital programming for consumers around the world. Numerous phone apps have capitalized on cellphone owners' thirst for exploiting the capabilities of the sophisticated, pocket-sized hardware in their pockets. Many radio stations promote their own dedicated apps for local smartphone owners. Those apps can help build dedicated listeners. But other apps afford radio listeners the opportunity to access radio stations and podcasts from around the world.

TuneIn, for example, is an app for both the Android and the iPhone markets. It offers worldwide access to streaming radio stations and podcasts. There is a free version of the app as well as a paid version that allows listeners the ability to record the programs on their phones. Sirius-XM also offers an app for allowing its customers the chance to listen to its programming via smartphone. Such a strategy provides another revenue stream for the company while encouraging greater brand loyalty.

Switching Places

In some ways, the digital broadcast world of tomorrow flip-flops the relationship between the broadcast entities and their audiences from the one seen just a few years ago. Today's younger audience is growing up in control of its viewing environment in stark contrast to those who grew up in the limited push TV environment of the 1960s. In its assessment of broadcast's future, Accenture Consulting characterized the changing landscape:

> Where broadcasters once held power, with exclusive command over the viewing experience, consumers now rule. They want to be in control of what they consume and when they consume it— creating their own new digital experiences across channels and devices, planning their own entertainment schedules, and finding new ways to interact with content itself.
>
> (Venturini et al., 2013, p. 15)

149

Astute broadcasters are making changes and so are television manufacturers. For example, the *Connected TV Forecasts* report predicts that, worldwide, almost one billion TVs will be connected to the internet by 2020, approximately 30 percent of all televisions. That compares to just over 4 percent of all televisions at the end of 2010. In South Korea and in the UK, that will amount to over 50 percent of all TVs (Digital TV Research, 2014). That internet connection, of course, will allow hundreds of millions of video creators to view their works on bigger screens, perhaps a way to entice back younger viewers to some form of broadcast television distributed along with internet programming.

Broadcast Strategies to Adapt to Audience Change

Actively monitoring social media has clear benefits for broadcasters. Traditional means of measuring and defining an audience via traditional research methods (such as focus groups or surveys) can cost five times as much as acquiring that data via social networking sites (Chui et al., 2012). Numerous TV shows and television networks have come to embrace internet technologies that serve to draw show producers closer to the audiences they so covet. They do that with the recognition that many viewers are watching television on one screen while talking back to it on another.

Shapiro argues that multiple offerings are clearly in the interest of broadcast programmers: "The more you can feed that passion with second-screen experiences, communal experiences, live complementary experiences, the more loyal that audience will wind up being" (Zammit, 2012). The former IFC-TV President said shows like Portlandia are fostered by social media interactions: "While we do control our own Twitter output, we don't try to mandate a curative experience over Twitter or even on Facebook. We really do allow the consumers to drive a tremendous amount of the conversation" (Zammit, 2012).

In a 2014 entry, the website Social Media Today (Cohen, 2014) outlined how six top broadcast shows purposely engaged their viewers via social media. For example, CBS's *Big Bang Theory* dominated network ratings for much of the early 2010s in the United States. The show used several strategies to promote itself, including providing episode teasers on Facebook, and promoting the GetGlue app for its viewers. The mobile app lets viewers clue in their friends on the shows they watch, serving as promotion agents for these shows.

Competition shows such as *American Idol* and *Dancing With the Stars* have made audience polling and feedback part of the formula for winning the competitions. Cognizant.com consultant, James Benedict, concludes, "The true power of social media is in the information it provides. Millions of users, generating thousands of messages every minute, freely give away valuable insights in public forums" (Benedict, 2013). When those prompts, tweets and posts help promote programs, the peer-to-peer promotion is typically more persuasive than any message the program developer could provide itself.

Broadcasters are now using social media to also attract viewers to new shows. In 2014, the Starz network aired the first episode of its series, *Power*, on Twitter. Starz touted the show's interactive capabilities as the "first-ever television show to premiere on Twitter using the service's new in-line video feature ... make(ing) it possible for people to do things like watch videos, download apps, or view articles and photos—all from within a Tweet" (Starz, 2014).

The year 2014 also witnessed the rebranding of the TV app, Zeebox, to Beamly—a platform designed to function as both a source of information about television and as a social media networking site for television viewers (Wikipedia, 2014a). The site's CEO, Jason Forbes, argues that television's interaction with its audience will soon be nonstop:

> I think you're going to see even higher levels of interactivity and inter-leaving between the TV show and its audience, pointing to a 24×7 cadence that in many cases continues after the season has ended for episodic content. There is also more permeability than ever before as super fans become influencers in shaping broader TV behaviours and in some cases come to shape the content of the TV itself.
>
> (Informa Telecoms and Media, 2014)

Radio programmers have also explored ways to promote audience interaction via social media. Some believe the "social function" of radio fits naturally with the inherent abilities of social media, tying audiences to radio stations and developing a strong sense of listener loyalty. Media strategist Loyd Ford believes social media interactions among radio listeners can lead those listeners to greater station loyalty, enticing them to visit station websites and listen even more:

> We have the same opportunities to engage listeners using visuals to grab attention, local weather to create alerts, specifics on local stories important to listeners (or at least topics), and to engage them in a fairly constant variety of content that keeps us in the conversation with listeners we most want to attract.
>
> (Shapiro, 2014)

Behemoth radio conglomerate Clear Channel is allying itself with Facebook to make that connection.

Similar changes are taking place around the globe. Paul Cordeiro studies radio in Portugal and the message there mirrors the image in the United States: "The radio industry is currently striving to become a more web-based and multimedia business" (Corderio, 2012, p. 494). For Cordeiro, those new capabilities may be key to keeping radio alive, despite pressure from so many competing sources of information and entertainment: "Multimedia takes radio out of its traditional business and broadcasting model, updating a medium with a history of more than eighty years, and giving the listener a broad set of capabilities" (Corderio, 2012, p. 495).

Indeed radio is free to utilize new capabilities and employ new production and distribution technologies. Just as YouTube has allowed novice film makers the opportunity to get their materials "aired" to a large number of people, audio sites such as the Berlin, Germany-based SoundCloud, have opened the door for audiophiles to present their mixes, musicians to record their own music, and individuals to stream their own works. Many college radio stations are shedding their broadcast costs and simply streaming their programming to listeners around the world.

Viewing the Digital Broadcast Audience Through Another Lens

Technological innovation and evolving audience expectations are forcing all those involved in the modern television enterprise to rethink the way programming is used and consumed. Dan Tucker is a freelance producer who recognizes in himself the changing viewing patterns he needs to account for in his own work, "Most of the comedy content I watch from TV I watch whilst commuting," says Tucker. "Then I'll sit down with my wife and watch back-to-back episodes of a drama. Big documentary series are often watched on long rail or plane journeys" (Geere, 2013).

The digital broadcasters of tomorrow will likely never earn the audience share enjoyed by the TV networks in the 1960s and 1970s. There are just too many alternatives available to contemporary and future TV viewers. And just tuning into a show does not necessarily indicate passion for a show or consistency in audience attention. Audience members may interpret programming in ways inconsistent with media producers. Scholar Phillip J. Hanes contends no two members of an audience perceive messages in the same way: "This alerts users of the various media to the ambiguity of meaning and the richness inherent in the medium, aspects that producers need to be aware of in the construction of their texts" (Hanes, 2014, p. 8).

Of course, from the perspective of traditional broadcasting, viewer ambiguity and content richness is of minor concern. In the advertising-supported model, networks focus on delivering the greatest number of viewers or listeners to advertisers; the audience is essentially viewed as a commodity. Yet such a view is inherently limiting and may not even be the most productive model for garnering profits. José Alberto García-Avilés argues for a broader model—viewing listeners or viewers as "citizens" within the multi-platform world of the future:

the image of the citizen before the television set goes beyond the reductionist concepts of spectator and consumer. A citizen is not only the subject of the reception, nor the mere consumer of images and/or products, but a subject implicated in different kind of processes: communicative, cultural, social, political, etc.

(García-Avilés, 2012, p. 432)

In his analysis of Spain's television system, García-Avilés outlines eight different ways of envisioning the TV audience: as consumers, as players, as followers, as commentators, as citizens, as collaborators, as benefactors, and as activists (p. 435).

In broadening the perspective of the modern digital broadcast audience, one recognizes that today's viewers and listeners are no longer simply passive receivers, nor are they capable of just incidental feedback. Instead, the audience needs to be considered a dynamic component of future broadcast models. Increasingly, engaged viewers and listeners can provide instant programming analyses, promote programs they like, recommend program modifications, and generate their own materials for distribution.

When one confines oneself to considering the future of digital broadcasting only in respect to projected technological developments or in business forecasting, the prognostications can be perplexing. There are just too many variables at play. Yet, when one takes a step back and considers audience needs and behaviors, the likely scenarios are easier to anticipate.

Television and radio entities will increasingly encounter viewers and listeners who actively engage with the material they hear and see. They will do this via direct contact with broadcast distributors and by offering feedback through a multitude of social media outlets and tools. They will also create their own programs and media products and distribute them through a growing array of platforms and software programs. Some will simply share materials with close friends, while others will share the materials with the world. Some of this sharing will be done for fun and self-expression, while some will be done in efforts to profit financially.

The technological capabilities of this sharing will undoubtedly allow some to illegally profit from others' efforts and to break copyright laws—regulations that may be enforced in some countries while not in others. Attempting to safeguard producers' rights will likely turn out to be unmanageable, just as early efforts to prosecute early peer-to-peer sharing on Naptster led listeners to share the music in different ways. While attempting to operate exclusively within the traditional confines of the advertising-supported broadcasting model is continuing to prove more difficult, broadcasters who keep their focus on audience usage patterns and capabilities will likely come out ahead.

The Bigger Picture

In his "Vast Wasteland" speech in 1961, new FCC director, Newton Minow, admonished the US National Association of Broadcasters to do better by its audience and offer programming alternatives:

> You must provide a wider range of choices, more diversity, more alternatives. It is not enough to cater to the nation's whims; you must also serve the nation's needs. And I would add this: that if some of you persist in a relentless search for the highest rating and the lowest common denominator, you may very well lose your audience.
>
> (Minow, 1961)

Now, over 50 years later, the message appears prescient. Of course, American programmers were not readily accepting of Minow's message and flagrantly aired more than their share of "lowest common denominator programming." Decades later, however, the development and subsequent growth of cable, the internet, and satellite transmission have led to far greater choice for both radio listeners and TV viewers. Growing audience segmentation approaches naturally led programmers to innovate in a variety of both profound and insignificant ways.

As FCC Commissioner, Minow's focus seemed less concerned with the broadcast industry and more targeted on the audience it served. While his orientation likely stemmed from the period's emphasis on broadcasting's "social responsibility" to operate in the public "interest, convenience and necessity," it also makes good sense today and for the foreseeable future. Radio that will still address local or vital concerns or that will cater to unique tastes and lifestyles can naturally develop loyal listeners. When television allows for multiple creators and gives genuine credence to audience discussion and chatter via social media outlets, it will likely develop a base of engaged viewers.

Learning how to authentically tap into the expressed concerns and input of an active audience will be of value not only to those who watch or listen to a particular program, but to the greater society. The engaged audience of today and tomorrow can be further activated to pursue greater purposes of society at large. And in that greater engagement, the broadcaster will undoubtedly come to benefit as well.

References

Abbruzzese, J. (2014). HBO to offer standalone streaming service in U.S. in 2015. *Mashable.com*, October 15. Online at http://mashable.com/ (retrieved October 24, 2014).

Ang, I. (1991). *Desperately seeking the audience*. London: Routledge.

Auletta, K. (2014). Outside the box: Netflix and the future of television. *The New Yorker*, February 3. Online at www.newyorker.com/magazine/2014/02/03/ outside-the-box-2 (retrieved August 14, 2014).

Benedict, J. P. (2013). Embracing the power of social media for broadcast business insight. *Cognizant*, April. Online at www.cognizant.com (retrieved August 14, 2014).

Chui, M., Manyika, J., Bughin, J., Dobbs, R., Roxburgh, C., Sarrazin, H., Sands, G., & Westergren, M. (2012). *The social economy: Unlocking value and productivity through social technologies.* McKinsey Global Institute report, July. Online at www.mckinsey.com (retrieved September 14, 2014).

Cohen, P. (2014). 6 TV series that integrate social media with their broadcast. *Social Media Today*, March 15. Online at www.socialmediatoday.com (retrieved September 30, 2014).

Corderio, P. (2012). Radio becoming r@dio: Convergence, interactivity and broadcasting trends in perspective. *Participations: Journal of Audience & Reception Studies, 9*(2), 492–510. Online at www.participations.org/ (retrieved October 1, 2014).

Crupi, A. (2013). Fifty shades of grey: Broadcast audience older than ever. *Adweek*, October 16. Online at www.adweek.com (retrieved October 23, 2014).

DeWerth-Pallmeyer, D. (1997). *The audience in the news.* Mahwah, NJ: Lawrence Erlbaum Associate.

Digital TV Research. (2014). *Connected TV forecasts.* Press release, September. Online at www.digitaltvresearch.com/products/product?id=108 (retrieved September 20, 2014).

Ettema, J. S., & Whitney, D. C. (1994). *Audiencemaking: How the media create the audience.* Thousand Oaks, CA: Sage Publications.

García-Avilés, J. (2012). Roles of audience participation in multiplatform television: From fans and consumers, to collaborators and activists. *Participations: Journal of Audience & Reception Studies, 9*(2), 429–447. Online at www.participations. org (retrieved September 9, 2014).

Geere, D. (2013). Origin of the series: How TV producers are adapting for on demand. *TechRadar*, December 14. Online at www.techradar.com (retrieved October 10, 2014).

Goldstein, P. (2014). The future of the music industry: Selling audiences to advertisers. Web log post, April 4. Online at http://recode.net (retrieved September 15, 2014).

Graser, M. (2013). Epic fail: How Blockbuster could have owned Netflix. *Variety*, November 12. Online at http://variety.com (retrieved October 5, 2014).

Hanes, P. J. (2014). The advantages and limitations of a focus on audience in media studies. *A Level Media*, April 17. Online at alevelmedia.wikispaces.com (retrieved October 21, 2014).

Hill, B. (2014). Streaming music listening rose by 32% in 2013 (Nielsen). *Rain News*, January 9. Online at http://rainnews.com (retrieved October 25, 2014).

Informa Telecoms and Media. (2014). Beamly: "Our vision is to be the leading social network for TV." *TVXperience World*, August 22. Online at http:// tvxperienceevent.com/beamly-our-vision-is-to-be-the-leading-social-network-for-tv/ (retrieved October 15, 2014).

MarketingCharts Staff. (2014). Are young people watching less tv? *MarketingCharts*, September 15. Watershed Publishing. Online at www.marketingcharts.com (retrieved September 30, 2014).

Marshall, M. (2006). They did it! YouTube bought by Google for $1.65B in less than two years. *VentureBeat News*, October 9. Online at http://venturebeat.com (retrieved October 10, 2014).

Miniwatts Marketing Group. (2014). Internet growth statistics. *Internet world stats: Usage and population statistics*, October 9. Online at www.internetworldstats.com/emarketing.htm (retrieved October 10, 2014).

Minow, N. (1961). *Address to the National Association of Broadcasters (television and the public interest)*. Speech, Washington DC, May 9. Online at www.americanrhetoric.com (retrieved October 25, 2014).

Neuman, W. R. (1991). *The future of the mass audience*. Cambridge: Cambridge University Press.

Pisharody, A. (2013). The future of television: Will broadcast and cable television networks survive the emergence of online streaming? Unpublished master's thesis, Leonard N. Stern School of Business, New York.

Sass, E. (2014). Half of U.S. listeners tune into online radio. *MediaPost*, March 5. Online at www.mediapost.com (retrieved October 5, 2014).

Shapiro, E. (2012). *01—History of TV—TV101*. Lecture presented in The Cable Center, October 23. Online at www.youtube.com/watch?v=mnKcnVWdFrk (retrieved October 25, 2014).

Shapiro, G. (2014). Learning from TV social media. *Radio Ink*, May 2. Online at www.radioink.com/ (retrieved September 15, 2014).

Starz. (2014). *Starz previews new original series "Power" with premiere episode sampling initiative*. Press release, May 30. Online at http://ir.starz.com (retrieved September 20, 2014).

Venturini, F., Marshall, C., & Di Alberto, E. (2013). *The Future of Broadcasting Issue III: Strategy delivers*. Online at www.accenture.com (retrieved September 12, 2014).

Webster, J. G., & Phalen, P. F. (1997). *The mass audience: Rediscovering the dominant model*. Mahwah, NJ: Lawrence Erlbaum Associates.

Webster, T. (2014). *The infinite dial 2014*. Edison Research, Web log post, March 5. Online at www.edisonresearch.com (retrieved October 17, 2014).

Wikipedia. (2014a). *Beamly*. Online at http://en.wikipedia.org/wiki/Beamly (retrieved October 24, 2014).

Wikipedia. (2014b). List of original programs distributed by Netflix, October 24. Online at http://en.wikipedia.org (retrieved October 25, 2014).

Zammit, D. (2012). *Q&A*. Evan Shapiro, former president, IFC TV and Sundance Channel; president, Participant Television. Online at www.jwtintelligence.com (retrieved September 9, 2014).

10

CONFRONTING THE CENTRAL PARADOX OF MEDIA STUDIES

The Network Society, Digital Technologies, and the Future of Media Research

Randolph Kluver

In recent years, the developed world has become accustomed to the idea and the reality of a "globalized" world, in which cultural, political, economic, and social trends circulate widely across a wide portion of the earth. The processes of technological change, primarily driven by new technologies, including communications, travel, and digital technologies, and the increase in global interaction are deeply intertwined, making it difficult to sort out where one process begins and another ends. While there is significant scholarly divergence in opinion as to the "essence" of globalization, there are a few key characteristics upon which most observers agree, and which have implications for media studies and education. The purpose of this chapter is to highlight specific theoretical and methodological developments that have implications for re-casting global media studies away from a local or regional scale to a global scale. I will first outline the key theoretical paradigms that have emerged that challenge traditional global media studies, then focus on some of the ways in which new research methodologies offer promise to provide a fuller picture of global media. Finally, I will articulate a number of potential research agendas that emerge from these developments.

One of the key arguments of this essay is that, in this globalized age, media research needs to reflect a global perspective, but rarely does. Moreover, when it is attempted, global media research usually focuses narrowly on single country case studies. There are numerous reasons for this, including the difficulties in obtaining consistent data across multiple nations and regions, difficulties in translating the data to do accurate comparisons, and, finally, just the limitations of cross-national research. When comparative research is attempted, it often moves from the familiar (US or UK media) to the unfamiliar. This research is undoubtedly helpful in illustrating the ways in which media content and production varies across various economic, cultural, social, and political contexts. The drawback, of course, is that it roots comparative research in the experiences and production contexts of the developed world. This has a theoretical and practical effect of centering global media studies within a narrow context, namely, the Anglophone world of the US and UK. Likewise, research that develops comparative studies of the large Western media corporations (such as CNN or the BBC) end up positioning these global players as the de facto standards by which the rest of global media are measured and understood. Thus, in spite of the intention to de-center and de-privilege Western media, much global media research ends up reinforcing the prevailing dominance of these large, primarily Western corporations, not just in their place of primacy in global media production, but also in academic scholarship.

As Kluver et al. (2013) argue, academic analysis of "global" media remains focused on primarily English language broadcasters, with little academic analysis of some of the most important media outlets, which collectively speak to 80 percent of the global population. China Central Television, for example, operates over 40 different channels, perhaps the largest number of subchannels in the world, and its audience is probably well over one billion people. The network's annual Lunar New Year show, or Spring Festival Gala, is viewed by over 700 million people. And yet academic analysis of the channel remains sparse, with only a handful of either journal articles or books appearing in international journals in recent years.

The study found that, as of 2012, the pages of academic journals dedicated to media were overwhelmingly focused on studies of CNN, the BBC, and other Western broadcasters. That research showed that, within the pages of the *Journal of Broadcasting and Electronic Media* (JBEM) arguably the most important academic journal dedicated to media studies, the Fox network was featured in 246 studies, CNN (and its counterpart CCNI) in 128 studies, and the BBC in 177 studies. These "big three" accounted for 551 academic studies in the journal, fully 90 percent of the total number of essays dedicated to "global" broadcasters. These results reflect articles that only mention the broadcasters, and not necessarily full and complete studies of the outlets.

The next most prominent global broadcaster in the list (Deutsche Welle) was only mentioned in 12 articles, less than 5 percent of the number inspired by Fox. When the other Western broadcasters (Deutsche Welle, Sky News, Univision, Telemundo, and TV Globo) are added to the number of articles that mention the big three, it leaves only 18 out of 611 essays (less than 3 percent of the total) dedicated to non-Western broad-casters, and the only broadcasters featured were Al Jazeera, Al Arabiya, and Chinese Central Television.

By contrast, the most studied non-Western news source (Al Jazeera), with an estimated audience of over 40 million people, had prompted only eight studies, while the broadcaster with the largest global audience, CCTV, had only been mentioned (not featured) in nine studies. Admittedly, CCTV's audience of approximately 500 million viewers is concentrated primarily within the People's Republic of China (PRC), which boasts few readers of JBEM. In the two years since that publication, JBEM has pub-lished a small number of studies examining global topics, but not enough to alter this base calculus.

My intention here is not to critique one journal, because my argument is that the imbalance in academic analysis of global media illustrated through this one example is symptomatic of a fundamental flaw in media studies, which is its overwhelming emphasis on the immediately visible, which in this case means the dominant Western broadcasters. Globaliza-tion has changed everything, except media studies.

To be sure, there are journals with an exclusive focus on global media that reflect far more diverse geographical content, such as the *International Jour-nal of Press/Politics*, the *Journal of International Communication*, *Global Media and Communication*, and the *Asian Journal of Communication*, among others. Each of these contributes greatly to the scholarly literature in global media, but generally speaking, these journals don't speak to media studies as a discipline, but to the smaller subset of scholars who identify as primarily interested in global communication and media. It isn't that the JBEM is unbalanced and parochial; it is that media studies as a whole is unbalanced and parochial, in outcomes if not in intent.

In one sense, this dearth of analysis of global media is surprising, because digital technologies have indeed created far greater access to diverse global media. As noted earlier, most media from around the world are now easily accessible, especially to researchers in the developed world, who usually have access to the state of the art in digital technologies.

But in other ways, it isn't surprising, because the underlying factors that drive research into media haven't changed fundamentally in the past two decades. As Chang and his colleagues found over two decades ago, international news coverage tends to reflect four socio-historical factors, including the normative deviance of an event (i.e., how "strange" the event is), the relevance of the foreign nation to the United States, the potential for long-lasting social change in foreign events, and geographical distance from the US (Chang et al., 1987). Although this essay doesn't attempt to document the factors that drive academic research, it is evident that aca-demic researchers in the social sciences, like anybody else, tend to focus on research subjects that are visible, and whose relevance is immediately obvious. Broadcasters or other global media outlets that aren't immediately "visible" in the daily life of an academic researcher are highly likely to be overlooked, not only because they don't immediately come to mind when developing research agendas, but also because it is harder to convince others (such as editorial reviewers) of the relevance of media outlets that have smaller or distant audiences, that seem irrelevant to the pressing political agenda of the day, or that don't reflect threatening change.

The central paradox of global media studies, then, is this; that by focusing our attention (whether in the form of news or academic analysis) on that which is "immediately" relevant, researchers miss the underlying issues and trends that are fundamentally reshaping global economic, cultural, and political realities. Let me illustrate by way of a geopolitical analogy. It is often argued that once the Soviet Union pulled out of Afghanistan, due in some part to US involvement in fomenting resistance to the Soviets, the US turned its attention away from the nation, and it soon became a haven for the Taliban and Al Qaeda, which in turn soon became threats to the US, exemplified in the September 11 attacks of 2001. Because Afghanistan no longer seemed "relevant" after the Soviet pull-out, the US ignored important trends and developments that occurred in the nation (namely, the willingness of the Taliban government to create a safe haven for Al Qaeda) and that made it a bigger threat to the US than it had ever been during the days of Soviet occupation.

In the same way, academic researchers focus on the "big three" broadcasters (CNN, the BBC, and Fox) because they seem immediately and undoubtedly important. But, in so doing, the media studies community neglects the dynamics driving the development, evolution, and impacts around the world, which will undoubtedly have significant impact upon not just the media themselves, but the larger geopolitical world. Although the big three undoubtedly have global influence, their relevance is continuing to shrink, even as other national and regional networks continue to spring up and gain audience share. In some cases, such as Al Jazeera, these are networks that explicitly seek to "influence the global news agenda," while in other cases, such as Russia Today (RT), these new media voices take on an explicitly geopolitical tone, and actively seek to undermine the ability of the Western media sources to define the global news agenda, creating openings for alternative ideological points of view.

To be sure, media scholars have always recognized the importance of global influences that impact media, and at least since the "propaganda studies" of the 1930s and 1940s, researchers have attempted to articulate the role of political context and culture in the development of media systems. But, academic research has suffered from a sort of "methodological nationalism," in Ekecrantz's phrase, in which analysis of media draws fairly tight parameters over the object of study, and thus ignores the global context in which media production is enacted (Ekecrantz, 2009).

Some recent work in media studies demonstrates significant steps forward in examining global media through a truly "globalized" framework, which sees particular media instantiations as an outgrowth of multiple global inputs and forces. For example, a recent volume by Hallin and Mancini features work that privileges "comparative" media systems, by highlighting multiple approaches to understanding media systems, and highlights multinational influences on media production and content (Hallin & Mancini, 2012). Even that work, however, is primarily a set of national case studies, although the contributors do attempt to take into account the processes of convergence, often seen as a characteristic of globalization, and to account for whether or not media systems should be seen as primarily national or transnational.

The rest of this chapter will seek to confront the central paradox by drawing from recent theoretical and social developments to articulate a more expansive understanding of global media influence, particularly by drawing upon the network society theories of Castells and others, as well as the opportunities provided by new technological developments for gaining greater access to global media. The chapter will then briefly consider how new digital technologies create the possibility for developing expansive methodologies of media analysis, enabling research that would greatly enhance our understanding of the evolution of global media. Finally, the chapter will articulate promising new research agendas and projects that might better reposition media studies as an essential element for understanding larger geopolitical shifts.

The "Network Society" and Global Media

In recent years, a number of innovative social theories have emerged that attempt to capture both the highly globalized nature of human society, particularly in the developed world, and the role of technologies in creating and sustaining that global interconnectedness. One of the earliest theories was that of a knowledge or "information" society, in which the information sector takes an inordinately large role in society. Daniel Bell, for example, argued that, in a modern society, "what counts is not raw muscle power, or energy, but information" (1973, p. 127). Bell's formulation of the information society privileges not just the production, but also the manipulation, processing, or transfer of information, and reorients our understanding of the economics of information.

Later theorists have expanded on this concept and called attention to the development of a "network" society, in which information and communication technologies have created widespread social, cultural, and economic changes, embodied by the logic of technological networks. These networks have reshaped and, in some cases, even reconstituted entire social structures, and social, political, and economic processes.

Wellman and Berkowitz's (1988) work argued that societies are best considered as networks, and networks of networks, rather than a traditional conception of societies as collectives, bounded by geography and hierarchy. Wellman was among the first scholars to recognize the reconfiguration of social order and, especially, the ways in which individuals developed networks to replace traditional group, and local, sources of authority and relationship. More recently, Rainie and Wellman argue that the "triple revolution" (the social changes wrought by social networks, the internet, and mobile technologies) continues to have far-reaching consequences (Rainie & Wellman, 2012, p. 276). This work also highlights the further empowerment of individuals vis-à-vis social groups, in terms of defining meaning.

Manuel Castells, one of the most important theorists of the network society, focuses attention on the network at a geopolitical scale, and argues that networks have a nature and capacity far beyond the meaning of what the term "network" ordinarily means within the field of media studies. Rather than envisioning a "network" as a commercial or non-profit entity operating a single information source, or even a handful of media outlets, under a single logo (such as the BBC or CNN), Castells understands "networks" as being at the heart of a new form of society, "made up of specific configurations of global, national, and local networks in a multidimensional space of social interaction" (Castells, 2009, p. 19). It isn't that a society *contains* networks, along with other social institutions such as governments, schools, or corporations; rather, societies *are* networks, and the characteristics of networks are the characteristics of societies.

Although "networks" in the network society theories are more than just the technological networks that facilitate them, and incorporate institutions, organizations, and social relationships, it is digital technologies that lie at the heart of the "network society." The technologies give rise to what Latham and Sassen call "digital formations," or "formations of varying scales that depend on digital technologies, cross a variety of borders (national or otherwise), and engender a diverse array of spatial, organizational, and interactive practices" (2005, p. 2). These networks have multiple participants (nodes, in Castell's term), modes of interaction, goals, and values, but what unites them is that they serve as communicative infrastructures, as well as contexts of action. They provide both the infrastructure and the means by which meaning is generated, shared, and adapted for the goals of the network.

These digital formations transcend the local and the technological, and now incorporate geopolitical relationships as well. The isolation from one another that once characterized entire groups of nations during the period of the Cold War has become unimaginable for most of the globe. Whatever ideological differences exist between the US, Russia, and China, it is unimaginable that the networks that bind these nations would be unraveled. The "network" that binds these nations together introduces unprecedented complexity to geopolitical relationships, as nations are now linked together through cultural, financial, social, and political networks that transcend our ability to act on the purely "political" motive. Regardless of the authoritarian political relationships within any nation, the economic, business, and social ties that now transcend nations tend to remain open, in spite of geopolitical tension. This creates a type of complexity that is difficult to unravel, and creates a different world in which global media operate.

This insight (the network society) has multiple implications for how we think about "global media," but let me just highlight two at this point. First, whereas global media studies has tended to look either at a single entity, whether governmental or commercial, local, regional, or national (such as CNN, CCTV, or the BBC), a network society perspective would focus on the role of any single entity as but one node in an overall network of influence and of purpose, which operates in a multidimensional space. Latham and Sassen argue that an important theoretical feature of these digital formations is that what has tended to operate at a "local scale," such as a regional or national media outlet, can now be conceptualized at a global scale, with "thick" local settings (Latham & Sassen, 2005, p. 2). A network society perspective, for example, would examine the BBC as just one node of a larger network of other institutions, organizations, or even informal collaborations. Potential network participants might be other UK governmental agencies, non-governmental agencies, English language global information sources, or even the larger constellation of international broadcasters, which observes, occasionally mimics, and often challenges the BBC itself. The BBC is aligned with and operates in a type of harmony (which does not imply agreement) with other nodes of geopolitical meaning, including financial, governmental, and commercial.

There are a few exceptions, of course, to this networked model of global media. North Korea's media still seem largely isolated from larger global trends and forces, but that is by political imperative, and is reinforced by deliberate attempts to remain "network-free" in all aspects of modern governance, with a few notable exceptions. North Korea even limits its engagement with its patron and biggest financial supporter, the PRC, in an attempt to avoid the globalizing tendencies that China exhibits.

This offers significant potential to global media studies, in that it allows researchers to scale up the level of analysis, beyond the local or national context, and allows us to move beyond earlier dichotomizations of media content. In their important book, *De-Westernizing Media Studies* (2000), Park and Curran highlighted how global media studies in the 1950s was overly driven by the work of Siebert and his colleagues, which conceptualized four "theories of the press" primarily from a perspective that categorized global media practices in reference to three ideologies: liberal democracy, Soviet totalitarianism, and the authoritarianism that characterized much of the developing world (Park & Curran, 2000; Siebert et al., 1956). Park and Curran were undoubtedly correct in their indictment of the easy simplicity of the Siebert et al. framework, and their book detailed a number of case studies that dramatically improved upon the overly simplistic model of the earlier work. Each of those case studies explored media systems within purely local contexts, highlighting the political and economic context of those national systems. But each national media system was examined *sui generis*, without acknowledgment of the larger global context or, indeed, of the larger global networks of media that undoubtedly help to shape the systems as they exist.

Second, a network society perspective undermines much of our traditional conception of "national" media, in that networks (in Castell's sense) are rarely defined by or limited to national boundaries. Financial networks, for example, serve for the cross-border movement of capital flows, and if national governments want to be in that game, as it were, they must think very carefully about how any proposed regulatory or legislative changes will impact the global financial network's perception of that nation, as one wrong move can alienate the very network that provides needed capital infusions. The global physics community, to take another example, recognizes few national borders, other than having some correspondence to funding agencies, and the movement of personnel and ideas across national borders is highly fluid and rapid. Thus, a network society perspective would envision "media networks" as open systems, with multiple nodes, channels, financial models, production standards and practices, and global influences and impacts. Moreover, any particular media outlet would be considered in relation to the ways in which content, production practice, and impact are contextualized in relationship to the other political, financial, and cultural practices within which these are embedded.

Global Digital Engagement

A second key characteristic of the globalized world is that much of that world, although by no means all, has access to instantaneous communication from around the globe. In early 2014, Tim Berners-Lee, one of the inventors of the World Wide Web, observed that approximately 40 percent of the globe was now connected, and created billions of dollars of economic value, transformed entire industries and social sectors, and activated new political movements around the world (Berners-Lee, 2014). An observer in Cleveland, Calcutta, or Cairo can use digital technologies to call up local news items, gossip, or weather reports from most places in the world. This is really quite unprecedented in human history. Although human migration and communication have been growing in intensity and scale for centuries, the ability to instantly find information from almost any locale globally, in an instant, is less than two decades old.

To be sure, some information from far flung places has long been accessible to political economic elites, even if not in real time. As global information networks developed along with communications technologies, such as maritime and economic technologies, communication tended to be limited to key cities and regions, and the conduits of that communication tended to have similar cultural, educational, and linguistic backgrounds. For example, as France, Britain, and the other European nations built communication networks to facilitate economic control over their colonies in Africa, those networks relied heavily on French, English, and other European languages, and depended largely on the ability to produce personnel (either European or local) who were educated in a familiar educational setting, spoke its language, and could contribute to the development of an infrastructure that largely resembled the one that existed in the colonizing power.

What this resulted in was not a "global" media system, in which information from around the globe diffused at an equal rate in a widely distributed pattern, but rather a number of parallel, but different media systems, each of which developed in response to primarily local conditions. For example, Hallin and Mancini's (2004) study found that even within Europe itself, a number of different media models arose, influenced by dimensions of the media environment and political culture. At the international level, these national-level systems were extended to include nations under political control, such as the colonies of the former colonial power. Thus, an English-language set of networks arose out of the former colonies of the UK, while others emerged out of the legacy of other colonial powers (French, German, Dutch, Spanish, etc). These "international" networks largely reflected the interests of the original colonial power, and information flow from one language framework to another was limited. Thus, although it might be fairly easy for a citizen of France to learn "the news" from Algeria, that information was not so easily accessible in London, Berlin, or New York (centers of information for different language spheres), and likely to be unavailable at all in towns and cities of lesser importance. Specialized information, such as weather reports that might impact agricultural production and the financial impact of droughts or monsoons, was even harder to obtain.

Digital networks, however, have completely changed this dynamic. The volume of information easily available overwhelms any other era of human history. A 2013 report found that 90 percent of "all data" had been generated over the last two years, in reference to the rise of "big data," or the ability to generate data by capturing, logging, and analyzing information that previously had been inaccessible (SINTEF, 2013). Although this certainly includes a concept of "information" that is distinct from information about foreign countries, the principle remains the same; that at no time in history has there been greater access to information about the most diverse parts of the globe. According to the International Telecommunication Union (ITU), 40 percent of the world's population is using the internet (ITU, 2014), creating an unprecedented access to information that previously had been the exclusive province of elites.

Obviously, the presence of a global, transnational digital communication network does not in any way compel attention to, or even knowledge of, the rest of the world, nor is access to these data uniform around the globe. Indeed, I have argued elsewhere that the logic of digital media in many ways hinders learning about the rest of the world (Kluver, 2002), a point echoed by Halavais (2000) and others. It is not really typical that a citizen of any nation spends much time looking at global news, but within any society, there are those who actively seek out information from foreign nations. In fact, work by Kwak et al. (2006) found that readers of international news on the internet tend to be more internationally engaged, and this is especially true of younger users. The authors noted that the relationship might not be causal, but regardless, the ability to access international news must be seen as important in reinforcing an interest in the outside world (Kwak et al., 2006).

Implications for Global Media Research

But what are the implications of this reality for the study of global media? Should it fundamentally change how we study global media? I would argue that indeed it should, for several reasons. First, much of the research trajectory of global media studies since the 1970s sought to explore the impact of Western media outlets on the rest of the world, and to explore the voices of media outlets from the developing world. Academic interest particularly increased in the wake of the "McBride Report," which was issued by the UN in response to concerns about Western domination of global news flow. Much of this research focused on media in the developing world, especially Latin America, Africa, and Asia, providing a necessary corrective to theories and studies that largely considered the large, multinational news agencies of the West as exemplars of media production, reception, and impact.

However, the easy availability of digital resources online means that for many important media outlets, online audiences become far more important, and vocal, than do local audiences. Although the citizens of any particular country might not be consuming media from neighboring countries, it is a good assumption that the journalists and other media practitioners are. Thus, media content that might have been produced for only a local audience can instantaneously develop an international following. The astounding success of South Korean singer PSY's "Gangnam

Style" video illustrates the impact of a global media infrastructure, in this case YouTube, in providing a mechanism for global interest in local content. Released in mid-2012, the video became the fastest YouTube video to attract over one billion views and, by May of 2014, it had become the most popular ever on the site, with over two billion views. The video generated dozens of responses, parodies, and video replies, in dozens of languages. Given a worldwide Korean language speaker base of approximately 77 million, this is a phenomenal achievement (Lewis et al., 2014). Although there is little doubt that the song, and video, were developed with the idea of capitalizing upon the increasing interest in Korean culture, or the Hallyu, or Korean wave, there is little indication that PSY or his producers had any idea how viral the video would become (Oh & Park, 2013).

A second important reason for refining our global media research approach is that, as digital content is now globally available, there is far more potential for examining the role of local culture in assigning meaning to content that emerges from transnational producers. To be sure, there is much to be said for a close analysis of local readings of local media. But this trees-before-the-forest approach also obscures the bigger picture, the ways in which multiple local, regional, or national responses develop in response to information flow. Whereas earlier generations of media research profited greatly from individually driven analysis of local responses, now there is far greater potential to access and analyze larger scales of media phenomenon. Whereas earlier research has tended toward a focus of reactions to global media in a local context (Kraidy, 2005), we now have the ability to focus on how global media play in a host of local contexts. One consequence of this strain of research, however, has been an over-reliance on methodologies of case studies, in which single news sources, within a limited cultural and political context, are analyzed, with the theoretical implications largely unexplored. In other words, studies focused on important political, economic, or cultural issues, but only to provide another perspective. Indeed, the consideration of these minor and often marginalized voices is critically important, especially in an age in which a handful of global information organizations maintain an inordinate influence.

Another significant problem with the case study approach to global media is that it portrays various national media systems or broadcasters as discrete, isolated actors producing content for an audience, also largely isolated from larger global trends. But that is not how global media work. Rather, media producers in most of the world are part of a highly networked, complex system, drawing inspiration, production practices, and content ideas from other global media sources.

As noted earlier, a network society approach to global media studies would ground analysis of news outlets within larger geopolitical, cultural, linguistic, or even "cause-oriented" networks, rather than traditional media metrics-oriented approaches to national media. For example, the rise of digital and satellite technologies has prompted the development of regionally grounded competitors to broadcasters such as CNN and the BBC. At least half a dozen different English language channels have started since (2005), including CCTV 9 (which has become CCTV News), NHK English, Russia Today (RT), Al Jazeera English (AJE), and Al Jazeera America (AJAM). Most of these channels exist primarily because they are attempting to engage in a global conversation, influencing Anglophone or other audiences, and attempt to present domestic and international news with an editorial slant alternative to those of CNN and the BBC. Some, like RT, are openly derisive of Western policies and leadership, and usually present a perspective on news highly sympathetic to the Russian government. Others, such as AJE, maintain a much higher degree of editorial independence from the sponsoring government (el-Nawawy & Powers, 2013; Powers & el-Nawawy, 2009).

In August of 2014, a media group in the Ukraine started its own English language network, broadcast from satellite and streamed via the internet, to try to shape international public opinion about that nation's conflict with Russia, and to offer "Ukrainian news, from a Ukrainian perspective." The network was developed by the 1+1 media network, a Ukrainian media conglomerate, and the network's immediate agenda was to try to create a firewall that would help it to resist Russian encroachment, and to present a pro-Western, pro-EU perspective from the region. In an attempt to move quickly, the channel began broadcasting even before it had its own studio space, and didn't move to a fully functioning studio until early September. The channel stressed that it was "Europe's largest country," based on the fact that it has the largest land area within the European continent. Not surprisingly, a number of early broadcasts were focused primarily on countering the narratives presented on RT, and challenging Russian policy and actions across Eastern Europe.

In addition, there are a number of non-state, private media organizations that operate, often in opposition to official state apparatus. The "New Tang Dynasty Television" organization, for example, is intended to counter official Chinese government channels, and provide an alternative take on Chinese culture, history, and society. The organization, along with a partner print publication known as *The Epoch Times*, grew out of the Falun Gong religious movement after the Chinese government banned the movement in 2001, although the broadcaster takes pains to obscure this fact. In addition to Mandarin, the broadcaster now offers programming in English, Spanish, Japanese, French, Russian, and other languages. *The Epoch Times* publishes editions in 21 languages in 35 countries, and claims a circulation of over 1.3 million copies (*The Epoch Times*, 2014).

A final example was the creation in the spring of 2014 of the "Novorossiya News Agency," an effort to create a news agency to bolster the legitimacy of the territorial and cultural claims of pro-Russian separatists and nationalists in Eastern Ukraine and elsewhere (Novorossiya News Agency, 2014). Although the agency did not operate a broadcast outlet, it was transparent in its efforts to translate news and other pieces into key European languages to lend legitimacy to the concept behind the geographical construct of "Novorossiya." As might be expected, the news feed from the group stressed a strongly pro-Russian view of regional conflicts.

For the most part, these high-profile attempts at public diplomacy have gone unnoticed in academic literature. As of late 2014, for example, no academic analyses of New Tang Dynasty, *The Epoch Times*, or RT have appeared on Google Scholar, and there were fewer than half a dozen results for Al Arabiya. A similar search on Academia.edu also yielded no results. Certainly, these relatively new networks have neither the audiences nor the history to justify an extensive body of research, but their geopolitical importance alone would justify some attention from the academic community.

Digital Media Technologies and Methods

The rise of new digital technologies brings significant new potential to global media studies, helping to broaden both the types and range of content available. As noted earlier, if 90 percent of "knowledge" has been created in the last few years, much of that knowledge is solely capable of being discovered through digital technologies. In other words, data capture and processing allow researchers to sift through far more content, and potentially see trends and themes emerge from larger quantities of data than previously possible. Through digital technologies that allow automatic harvesting and translation of important global media sources, it is possible to dramatically expand the scope and trajectories of new media outlets, including those that are available only via the web or satellite. The problems of access to global media have been largely resolved, as even minor media outlets now seek to move content online. The use of digital technologies to harvest, archive, and search media content creates a potential for a big data, quantitative approach to media studies that seems truly unprecedented. But that doesn't mean that all the problems are solved. As Kluver et al. (2013) have argued, the "boundaries" of global media research have expanded greatly because of new digital technologies that have allowed for instantaneous translation of media content, as well as the ability to archive and search that content for trends that might be missed through more traditional media analysis techniques.

One such project is the GDELT Project, an audacious attempt to capture global media content from around the world, run analytical methods through the data, and "quantify global human society," especially as expressed in global news sources (Leetaru, 2014). But the GDELT Project attempts to do more than just document every news story; it seeks to create knowledge databases along a set of pre-determined themes (war, disease outbreaks, etc.) and to record "how the world feels about it," by performing sentiment analysis of that content.

The sheer scale of the GDELT Project raises interesting possibilities, but also serious concerns about the quality of analysis that can be handled exclusively by databases. Media content, after all, is produced by humans (although with digital tools), for humans, and can best be understood by humans. Computer analysis, even the highly sophisticated content and sentiment analysis that emerges from advanced computing technologies, cannot replace the human interpreter of communication content. Word choices matter, as to stylistic presentation of content, whether verbal, visual, or other, and at this point, computer-driven technologies fail to detect humor, irony, sarcasm, or the truth or falsehood of a statement. Moreover, as Mahrt and Scharkow (2013) argue, big data approaches might actually provide less validity and scope, when used improperly.

Thus, there are certain limitations to what digital technologies can provide to media studies, although there is little doubt that they can provide much. Indeed, I would argue that new digital technologies enable new research agendas to develop that can significantly enhance our understanding and analysis of global media. For the final section of this chapter, I focus on just three such areas that have tremendous potential to expand the scope and salience of global media research.

Comparative Research Across Cultural/Linguistic Worlds

As noted earlier, a number of scholars have sought to incorporate comparative approaches to media, hoping to illustrate important national differences in media production and content. The most successful of these have tended to focus at the system level; i.e., the way in which financial, regulatory, ownership, or other system-level influences have constrained the operation and development of media outlets (Hallin & Mancini, 2004, 2012). Others have sought to do more content-level analysis, such as comparing news framing and political agendas across national boundaries. These studies tend to be a bit more difficult to conduct, however, because of the difficulty in articulating the meaning of content in different cultural frameworks.

As noted, there is undeniable utility in these approaches and their outcomes. But the vast majority of these studies are contextualized as comparisons between highly developed media systems, or how new broadcasters (such as Al Jazeera) compare to one of the big three (Barkho, 2010; Johnson & Fahmy, 2008). Although valuable, this approach assumes (and reifies the assumption) that the multinational news corporations of the West serve as an adequate standard for media production and content, and that other global broadcasters are best understood in those terms (i.e., Al Jazeera as the CNN of the Arab World).

Thus, one potential research agenda that would offer great potential, both from a theoretical and a pragmatic perspective, is research that would explore the ways in which media from outside of the West might draw from, or reflect to, media from other regions, also outside of the West. For example, although the Western world is well aware of the ways in which China's increasing economic strength is giving the nation significant new capacity in manufacturing, resource development, and even military power, there is little understanding of the ways in which China's investments in an African media networks might give the nation greater geopolitical pull, not just in Africa, but globally, or the ways in which the Chinese development of these systems might ultimately change the nature of media in Africa itself. One promising development looking at this specific issue is a research team funded by the Research Council of Norway, the Voice of China in Africa, which seeks to explore and document the potential and likely long-term impacts of China's investments in Africa's media sector (Chr. Michelsen Institute, 2014).

A related research agenda that would draw upon these new theoretical and technological developments as well as increase our understanding of global media would be research that seeks to map out information flow across cultural, national, or regional boundaries, but that doesn't begin with the West (Hermann & McChesney, 2004). Media content, production techniques and standards, themes, and values all "flow" across a variety of borders, cultural, linguistic, and national. And yet, we have little understanding of the impact of this flow, as the primary assumption seems to be that media flow happens only from the developed nations to the developing, from North to South, from West to East.

In many cases, there are important markers of socio-economic, ethnic, or religious identity that serve as the carriers of media flow. The #Occupy movement, for example, which began in a small park in Manhattan, captured the imagination of protesters with a huge variety of grievances around the world, who appropriated the #Occupy brand, as it were, reinterpreted it, and gave it a whole new cultural resonance in vastly different contexts. During the summer and fall of 2014, for example, the #Occupy Central movement of Hong Kong mounted a significant challenge to Hong Kong's rulers and, by extension, the government of the PRC. But the inspiration and theme of that movement was not the strong critique of capitalism that drove the New York movement some two years previously; it drew far more inspiration from, and more closely resembled, the #Occupy movement that occurred in protests over Gezi Park in Istanbul in the summer of 2013. The movement had radically changed its focus of protest, from the original anti-corporate orientation of New York, to a protest against authoritarian government in Turkey, to a critique of the "colonial" actions of the PRC, which refused to allow candidates to stand for election to the Legislative Council, unless they had been previously approved by Beijing, with multiple stages in between. Thus, what began as a critique of corporate power, focused largely on the Wall Street elite (#OccupyWallStreet), became a movement which was re-energized with local meanings in every distinct locale, and the unique Western characteristics of the movement had long since been forgotten. Certainly, there were common themes among all the #Occupy events, including greater democratic governance and a flattening of economic inequalities, but those themes have been prominent in almost every protest movement across history, so can't be seen as uniquely characteristic of the #Occupy movement itself.

A second example of media flow that helps to illustrate this potential research agenda might be the way in which political or religious agendas flow, or don't flow, across linguistic and cultural divides, when there are identity markers to facilitate that flow. For example, the world's largest Muslim country, Indonesia, maintains only informal and lower-level ties with the state of Israel, not because of any historical or current enmity between the two nations, but rather because of Indonesian solidarity with Palestine. And yet, Israel maintains much closer relations with a number of Arab states, including Jordan, Egypt, and Morocco. Clearly, Indonesian sentiment toward Israel is drawn from media characterizations of Israel that emerge from the Arab world, but that is inconsistent within the Arab world itself. One study (Chinn, 2014) found that Urdu and Arab language media largely ignored Iranian interpretations of Israeli actions, regardless of the propensity of the Iranian media to speak for the Islamic world. These are interesting examples of media flow and influence that have largely been invisible in media studies, and new technologies create the possibilities for exploring many variations of these themes.

Cultural Framings of Geopolitics

A third potential research direction facilitated by the rise of a networked society and digital technologies emerges from the capacity to draw more culturally nuanced and sophisticated readings of geopolitical events. Global news framing has long been heavily shaded by elite news agencies, typically from advanced capitalist democracies. A recent study by Watanabe (2003) discovered that even online news aggregators, such as Yahoo! News and Google News drew samples disproportionately from these same sources. The power of defining a global news agenda remains strongly in the hands of Western news agencies, as these agencies are seen as arbiters of what is important.

However, even if the news agenda remains skewed to the developed world, there are multiple ways in which the specific framing of geopolitical events might be framed, and uncovering these cultural and national framings of global geopolitics can be of great value in revealing multiple interpretations of events. News frames reflect not just political and ideological positioning, but also important cultural components. As Van Gorp argues, frames are at times best viewed as extrinsic to the individual, and media outlets draw upon this cultural repertoire to frame important issues, which shapes audience responses to media coverage (Gorp, 2010).

To be sure, media scholars have often attempted studies that show alternative perspectives to great geopolitical events, such as the Iraq war or the NATO invasion of Afghanistan. But, the case of the Iraq war reveals a decidedly one-sided analysis of global news coverage. At least a dozen studies appeared in the pages of academic journals on the framing of the Iraq war, with the bulk of them focused solely on news coverage in the West (see, for example, Aday et al., 2005; Entman, 2003; Schwalbe, 2006). Several studies, however, by comparing how the war itself was covered from multiple perspectives, demonstrated the intrinsic value of seeing the events of the war from very different eyes (Aday et al., 2005; Dimitrova & Connolly-Ahern, 2007). But even those studies focused primarily on the large, Western news agencies, with Al Jazeera presented as a point of contrast. As noted earlier, although the comparison is valuable, ultimately this sort of study continues to center the Western press outlets as the norm, rather than representing a particular viewpoint within the global conversation. Only one study brought in multiple perspectives on the war, and demonstrates the greater utility of studies that take into account a truly global perspective. Kolmer and Smetko's (2009) analysis examined coverage from six national perspectives, revealed a more nuanced interpretation of the various news feeds, and demonstrated the ways in which even political allies interpret important geopolitical events (Kolmer & Smetko, 2009).

Another example of such a research agenda would be to examine the ways in which news is presented across the variety of language channels of the global media outlets mentioned earlier. Many of these outlets have created multiple language channels, including Spanish, Arabic, Farsi, French, and others. CCTV, for example, offers dedicated channels in most of the above, as well as Russian. Russia Today has sister sites in Arabic and Spanish. Al Jazeera has already launched a service in the Balkans, and is planning for new services in Turkish and in Kiswahili, targeted to East Africa.

These studies demonstrate the value of a comparative perspective on an event that is widely interpreted as an event of global significance, the Iraq war. But, as noted earlier in this chapter, often it is the long-term economic, cultural, and political trends that create the most important long-term changes. One example of such a research agenda might be climate change, where significant research has gone into media frames in the US and UK, with decidedly less coverage of other nations (Anderson, 2009).

Re-imagining Media Ecology

A final research agenda that fully embodies a network society perspective, as well as fully utilizing digital tools at our disposal, would be a reimagining of the tradition of media ecology. The "media ecology" school of media studies, associated with thinkers such as Marshall McLuhan, Neil Postman, Walter Ong, Jacques Ellul, typically focuses on the ways in which different media formats impact the ways in which a message is perceived (Kluver, 2005; Lum, 2005), and demonstrates the ways in which differing formats might impact message reception.

During the decade of the 2000s, the buzzword of many in the media industry was "convergence," which typically used to refer to how merging companies, each with a different platform dominance (such as telecommunications, television, print media, for example), could build upon their respective areas of dominance to create new areas of collaboration and growth. Another way of interpreting the concept, however, was that content created for one platform (such as print) could be repurposed, enhanced, and deployed across multiple platforms, such as websites or social media. For example, a journalist writing a story on a topic could write one version for a print outlet, provide a (typically shorter) version for an online outlet, and create video for broadcast. In fact, journalists began to be trained to develop content across these multiple platforms, and every media company sought to extend the span of content across multiple platforms.

A line of thinkers within media ecology would argue that each platform, or channel, will transform content into something new. This is particularly true when these different formats have their own values. When nuanced and well-argued print opinion columns, for example, are presented on television, the format of the broadcast distorts the "reasonableness" of the opinion piece into something more like a spectacle, as can be demonstrated nightly on television debate shows.

Global media studies, however, tends to remain focused on specific platforms, with little recognition or analysis of the ways in which global media organizations are seeking to maximize the utility of content across multiple platforms. For example, Al Jazeera is analyzed in the academic media studies literature primarily for its Arabic language news broadcast, with some lesser amount of attention on the English language broadcast. The Arabic channel and the English channel are administered separately with different talent and news production staffs. The introduction of Al Jazeera America created something altogether different, with a primary focus of creating an alternative news channel focused on US news.

As noted earlier, however, the rise of digital media platforms enables access to each of these outlets, and more, and can contribute greatly to an ecological understanding of media that not only takes into account just channel or platform characteristics, but that also captures the ways in which media content is transformed by its venue of production, its audience, and its counterparts. We have earlier noted the importance for a number of global broadcasters in developing English language versions of their news services, but these services are still largely invisible within the academic literature. One important future direction for media studies, therefore, is a recognition of the ways in which the ecology of media has changed to include more diversity of production, of audience, and of impact than has traditionally been anticipated.

Conclusion

I have sought in this chapter to demonstrate the ways in which media studies might reposition itself, as a field and as a practice, within a reinterpreted context, both in a geopolitical context that is largely network driven, and in a cultural context in which access to global media is far more abundant. The traditions and processes of media studies, including its methodologies, have largely arisen from a historical context in which neither of those was as pronounced as it has become in the last two decades and, thus, they need to be re-examined and reinterpreted within a changed global dynamic.

It is obvious that digital technologies have transformed the nature of media themselves, from production, to delivery, to reception and response. My argument is that these technologies offer much to the globalization of academic media studies, which still remains primarily focused on a few Anglophone touch points, and assumes the primacy of Western media, in terms of both global impact and as a foundation for theory development.

References

Aday, S., Cluverius, J., & Livingston, S. (2005). As goes the statue, so goes the war: The emergence of the victory frame in television coverage of the Iraq War. *Journal of Broadcasting & Electronic Media, 49*(3), 314–331. doi: 10.1207/s15506878jobem4903_4.

Aday, S., Livingston, S., & Hebert, M. (2005). Embedding the truth: A cross-cultural analysis of objectivity and television coverage of the Iraq War. *The International Journal of Press/Politics, 10*(1), 3–21. doi: 10.1177/1081180X05275727.

Anderson, A. (2009). Media, politics and climate change: Towards a new research agenda. *Sociology Compass, 3*(2), 166–182. doi: 10.1111/j.1751-9020.2008.00188.x.

Barkho, L. (2010). *News from the BBC, CNN, and Al-Jazeera: How the three broadcasters cover the Middle East.* New York: Hampton Press.

Bell, D. (1973). *The coming of post-industrial society.* New York: Basic Books.

Berners-Lee, T. (2014). On the 25th anniversary of the web, let's keep it free and open. *Google Official Blog,* March 11. Online at http://googleblog.blogspot. co.uk/2014/03/on-25th-anniversary-of-web-lets-keep-it.html (retrieved March 17, 2014).

Castells, M. (2009). *Communication power.* Oxford: Oxford University Press.

Chang, T.-K., Shoemaker, P. J., & Brendlinger, N. (1987). Determinants of International News Coverage in the U.S. Media. *Communication Research, 14*(4), 396–414. doi: 10.1177/009365087014004002.

Chinn, J. (2014). Transnational media flows: Exploring the case of Iran and pan-Arab media outlets. Manuscript submitted for publication.

Chr. Michelsen Institute (CMI). (2014). Voice of China in Africa: Media and soft power. *CMI News.* Online at www.cmi.no/research/project/?1686=voice-of-china#home (retrieved October 10, 2014).

Dimitrova, D. V., & Connolly-Ahern, C. (2007). A tale of two wars: Framing analysis of online news sites in coalition countries and the Arab world during the Iraq War. *Howard Journal of Communication, 18*(2), 153–168. doi: 10.1080/10646170701309973.

Ekecrantz, J. (2009). Media studies going global. In D. K. Thussu (Ed.), *Internationalizing media studies* (pp. 75–89). New York: Routledge.

el-Nawawy, M., & Powers, S. (2013). Al-Jazeera English: A conciliatory medium in a conflict-driven environment? *Global Media and Communication, 6*(1), 61–84. doi: 10.1177/1742766510362019.

Entman, R. M. (2003). Cascading activation: Contesting the White House's frame after 9/11. *Political Communication, 20*(4), 415–432. doi: 10.1080/ 10584600390244176.

The Epoch Times. (2014). Worldwide distribution. Online at http://ads.epochtimes. com/pages/distribution-pricing-newspapers-distribution.htm (retrieved January 3, 2015).

Gorp, B. V. (2010). Strategies to take subjectivity out of framing analysis. In P. D'Angelo & J. A. Kuypers (Eds.), *Doing news framing analysis: Empirical and theoretical perspectives* (pp. 84–109). New York: Routledge.

Halavais, A. (2000). National borders on the world wide web. *New Media & Society, 2*(1), 7–28. doi: 10.1177/14614440022225689.

Hallin, D. C., & Mancini, P. (2004). *Comparing media systems: Three models of media and politics.* Cambridge: Cambridge University Press.

Hallin, D. C., & Mancini, P. (2012). *Comparing media systems beyond the Western world.* Cambridge: Cambridge University Press.

Hermann, E., & McChesney, R. W. (2004). *The global media: The new missionaries of corporate capitalism.* New York: Continuum.

ITU. (2014). *The world in 2014: ICT facts and figures.* Geneva: International Telecommunication Union.

Johnson, T. J., & Fahmy, S. (2008). The CNN of the Arab world or a shill for terrorists? How support for press freedom and political ideology predict credibility of Al-Jazeera among its audience. *International Communication Gazette, 70*(5), 338–360. doi: 10.1177/1748048508094290.

Kluver, A. R. (2002). The logic of new media in international affairs. *New Media and Society*, 4(4), 499–517. doi: 10.1177/146144402321466787.

Kluver, A. R. (2005). Jacques Ellul: Technique, propaganda and modern media. In C. Lum (Ed.), *Perspectives on culture, technology and communication: The media ecology tradition*. Cresskill, NJ: Hampton Press.

Kluver, R., Campbell, H., & Balfour, S. (2013). The limits of language: Media monitoring technologies and emerging research methodologies. *Journal of Broadcasting and Electronic Media*, 57(1), 4–19.

Kolmer, C., & Smetko, H. A. (2009). Framing the Iraq War: Perspectives from American, U.K., Czech, German, South African, and Al-Jazeera News. *American Behavioral Scientist*, 52(5), 643–656. doi: 10.1177/0002764208326513.

Kraidy, M. (2005). *Hybridity, or the cultural logic of globalization*. Philadelphia: Temple University Press.

Kwak, N., Poor, N., & Skoric, M. M. (2006). Honey, I shrunk the world! The relation between internet use and international engagement. *Mass Communication and Society*, 9(2), 189–213. doi: 10.1207/s15327825mcs0902_4.

Latham, R., & Sassen, S. (Eds.). (2005). *Digital formations: IT and new architectures in the global realm*. Princeton, NJ: Princeton University Press.

Leetaru, K. (2014). *GDELT Project*. Online at http://gdeltproject.org/ (retrieved October 13, 2014).

Lewis, M. P., Simons, G. F., & Fennig, C. D. (Eds.). (2014). *Ethnologue: Languages of the world* (17th ed.). Dallas, TX: SIL International.

Lum, C. (Ed.). (2005). *Perspectives on culture, technology and communication: The media ecology tradition*. Cresskill, NJ: Hampton Press.

Mahrt, M., & Scharkow, M. (2013). The value of big data in digital media research. *Journal of Broadcasting & Electronic Media*, 57(1), 20–33. doi: 10.1080/08838151.2012.761700.

Novorossiya News Agency. (2014). Novorossia today. Online at http://novorossia.today/ (retrieved October 15, 2014).

Oh, I., & Park, G.-S. (2013). The globalization of K-pop: Korea's place in the global music industry. Paper presented at the international conference: The "Miracle" Narrative of the Korean Cultural Industries: Perspectives from the Middle East, Jerusalem, May 7–9. Online at http://iwahs.org/research/data/research_file_07.pdf (retrieved August 10, 2013).

Park, M.-J., & Curran, J. (Eds.). (2000). *De-Westernizing media studies*. New York: Routledge.

Powers, S., & el-Nawawy, M. (2009). Al-Jazeera English and global news networks: Clash of civilizations or cross-cultural dialogue? *Media, War & Conflict*, 2(3), 263–284. doi: 10.1177/1750635209345185.

Rainie, L., & Wellman, B. (2012). *Networked: The new social operating system*. Cambridge, MA: The MIT Press.

Schwalbe, C. B. (2006). Remembering our shared past: Visually framing the Iraq War on U.S. news websites. *Journal of Computer Mediated Communication*, 12(1), 264–289. doi: 10.1111/j.1083-6101.2006.00325.x.

Siebert, F. S., Peterson, T., & Schram, W. (1956). *Four theories of the press: The authoritarian, libertarian, social responsibility and soviet communist concepts of what the press should be and do*. Urbana, IL: University of Illinois Press.

SINTEF. (2013). Big data, for better or worse: 90% of world's data generated over last two years *Science Daily*, May 22. Online at www.sintef.no/home/corporate-news/big-data--for-better-or-worse/ (retrieved June 1, 2013).

Watanabe, K. (2003). The Western perspective in Yahoo! News and Google News: Quantitative analysis of geographic coverage of online news. *International Communication Gazette*, 75(2), 141–156. doi:10.1177/1748048512465546.

Wellman, B., & Berkowitz, S. D. (Eds.). (1988). *Social structures: A network approach*. New York: Cambridge University Press.

11

CONNECTING IN THE SCANDALVERSE

The Power of Social Media and Parasocial Relationships

Naeemah Clark

Introduction

Like pioneers who settle a new land, users of social media connect to create a universe that is all their own. One of the most popular and, frankly, fascinating online worlds to explore is that of *Scandal* fandom, found on the short messaging site Twitter, video distributor YouTube, and microblogging site Tumblr. The "Scandalverse," as it is known online, is populated and led by women—many of color—who use social media to celebrate the ABC hit drama.

This case study analyzes one of an array of emerging phenomena involving the cross-sectioning of broadcast and digital media. It investigates how the *Scandal* audience turned to the internet as a way to connect with the program, demonstrating how the internet enhances parasocial relationships whereby audiences believe mediated personalities are their friends. Television viewers use social media to deepen their relationships with primetime television by communicating with and about casts and crews. In turn, social media interaction not only encourages viewership, but also promotes the all-important real-time/live television viewing that produces higher ratings.

The initial success of *Scandal* was tied directly to its social media campaigns. These campaigns laid a social media foundation for creative, technologically savvy women to share their wit, talents, and strong opinions in ways that are frequently as dramatic as those portrayed on the program itself. This chapter examines how the parasocial relationships in the Scandalverse blur lines between fact and fiction, producer and consumer, and celebrity and fanatic. The discussion also highlights the ways in which language and symbols related to race and gender become common tropes in this community.

But First, a Primer on *Scandal*

Scandal, an hour-long drama, premiered on the ABC network on Thursday, April 5, 2012 (Levin & Bianco, 2012). The program's showrunner, Shonda Rhimes, along with her producing partner Betsy Beers, created the program based on the career of real-life political strategist Judy Smith. On the show, Kerry Washington stars as Olivia Pope, a fast-talking, fashionable woman whom the Washington, DC elite call on to fix their problems. She runs a crisis management firm with her team, known as "Gladiators in Suits." Also integral to the storyline is the fact that Pope, a 30-something African American woman, is intertwined in an on-again, off-again love affair with the 50-year-old President of the United States, Fitzgerald "Fitz" Grant (Tony Goldwyn), who is white, Republican, and married. President Grant's first lady is the formidable Melody "Mellie" Grant (Bellamy Young), who wants her husband in the White House more than he wants to be there himself.

The seven episodes of the first season revolved around Pope handling a scandal involving President Grant's Oval Office trysts with aide Amanda Tanner. When Tanner is found murdered, Pope and Associates solve the crime while Olivia and Fitz reminisce about how they fell in love, dance a little too close at a state dinner, and make out in full sight of the White House's security cameras. The audience for the first season averaged around 6.5 million viewers on Thursday nights and increased to almost 9 million when DVR viewing was measured (Gonzalez, 2013). Although the Nielsen ratings for the first season were tepid, they were strong enough to garner a full season in the fall of 2012. The May cliffhanger inspired the hashtag #whoisquinn and drove a marketing campaign for the show over the summer months.

Along with Christmastime binge-watching on ABC.com, steamy chemistry between the lead characters and twisting storylines including a Presidential assassination attempt (#whoshotfitz) created a sensation for *Scandal*'s second season. By January 2013, the grassroots buzz for the show created a loyal following of fans, who called themselves Gladiators. On average, more than 8.5 million watched in real time and an additional 2.5 million caught up via DVR (Gonzalez, 2013). The cast's and crew's live tweets also generated energy for the program, with the February 7, 2013 episode, in which the President suffocates a Supreme Court justice (#holyfitz), spawning more than 350,000 tweets (Keveney, 2013).

In the months before *Scandal*'s third season, star Kerry Washington had a secret wedding (news of which was first leaked on the user-edited Wikipedia.com). Directors then worked for 22 episodes to conceal her ever-growing pregnancy with strategically placed designer handbags and Oval Office furnishings. The season also introduced a love triangle involving Olivia, Fitz, and super spy Jake (Scott Foley); the revelation that Fitz's father raped Mellie and may have fathered one of her sons; and the murder of Chief of Staff Cyrus Beene's husband James. Season 3 concluded with *Scandal* as the week's number one program in the coveted 18–49-year-old demographic (Harris, 2014).

The diverse nature of the reputedly close cast and crew has been reported in the media. For the first three seasons, the primary characters included two African American actors: Pope and her Gladiator Harrison. Pope's parents joined the cast in Season 3. President Grant's Chief of Staff Cyrus Beene is a gay man married to another man who tricks him into adopting an African American daughter. Olivia Pope's most trusted confidante is trained assassin Huck, played by openly gay Hispanic American actor Guillermo Diaz. Showrunner Shonda Rhimes is an African American woman who produced every program airing during ABC's Thursday 2014 primetime schedule. The drama on and off the screen generated widespread attention and discussion and provoked enormous creativity in the social media Scandalverse.

Social Media Communities

Early scholarship on interactive social media sites found that comments from members of online communities can act as catalysts in prompting agreement or disagreement from other members, stimulating virtual conversation and debate (Blood, 2002). These online exchanges allow readers to transform what was initially a one-way communication source (i.e., online bulletin boards, email) into a platform that empowers them to contribute to its content. With very little training or know-how, an online user can join a discussion simply by offering a provocative comment (Dippold, 2009).

Twitter, a short messaging system application, and Tumblr, a microblogging site owned by Yahoo!Inc., are two platforms that enable such participation. Twitter allows users to write and reply to other users with 140 characters, photos, and video. Tumblr provides a multimedia space or Tumblrlog where users can share blogs, chats, gifs, videos, and links to other content. Tumblr went live in 2007, and has resulted in 108.4 million Tumblrlogs with nearly 51 billion posts (Aamoth, 2013). Additionally, Facebook and Instagram are popular sites where users share photos and short messages. Finally, YouTube, owned by Google, allows users to post videos and create channels for original video content. *Scandal* and most of its stars have official Instagram, Facebook, and Tumblr accounts. Promotions that run throughout the season encourage television viewers to visit the program's official social media sites.

Although all of these social media applications are used to create and maintain the Scandalverse, Twitter is the most successful of *Scandal*'s platforms. On average, Gladiators post more than 2,000 tweets per minute during new episodes. On Thursday nights, #Scandal and #AskScandal are frequently among the top hashtags trending on Twitter. Rhimes has more than 350,000 followers, and the program and all but one of the main cast members have official Twitter accounts with at least 200,000 followers; Washington leads the group with more than two million followers. These accounts, along with those of the makeup artists, main director, and set designers, have further built the audience for the program.

Scandal has viewers from all walks of life, but it is exceedingly popular in African American and other diverse households (Houston, 2013). The power of Twitter in the black community is one reason the marriage between Twitter and *Scandal* is so strong. In 2014, the Pew Research Center reported that blacks use Twitter more frequently than whites, noting that 22 percent of black internet users access Twitter at higher levels compared with 16 percent of whites. Overall, 73 percent of black internet users and 72 percent of white internet users use Twitter. The phenomenon of African Americans using Twitter to form a community has been dubbed "Black Twitter." Blogger Reagan Gomez characterized Black Twitter by commenting that she "Can't really explain #BlackTwitter other than 2 say, it's one big barbershop/beautysalon with a mix of church & the black table at HS lunch."

In its 2014 study of race and internet usage, Pew found that roughly 72 percent of blacks have a home broadband connection, a smartphone, or both. About 86 percent of black internet users ages 18–29 have home broadband access, about 88 percent are college graduates, and about 91 percent earn at least $75,000 annually. Nearly 96 percent of this group use some form of social media. While those who choose to post on social media about *Scandal* are generally considered to be fans or even Gladiators, the most fervent of the users have a deeper connection to the show and those who create it. In the case of the Scandalverse, social media usage, along with the compelling broadcast content, has triggered passionate and complex parasocial relationships.

Parasocial Relationships in the Scandalverse

Parasocial relationships are formed when viewers develop a bond with personalities they see only in the media. Horton and Wohl (1956) first addressed this phenomenon by demonstrating that viewers can develop feelings of close friendship with media figures, much like the relationships individuals have with each other in their real lives. Even though these relationships are one-sided, viewers are attracted to, or identify with, these media personalities in ways that foster authentic feelings. Such mediated friendships are likely to occur when viewers perceive that the television personalities are real and possess qualities that are attractive to the viewer (Rubin & McHugh, 1987). Early research into the phenomenon indicated that, in some cases, viewers use the mediated personalities and their behaviors as a way to understand their own lives. This research also suggested that those who experience these relationships may use them to compensate for voids in their personal lives (McQuail et al., 1972).

Previous research has explored parasocial relationships formed with fictional characters in situation comedies, romance novels, and soap operas. But particularly germane to the present study are the relationships viewers cultivate not only with the fictional characters, but also with the actors who play them. Because the actors are real people who share elements of their lives, habits, thoughts, and daily activities with audiences via social media, viewers can identify with these individuals more strongly than with fictional characters (Rubin & McHugh, 1987).

The parasocial relationships in the social media Scandalverse can be characterized in three distinct ways. First, the most ardent fans seem to have difficulty separating fact from fiction. Second, some fans take a turn at being producers of content, rather than just consumers. Third, in the most extreme cases, some fans use the shows' success to bolster their own names in the Scandalverse, hoping to transform themselves from fans to celebrities.

Fact Versus Fiction

The deep connection some fans experience with the program's characters and its stars creates an enthusiastic blurring of the distinction between real life and the on-air drama. This fuzziness manifests itself in several ways. First, discussions in various social media forums may seamlessly interweave elements of the TV storylines and participants' own personal experiences. Second, some members of the Scandalverse hope for and, in some cases, create romantic relationships (known as "shipping") for the actors on the programs.

A three-minute video clip of Fitz and Olivia (dubbed as "Olitz") arguing in a hospital room provided commenters with ample opportunity to compare the scene's contents with their lives. In January 2014, Super-Glorious44 wrote, "true love comes along once in a life time—twice if you're really really lucky. it's more powerful than pride and conscience. although this is fiction, i love their love, and it makes me believe and hope!!" Although some commenters acknowledge that they know the program is scripted, their feelings are nonetheless real and palpable. In January 2014, Charlene Jozefzoon wrote, "This is pure crack, I'm hooked on their love and it's freakin' fiction!! I need help or sex, whatever."

In December 2013, Lovepeacemusic18, in a response to a YouTube conversation about Olitz's encounter at a state dinner, agreed that the elements of race on the program resonate with her reality:

As a black woman from Australia, I am attracted to the show and am proud of the message the show is inevitably communicating, because it is the first mainstream tv drama that has a black woman as the protagonist lead character. The relationship between Fitz and Liv is one of great passion and excitement . . . who happen to be black and white. And this coincidence of different races is also sending a positive message as well.

Not all of the show's fans are Olitz shippers; in fact, some are disappointed in the relationship. Responding to a clip from the program's first season, 1bulma11 wrote that the adulation for the couple's interaction:

proves again the shallowness of this generation. their relationship is still ADULTERY. yes ADULTERY. there is no chemistry in that it is LUST and SEX ADDICTION. for you black women I hope you won't have a problem if the table was turned and a black president treats his black wife like crap for his white mistress. I hope black women will be cool and even watch that without any complaints.

There is no doubt that the fictional interracial affair has created some real-life animosity in social media. When the program began, there was much media attention highlighting Washington's status as the first African American woman to lead a network drama since the 1970s. While the program was lauded, some members of the African American community lamented that Olivia Pope's romance with a white President turned this triumphant character into little more than a sexual figure harkening back to the abuse of black female slaves by their white male owners. African American men voiced their concern through blogs. Damon Young, a blogger for VerySmartBrothas.com, noted that his Twitter feed was flooded with discussions about "bed wenches on Thursday night between 10:00 p.m. and 11:00 p.m." (Young, 2013). In other words, the men in his Twitterverse viewed the Pope–Grant relationship as a catalyst for deeper concern about black women being given to white men by show producers.

Individuals who genuinely identify with the characters and see aspects of the characters' experiences in their own lives often confess these connections via Tumblr. One of the most popular sites in the Scandalverse is "Sabia's Musings." Sabia is an African American woman who was one of the first to regularly posts gifs using images and photos of the cast and podcast synopses of each episode. Her Tumblr site is a must-stop destination for fans. One user expressed her appreciation with some self-identification:

Hi Sabia: I'd like to thank you for your blog, it's great & I enjoy the commentary on the episodes, also the characters. I was listening to your podcast & wanted to say I so agree with the comments re where Liv is emotionally, her insecurities. I identify with her issues, so scary—even her love for Fitz. I guess that's what draws me to her, I see myself in her.

This user found Tumblr to be an ideal vehicle through which to share the connection she feels with Olivia Pope. All of us have our own set of "truths." Confession is rooted in the desire to tell our truth to someone with whom we identify (Acosta-Alzuru, 2003). This commenter saw her own pain reflected in the Olitz relationship and used a social media outlet to convey it.

In such settings, individuals learn what others think and expect of them based on the responses to their posts. Individuals may feel comfortable sharing in these groups because they feel a kinship with others in this online community. Not only are the group members *Scandal* fans, but many are also women of color. References to Pope as a "sister," commiseration about the paucity of successful African American males, and their avatars indicate that the most frequent commenters are African American women.

It is apparent in the Scandalverse that some fans construct narratives to satisfy their own beliefs about the real lives of the show's actors. Tumblr users participated in conversations about the decision to use "granny jackets with large prints" as a means of distracting viewers from noticing Washington's pregnancy. A few Tumblr users (AliasVaughn and Scandal-Gladiators are frequent ringleaders) opined that the notoriously private Washington was not actually pregnant for the entire season and that she used the program's shot selection to conceal that she had given birth to her daughter. For several days in April 2014, Scandalverse pages were full of photos of Washington's face and commentary on whether or not it was round enough to be that of an expectant mother. Words such as "delusional" appeared on the sites, but more frequently, believers in the conspiracy delighted in the undisclosed discovery.

Shipping Fact and Fiction

Viewers hoping for love matches between television characters is nothing new. The off-again, on-again pairings of Sam and Diane on *Cheers* or Ross and Rachel on *Friends* kept audiences engaged season after season. The pairings on *Scandal*—Olitz, Huck/Quinn, Olivia/Jake (shipper names, respectively, Huckleberry Quinn and Olake)—are no different. Fans become invested in these relationships and enthusiastically hope for connections. When there is turmoil in these relationships, fans may become disgruntled. For example, in the program's second season, African American actor Norm Lewis was introduced as Senator Edison Davis, a love interest for Olivia Pope. Tumblr users began pejoratively referring to Lewis as "Senator Puddin' Pop" because he resembled Jell-O Pudding pitchman Bill Cosby. After an episode in which Davis challenged Pope's devotion to him, on October 22, 2012, alexleefitz posted on her Tumblr page, "ok puddin' pop. I see you . . . YOU AINT NO FITZ."

The viewers' anger in response to the discord can be attributed to genuine feelings of loss (Cohen, 2003). An extension of the research into the dynamics of parasocial relationships has found that parasocial "breakups" occur for viewers when their media friends are threatened with a departure of some type (Cohen, 2003). Although the theory has primarily been applied to the death of a character or a series cancellation, fans view Olitz as a character on the show. Therefore, when Olivia and Fitz argue or split, the effect can be the same.

Several key findings have emerged from the study of parasocial breakups. Simpson (1990) contends that the more committed a viewer is to tuning in to see a media character, the higher the level of distress in response to the media breakup. Similarly, Drigotas and Rusbult (1992) found that the more a viewer depends on a character to satisfy a need (i.e., living vicariously through the love of Olivia and Fitz), the greater the impact of the breakup. Eyal and Cohen (2006) found that factors other than the intensity of the relationship may also impact the feelings associated with a parasocial breakup. For example, the impact may be eased if viewers expect to have subsequent contact with the departing character. In the case of an Olitz breakup, for example, Fitz still appears on the program and viewers continue to see him struggling with his broken marriage and intermittent alcoholism.

In a persistent phenomenon, some fans not only ship Olitz, but also envision a real love affair between the show's stars, Kerry Washington and Tony Goldwyn. This match is given the shipper name "Terry." Although Goldwyn has been married since before the show began, Terry shippers contended that a real relationship must exist between the two stars because the actors' chemistry felt so genuine. Even when Washington married in the summer of 2013, true Terry shippers did not lose hope. Instead, they dismissed both partnerships as marriages of convenience, much like those staged in the era of the Hollywood Studio System. For those who held this view, the marriages were part of a "narrative" (an oft-used term) designed to placate members of the public who could not accept a real love affair between an older white man and younger African American woman.

However, some viewers did "jump ship" when confronted with the actors' real-life love affairs. Among these was Tumblr user Babycakesbriana, who confessed that learning of Washington's marriage made her so ill that she had to drink Pepto-Bismol to deal with the physical upset it caused. When news of Washington's marriage broke on July 3, 2013,

Goldwyn received four tweets from concerned fans asking if he was okay. Additionally, a year after Washington's marriage, three Tumblr posters (Aliasvaughn, Scandalbitchinheels, and Scandalgladiators) began trading stories of Washington's husband secretly visiting gay bars in Los Angeles and San Francisco. During the first week of February 2014, gossip blogs such as lipstickalley.com, bossip.com, and terezowens.com carried the story, which was seemingly picked up from the persistent Tumblr conversations.

Research about contributions to public forums demonstrates that those who write are unique and not the typical audience member in that they are more enthusiastic and vocal than others (Dahlberg, 2001). Moreover, research on parasocial relationships has found that television viewers who contribute to online forums often develop homophilic relationships with the lead characters (Eyal & Cohen, 2006). *Homophily* refers to the human tendency to form bonds and establish empathy with those who share similar characteristics. In the case of RL shipping (shipping in real life, or the belief that the actors themselves were engaged in a love affair) and the resulting backlash, the hurt reported as a result of the parasocial breakup was more intense than the responses typically reported for simple character shipping.

A key reason for these intense reactions is the heightened access to the lives of celebrities the internet provides. Photo agencies (i.e., Getty Images), entertainment blogs (i.e., Just Jared, Perez Hilton), and stars' personal Twitter, Instagram, and Facebook accounts offer almost daily glimpses into their lives. Now we can not only see stars sitting in the audience at the Emmy Awards, but we can also watch them select their dresses, have their makeup done, and walk the red carpet. Because these celebrities use online media to share aspects of their lives, habits, thoughts, and daily activities with audiences, viewers can identify with these individuals more than they do with fictional characters (Rubin & McHugh, 1987). This constant access creates a closer one-on-one relationship that heightens the power of parasocial interaction (Meyrowitz, 1994). Furthermore, like-minded people who frequently connect via social media can share and reinforce each other's beliefs—be they correct, incorrect, or just make believe.

Friends and Enemies

Before the advent of social media, the only recourse for those who disagreed with the direction of a televised storyline or the introduction of a new character was to write a letter to the network or to the fan club of one of the stars. With social media, audiences can reach out to a writer, producer, or star with a few keystrokes. Criticism can therefore be expected. *Scandal* showrunner Shonda Rhimes has more than 350,000 Twitter followers whom she warns, in her profile, "I make stuff up for a living. Remember, it's not real, okay? Don't tweet me your craziness." Still, the craziness finds its way to her Twitter page. After a scene in which Olivia Pope's on-and-off love interest puts his hands around her throat and demands information, Rhimes received dozens of tweets lamenting the glamorization of domestic violence on the program. Rhimes's response? "Maybe this show isn't for you."

When viewers get angry with a story, social media provide them the access and opportunity to give the writers some direction. Cherhonda Gunn commented on April 3, 2014:

> Write a presidential divorce! Does this mean Olivia and Fitz should be together right away? Absolutely not, because as mentioned above, they both need to go find themselves. That story is dead, let it rest in peace . . . just divorce them so WE can all move on!

Here, the parasocial relationship created by the Scandalverse engenders opinionated discussions. Because viewers feel a connection with the characters, they believe they know what's best for their lives—even if it's counter to what the showrunner has devised.

Much like siblings, members of the same *Scandal* community have squabbles, which often take the form of heated exchanges on YouTube. After watching a clip from Season 1, Nancydrew5 commented that Kerry Washington looked "scary thin." MichaelJfan4real's reply was impassioned: "No. Everyone's body is different. She does not look scary thin. That's ridiculous. Grow up and get an education."

Nancydrew5 replied aggressively:

> "Grow up and get an education." I am grown up and educated; perhaps you should take your own advice and grow up and not take personally other people's comments. After all you are not Kerry Washington and you are taking this way too personally as if i were talking about you. People can disagree with you and grown mature people accept that and realize that. You don't control me, I have every right to have my opinion on how Kerry Washington looks, you don't have to like it or agree, get over it.

The dissention between group members tends to be more fractious on this outlet than on others, because Tumblr and Twitter users can select sites that align with their particular point of view. YouTube, in contrast, is a clearinghouse for video clips and therefore open to a variety of perspectives. The selective exposure available on some sites can lead to an extreme polarization of views. Users cannot only prioritize the allegiances and storylines they prefer; they can also select the sources from which they will receive that information. In the Scandalverse, there is no limit to the number of groups available that appeal to the like-minded.

The stance of a social media forum is frequently clear from its name. Olitz4thewin or Olitz4ever offers a sure fix for those who crave images and content related to the Olivia and Fitz relationship. The popeandballard Tumblr site offers solace to those who want Jake and Olivia to find happiness together, although one commenter is "trying so hard to not get my hopes up about what Liv and Jake might be up to." The curl in the front of Goldwyn's hair has a few Twitter accounts of its own (i.e., Curl Gladiator), started by fans who worship it and him. Sites that compile video clips, gifs, and images that fit with fans' visions of the characters only strengthen these parasocial ties. The possibility that another scenario could be satisfying is not a possibility for these fans.

Celebrity and Fanatic

Parasocial relationships can exert a powerful influence that leads to demonstrative fan behaviors. Viewers may talk to their televised friends in the hope of reaching out to them in some way. In a dysfunctional example, those with strong parasocial ties may stalk a media personality (Norlund, 1978). More common demonstrations of parasocial feelings take the form of *fanwork*: creative or artistic work that consumes the time and, in some cases, financial resources of the user (fanlore.org/wiki/Fanwork).

These creative users have fashioned a culture with its own language, symbols, and rituals. *Scandal* fans have adopted Olivia Pope's term for her employees—Gladiators—to signify their own commitment to the show. "Mama Pope" and "Papa Pope" are monikers for Olivia's parents that began on Twitter. Fans have also created other language found in social media. For example, Goldwyn is frequently labeled and portrayed in artwork as a unicorn (he's white and magical), while Washington is portrayed as a mermaid (the female version of a mythical figure) on Tumblr and Twitter. Washington's husband is often drawn and referred to as "stringbean," in reference to his lanky build, by those who ship Terry on Tumblr. The time and effort invested in such fanwork stem from a connection that is experienced as more than just friendship.

A YouTube search for "Olitz videos" leads to dozens of user-made music videos comprised of edited clips from the show set to popular R&B music. For example, in December 2013, gunnysgirl posted "Fitz and Liv Making Love Song is What My Heart Says by Monica." In January 2012, SG Olitz posted an edited video set to the music of Beyoncé's "Drunk in Love." The videos received 51,889 and 36,427 views on YouTube, respectively. SkyBreezeProductions has created and posted several videos starring Olitz, and each has received at least 2,000 views. The most recent one, posted in August 2014, was captioned, "Finally finished an

Olitz video! It only took me nine months . . . Please watch in HD! It truly makes a difference. Also come follow me on Twitter."

Requests for followers on Twitter, Tumblr, or YouTube create large, loyal audiences for the most active social media contributors. Tumblr user babycakesbriana reported on March 21, 2013 that, "Like 99% of all the Tumblr Clouds (pages) I've seen had AliasVaughn's name in it!" prompting fellow follower visionarywateringhole to declare, "You are [Scandal] Tumblr famous!!!" Others become famous in the Scandalverse because of their fanwork. Perhaps best known is Tangela Ekhoff, an amateur stand-up comedian who posts episode recaps from her living room and markets herself as a "Video Visibility Expert" (www.tangelaekhoff.com). Tangela's fame prompted the *Scandal* cast and crew to create a video thanking her for supporting the show.

Additionally, all of the show's stars have responded in some capacity to fanwork sent to them electronically. Goldwyn has added some fanwork, including tributes to his hair, to his Twitter and Facebook pages. Washington has tweeted messages to fans about Goldwyn's hair, which is now just a part of the Scandalverse. For example, on October 31, 2013, Washington live tweeted during a scene in which President Grant was playing basketball: "That sweaty Fitz curl?!?! PERFECT. @tonygoldwyn #Scandal."

Fanfiction (stories written by fans using favorite characters for inspiration) is also rife with fans whose loyal followers request updates and suggest storylines. Popular fanfiction archive FanFiction.Net has a *Scandal* archive of more than 1,100 stories. Writers, readers, and those who do both are beckoned, "Do you like exploring the Fitz and Olivia phenomenon in alternative universes [AU]? Have you written a Scandal AU? If so, please enter this community." Steamy stories abound, with Olitz/Terry married and living in or out of the White House with children. In Melivia (Mellie and Olivia) fanfiction, the powerhouse women in Fitz's life become lovers and have trysts of their own. The power of Scandalverse fanfiction has even found its way into the mainstream. Media juggernaut *The New Yorker*'s Cora Frazier wrote a piece of *Scandal* fanfiction in which Olivia Pope agrees to handle the embattled administration of New Jersey governor Chris Christie, even though she's already busy with her powerful boyfriend (Frazier, 2014).

Conclusion

A significant finding that emerged from analyzing the Scandalverse is that the marriage of social media and parasocial interactions blurs the lines between consumer and owner of content. Viewers' connections with a show that are translated into blog posts, fanwork, or tweets give the audience a tangible grasp of their favorite programs and characters.

In the case of the RL shippers, their persistence results in their stories showing up in other media, which allows these creators to influence how others view the personal lives of the program's stars. Public arguments over storylines, racial tensions, and even wardrobes on the show engender a passion that can only come from viewers who are invested in the outcome of the production.

The frequency of character shipping or RL shipping is another trend that highlights the visceral nature of the audience's connection with the characters. Perhaps, the most loyal of these shippers connect to the program, its stars, and shipping itself because of the members' need for love and romance of their own. It would, then, stand to reason that shipping on Tumblr has become a form of "emotional pornography" for some of those in the community. While this conclusion is possible, however, the faceless nature of the internet makes it difficult to verify. In the Scandalverse, anonymity is commonplace, which allows frank exchanges to occur but also enables some users to adopt specious personas. The anonymity makes researching the motivations of users somewhat confounding. In particular, users of Tumblr, YouTube, and blogs use pseudonyms, avatars, or pictures of their favorite television star as identifiers.

Attempts to contact the heaviest creators in the Scandalverse for the present study were unsuccessful, which is not surprising. Online conversations can result in honest discourse because users feel safe in expressing their feelings without fear of retribution (Bloch, 2007). Conversely, the anonymity offered by these sites conceals authorship, thereby cloaking users' identities (Daniels, 2009). Their anonymity allows them to be more graphic in their use of language and sexual content, as well as to present gossip without credible evidence.

As Costello and Moore (2007) discovered in their qualitative study of online viewers of television, the internet allows fans to seek more information about programs they watch on television and to engage in discussion with other fans. These conversations convey an ownership that is certainly illustrated in the Scandalverse. This online group was started by women of color who spread the word and recruited others to watch. Their loyal viewership led to the program's success, which enabled this audience to take ownership of their favorite program, deepening their relationships with the program and its cast. The importance of the viewer's sense of ownership of a program cannot be overstated: the public's support of television programs has been known to breathe new life into struggling shows. In April 2009, for example, audiences united via the internet to save the NBC action adventure comedy program *Chuck* (France, 2009). The internet provides a particularly useful tool for coordinating such efforts. For example, the websites Savethatshow.com and savemyshow. com are devoted to making viewers feel they have a direct line to television programming executives through grassroots campaigns.

The *Scandalverse* offers an example of the power of social media among African American users. "Black Twitter," which it has been dubbed by African-Americans who use Twitter to share, lament, and laugh, is quickly becoming an online hub. The Pew Research Center reported that 96 percent of African American internet users between the ages of 18 and 29 connect through social media (Smith, 2014). The ease of tweeting and Twitter's easy-to-find @'s help fans connect more readily with network executives and decision makers. *Scandal* exemplifies the value to be found in the audiences and programs in which women of color do a lot of the talking.

References

Aamoth, D. (2013). What is Tumblr? *Time*, May 19. Online at http://techland. time.com/2013/05/19/what-is-tumblr (retrieved June 21, 2013).

Acosta-Alzuru, C. (2003). Change your life! Confession and conversion in Telemundo's *Cambia Tu Vida*. *Mass Communication & Society, 6*, 137–159.

Bloch, J. P. (2007). Cyber wars: Catholics for Free Choice and the online abortion debate. *Review of Religious Research, 49*, 165–186.

Blood, R. (2002). *The weblog handbook: Practical advice on creating and maintaining your blog*. Cambridge, MA: Perseus Publishing.

Cohen, J. (2003). Parasocial breakups: Measuring individual differences in responses to the dissolution of parasocial relationships. *Mass Communication & Society, 6*, 191–202.

Costello, V., & Moore, B. A. (2007). Cultural outlaws: An examination of audience activity and online television fandom. *Television & New Media, 8*, 124–143.

Dahlberg, L. (2001).The internet and democratic discourse: Exploring the prospects of online deliberative forums extending the public sphere. *Information, Communication & Society, 4*(4), 615–633.

Daniels, J. (2009). Cloaked websites: Propaganda, cyber-racism and epistemology in the digital era. *New Media & Society, 11*(5), 659–683.

Dippold, D. (2009). Peer feedback through blogs: Student and teacher perceptions in an advanced German class. *Recall, 21*(1), 18–36.

Drigotas, S. M., & Rusbult, C. E. (1992). Should I stay or should I go? A dependence model of breakups. *Journal of Personality & Social Psychology, 62*(1), 62–87.

Eyal, K., & Cohen, J. (2006). When good *Friends* say goodbye: A parasocial breakup study. *Journal of Broadcasting & Electronic Media, 50*, 502–523.

France, L. R. (2009). "Save Chuck" latest in campaigns to rescue favorite shows. *CNN.com/entertainment*, April 29. Online at www.cnn.com/2009/SHOWBIZ/TV/04/30/save.chuck.show/index.html (retrieved May 14, 2009).

Frazier, C. (2014). Olivia Pope fixes Chris Christie. *The New Yorker*, January 15. Online at www.newyorker.com/humor/daily-shouts/olivia-pope-fixes-chris-christie (retrieved February 21, 2014).

Gonzalez, S. (2013). Addicted to *Scandal*. *Entertainment Weekly.com*, April 5. Online at www.ew.com/article/2013/04/05/addicted-scandal (retrieved June 9, 2013).

Harris, M. (2014). Black star, white ceiling. *Entertainment Weekly.com*, May 9. Online at www.ew.com/article/2014/04/30/lupita-nyongo-jungle-book-oscar (retrieved June 10, 2014).

Horton, D., & Wohl, R. R. (1956). Mass communication and para-social interaction: Observations on intimacy at a distance. *Psychiatry, 19*, 215–229.

Houston, S. (2013). How *Scandal* reinvents TV's gay couple . . . and not how you'd think. *Hollywood.com*, October 19. Online at www.hollywood.com/news/tv/55037053/scandal-cyrus-and-james-reinvent-the-gay-couple (retrieved November 12, 2013).

Keveney, B. (2013). A social-media *Scandal* rocks ABC (in a good way). *USA Today*, February 19. Online at www.usatoday.com/story/life/tv/2013/02/19/abc-scandal-builds-momentum/1930963/ (retrieved March 6, 2013).

Levin, G., & Bianco, R. (2012). For two upcoming series, ABC flirted with the B-word. *USA Today*, January 11. Online at http://usatoday30.usatoday.com/LIFE/usaedition/2012-01-11-Press-tour-print-111-ABC_ST_U.htm (retrieved February 13, 2012).

McQuail, D., Blumler, J. G., & Brown, J. R. (1972). The television audience: A revised perspective. In D. McQuail (Ed.), *Sociology of mass communication* (pp. 135–165). Harmondsworth, UK: Penguin.

Meyrowitz, J. (1994). The life and death of media friends: New genres of intimacy and mourning. In S. Drucker & S. Cathcart (Eds.), *American heroes in a media age* (pp. 62–81). Cresskill, NJ: Hampton Press.

Norlund, J-E. (1978). Media interaction. *Communication Research, 5*(2), 150–175.

Rubin, R. B., & McHugh, M. P. (1987). Development of parasocial interaction relationships. *Journal of Broadcasting & Electronic Media, 31*(3), 279–292.

Simpson, J. A. (1990). Influence of attachment styles of romantic relationships. *Journal of Personality and Social Psychology, 59*(5), 971–980.

Smith, A. (2014). *African Americans and technology use: A demographic portrait*. Pew Research Internet Project. Online at www.pewinternet.org/2014/01/06/african-americans-and-technology-use (retrieved December 1, 2014).

Young, D. (2013). Why (some) men seem to hate *Scandal* so damn much. *VSB.com*, October 9. Online at http://verysmartbrothas.com/why-some-men-seem-to-hate-scandal-so-damn-much (retrieved November 21, 2013).

12

THE LEGACY OF DR. HORRIBLE

Potential Research into Second-Screen Intrusion, Coordination, and Influence

Tim Hudson

Two of my favorite cultural references regarding the decline of network television viewership are: Dr. Horrible's streaming mishap during his attempt to "take over" the 2009 CBS Emmy Awards telecast, and Susan Tyler Eastman's speculation that entertainment industry magazines stopped publishing weekly television ratings because they were so embarrassing to the networks.

The former was a hilarious salute to an auditorium full of old-media dinosaurs, allowing them a collective codgers' "harumph" at the technical limitations of internet video streaming even as Neil Patrick Harris's online alter ego accurately predicted the demise of their critical mass-dependent, schedule-oriented business model. The latter is a more realistic, if somewhat cruel, veteran communication professor's illustration of the same phenomenon.

But for most viewers it is not an either/or decision. Increasingly, media audience members are utilizing more than one screen at a time when consuming audio-visual media entertainment or information. If we refer to the traditional home television set as the first screen, then we can discuss simultaneous use of a smart phone, laptop or tablet device as the "second screen."

Each of the three student-written chapters comprising the first section of this book represents an early exploration into the nature of second-screen usage by audiences.

Early studies on the first-screen experience of television often split focus between "attention to" and "retention of" these multimodal messages. With "Double Vision," Guo and Holmes (Chapter 2) attempt to track one of the key components of image attention, the gaze of the human eye. Their questions are basic: Which screen are viewers looking at? When? And for how long?

One of many popular uses of the second screen is social media activity. With the "Olympic Games" project, Lim and Hwang (Chapter 1) attempt to analyze the motives for and quality of experience, while viewers are utilizing both screens, one (presumably) to observe games, and the second, perhaps, to enhance or supplement the experience.

Brouder and Brookey (Chapter 3) narrow the second-screen subject even further by focusing specifically on the phenomenon of Twitter use during television viewing. Before an experience can be enhanced or a message can be retained, attention must first be gained. The authors begin with a recent claim by Nielsen Media Research that Twitter patter influences attention to specific television programs (ratings) and vice versa.

Clearly a lot is going on here. The first screen, with its historical and psychological status as a "lean-back" technology, already requires a great deal of our senses and cognitive abilities: simultaneously offering moving images, text, and sound. The existence of the second screen doubles down on these modality experiences, then adds potential kinetic, interactive, and information-seeking activity. Whether all of this represents deeper immersion into the media experience or increased distraction from the intended messages is one of many initial questions to be addressed. But to take on this and other questions at this super multimodal, multi-experiential level can seem overwhelming. Fortunately, we can dial things back a bit to review what we already understand about some of the building blocks of the two-screen video experience.

These three studies are informed by prior work regarding multiple-modality message retention and the effects of interactivity on media attention and retention.

As a boy in primary school, one of my favorite sections of the library was the filmstrip collection. The combination of still images and recorded sound provided a multimedia experience similar to television, but with me in control. I could pause on a particular frame or rewind and repeat a section. I found the experience more fun than quietly looking at picture books. My classmates and I also looked forward to "story time," when the teacher would read fiction aloud to us while we read along in our own copies of the book.

Years later, in college, I ran across a body of research that confirmed my experiences scientifically—noting that, not only did most children enjoy dual-modality lessons, but that any combination of two of the three learning modalities (sound, images, and text) resulted in higher retention than any of the individual modes alone, provided there was high message redundancy in the two combined channels. As research progressed, we learned that, while two were typically better than one, having the information presented simultaneously in *all three* modalities did not further increase learning of the material. The term "information overload" had already entered the popular lexicon, helping to describe twentieth-century experiences where so many messages were distributed in so many new ways.

By the late 1980s and early 1990s researchers were measuring whether the addition of new types of interaction on the part of the user might increase retention. While students may have reported higher levels of enjoyment, faster completion, a feeling of increased convenience, and even a *perception* that they learned more from an interactive multimedia lesson as compared to a standard classroom seminar covering the same material, findings did not consistently support an increase (or decrease) in retention (without repetition of material).

Of course, the television industry doesn't always incorporate these lessons in the most logical manner. Professional journalists routinely emphasize the importance of effectively disseminating information. And certainly advertising sales professionals reassure their clients that viewers remember the imagery and information they see and hear on television. But despite the stacks of studies warning that added modality stimulation (especially with non-redundant content) was not helpful to either of these goals, in the 1990s the TV screen was carved up and overburdened with a variety of splits, corner boxes, captions and crawls, especially during news, political, business, and sports programming: attention-getting screen techniques perhaps, but antithetical to any retention-based goal.

The opening session of the BEA2014 Research Symposium brought these earlier findings in modality and cognitive learning back to my mind. We've come a long way and made great strides in the application of multimedia and interactivity, but we are still exploring some of the same questions regarding attention, experience, distraction, and learning.

Guo and Holmes, other academic researchers, and their industry counterparts measuring eye-gaze and biometrics at the impressive high-tech Time-Warner media lab in Manhattan will, no doubt, discover that variations in sound, noise, light, screen division, text presentation, and even device vibration can dependably attract and otherwise affect the attention of the audience member. But will this knowledge primarily result in a lot of gaze-bouncing/attention-shifting activity, heightening the "experience" without increasing message retention, or might there be more thoughtful practical industry application of what is being learned?

This kind of research is very much in its infancy, and certain limitations of "Double Vision" serve as stark reminders of this fact. The first is the absence of attention to sound. Isolation of eye-gaze from hearing and listening is operationally problematic, as changes in volume, pitch, source, type, pattern, or even existence of sound are known to influence attention and gaze. In addition to simply accounting for and measuring program audio changes in correlation to eye behavior, future researchers might ask if, when, and why audience members themselves raise, lower, or mute the sound from one source or the other.

There also seem to be some major technical issues remaining with close biological observation and measurement in general and eye-gaze software in particular. Guo and Holmes had to conduct supplementary manual observation and coding. Not uncommon in experimental and quasi-experimental research are concerns regarding the operationalized environment—in this case a simulated living room. And is 30 minutes really long enough for subjects to settle into normal viewing behavior? These issues, sample size, and the limitations raised by the researchers themselves suggest that the primary value of this study might be heuristic in nature. Like a well-conducted focus group, rather than offering gener-alizable conclusions, the work can point us to potentially fruitful avenues for further research.

Guo and Holmes speculate as to whether we might eventually see some evolution in the ability to multitask—perhaps first as disruption in our gaze patterns. Maybe the millennials in my classroom are right. Perhaps in the near future, multitasking will become less of a delusion and more of a reality.

In this context, the kind of work represented by Hwang and Lim takes on special significance. No doubt, some of us old curmudgeons will con-tinue to put down or turn off our portable devices when settling into the recliner for some quality lean-back media time. But those who choose to go to the second screen must be seeking something more from their down time. We learn in this study that some, especially male sports fans, are seeking convenient access to information, while others, including female viewers, are more interested in a shared social experience, an incorporeal yet empirical sense of community.

There aren't many surprises in these results, given prior research regarding motivation for consumption of broadcast sports as information, entertainment, and shared experience. The convenience factor, however, seems especially tied to the second-screen information seeking. And given the lack of other sports fans in the room, the extent to which viewers experience social presence via social media merits considerable attention.

Whether two-screen users remember more about their messages or not, findings of enhanced experience—excitement, social connectedness, supplemented knowledge—all represent rich avenues for further explora-tion of the multi-screen interactive experience. If consistent, findings such as the reportedly higher commitment levels for male sports viewers using social media will certainly perk up the ears of constituent programmers and advertisers.

It seems fairly straightforward to design sport-channel web sites and "apps" that capitalize on the community/social presence motivations of some viewers (possibly more women than men), while also providing convenient avenues to stats, facts, and figures to other viewers (perhaps skewing male). Of course, early forays into such second-screen enhancements already exist.

The studies under discussion confirm that attention to the second screen increases during commercial breaks. Whether it's to check on dinner, take in the view from the picture window, or browse a magazine, viewers have always had opportunity and tendency to look away from the television during commercials. However, as both the eye-gaze and the Twitter study illustrate, when the alternative experience is an interactive second-screen device, there is at least significant opportunity for program-related engagement.

A limiting bugaboo that casts a shadow over practical application of second-screen data is the commonsensical notion and research-supported observation that most of the time spent accessing the second screen is time spent cognitively, if not actively "away from" program-related material. In the case of one subject, Guo and Holmes observed, "While her visual attention pattern alone would suggest she was distracted by the second screen, she was reported being deeply engaged with the show . . . [and] . . . using her mobile device in support of parasocial interaction and identity attributes of that engagement" (page 40, this volume). In my media programming class, I recently asked students how they use their second screens. One woman indicated that during commercial breaks she checks out the efficacy of medical and science-related assertions made by characters in the police procedurals she enjoys.

In their chapter, Brouder and Brookey document several entrepreneurial efforts to coordinate television viewership and social media use, especially Twitter. But each is fairly specific to the company or client at hand. Can we soon expect an automatic gatekeeping service that guides the viewer to the most relevant source-supportive material ranging from predictable Google searches to movie-cast or sports-team Facebook pages, Twitter activity, network and product sites, fan-generated material, and viral multimedia—updated in real time to coordinate with the signals imbedded in mass-distributed audio and video materials?

If it pans out that there is a reliable change in gaze pattern when the second-screen opportunities have been purposefully crafted to complement the main-screen material, can it be long before development of a comprehensive "TV/multimedia Viewing App"? This might be a simple program that, much like a ratings "people-meter," monitors viewing/ listening and then directs the second screen to source-determined or source-recommended supplemental program, promotional, fan, social interaction, informational, and, of course, advertising material and experiences. Several popular second-screen fan support and social media apps already exist, and Shazam has been softening up the audience for an Arbitron-like "listening" function for many years. Think "Beamly" writ large. Viewers may soon be able to call upon a second-screen traffic cop (albeit a patrolman who is very much on the take). Free to the user, such a service could be advertiser-supported and/or funded via revenue coming in directly from the media companies themselves in exchange for their rich proprietary ratings and usage data collected passively from the ubiquitous smart devices. Because such an app will almost surely be triggered by audio "watermarks" in the programs themselves, the service would work equally well during live, real-time, time-shifted, video on demand (VOD), and over-the-top online program consumption.

As much fun as it currently may be to engage via Facebook or Twitter, and to search IMDb or thespread.com, it's easy to imagine many audience members occasionally choosing to "give up" partial control of the second screen during viewing sessions in exchange for an "enhanced" multi-screen experience. Perhaps this represents a future role for the beleaguered media "gatekeeper."

Taken together, the three studies that open this book point to an immense frontier of potential research into media activity and consumption. For the purpose of brevity, we might peer into one small valley of this frontier by continuing speculation about the application of such a second-screen "traffic-guidance" application.

Audience Behavior

Those who study television often comment on its role as a relaxing activity, while social media use and other internet-based activity requires users to lean forward and *work at it*. If television programmers, advertisers, and perhaps even journalists develop ways to create and predict (or at least estimate) the most rewarding and engaging Twitter hashtags, Facebook pages, web sites, aggregators, articles, games, etc. to associate with first-screen programs, documentaries, specials, and newscasts as they are being consumed, then audiences might find significant value (and potential relaxation) in the added convenience.

This kind of broad data-driven second-screen coordination is already very nearly possible for cord-severed audiences who enjoy their TV via internet streaming. But a pestering potential downside to an all-streamed video diet is the fact that internet bandwidth is neither infinite nor inexhaustible. If technology and economics dictate that for a significant portion of the near future much of the audience will still need or want fat-pipe-delivered and/or over-the-air broadcast content, then this second-screen interactive function of the smart device might be an important gap technology for measuring, enhancing, researching, and capitalizing on the second-screen experience. When we consider the proliferation of out-of-home multimedia opportunities, the shelf life of such a user-enacted second-screen enhancement might be significant.

A simple, straightforward early research application of such a device would be a series of comparisons of second-screen use by those who do not engage the application (beyond simple ratings measurement) with those who do. This would begin to answer some of the questions that challenge Guo and Holmes, and other contributors to this collection.

Advertising

Current new-media giants are competitors, of course, each working to become THE preferred destination for second-screen activity and to sell those eyeballs & eardrums to advertisers. But it wasn't so long ago that the leading pioneers of the WWW (ranging from legacy giants to tiny start-ups) jousted and parried to become THE preferred "portal" to the online world. Everybody wanted to supply the user's "home page." Just as those competitors came to concede the precious "home space" prize to quasi-personalized social media pages (Friendster, MySpace, Facebook), targeted research might reveal a similar need for a quasi-personalized, sponsor-influenced friendly interface between the recreational main screen in the home, and the second screen in the pocket or backpack. Some major internet businesses continue to operate without consistent profit. It might be more realistic and more profitable to refocus efforts from the objective of becoming THE ubiquitous second-screen activity to becoming a sometime second-screen activity of choice, particularly when and where viewers are most likely to find what they want and specific advertisers are willing to help pay for the connection that reels in the already motivated audience member.

Such a second-screen "traffic" app could provide some of that sought-after predictability-of-experience. At the least, some experimental research along these lines seems appropriate.

Cultural Sensitivity

Media pundits including Jon Stewart and John Oliver have criticized corporations and advertisers for "hijacking" social media conversations like unwanted guests at a cocktail party. But a less obtrusive role within the background of an invited, second-screen gatekeeping architecture might be better tolerated, even appreciated. Suppose, for example, a "traffic" app were to detect viewing of an extended cable news program commemorating victims and heroes of the 9/11 attacks. The properly tuned "traffic" app might direct viewers to a menu of second-screen options while simultaneously excluding sites and services often considered overly crass, commercial, opportunistic, or irritating. Is such a level of gatekeeping finesse even possible? Research is needed to explore the prospects and possibilities.

Journalism

Cass Sunstein, Bill Maher, and scores of other scholars, journalists, and personalities have bemoaned the negative consequences of allowing individuals to create their own personal bubbles, the internet user's "Daily Me" being more narrow and less conducive to serendipitous exposure and learning than the mass media of the twentieth century. Is there room for a twenty-first-century version of "Mr Gates"? Could a second-screen traffic service employ experienced journalists, salvaging and modernizing the roles of the old city editor and executive producer by contributing informed, fact and issue-based directional codes and algorithms to the second-screen process? Might this reinstate some of the shared media experience and perceived "understanding" of current events: the sense of commonality citizens lost to Web access, a loss often lamented by the over-50 crowd? Would media consumers even be interested in such a service? Online survey research might provide some useful feedback in short time at little expense. Guo and Holmes found shorter gaze patterns for news and reality programs than for entertainment and sports. Might this suggest a particular opportunity for second-screen guidance to supplemental story- or personality-related information?

Regulation

It's easy to imagine a variety of commercial partnerships offering a menu of differing versions of this "traffic" app idea (assuming more open access to imbedded audio program codes). We could end up with a "Fox News-ish" version pitted against a politically progressive version of the app, with the same false duality of content and popularization of charlatans plaguing the "cable news" business today. Perhaps this is an opportunity to explore adaptation of the "public service" model to new media technology. What might be the possibility of "traffic" app providers enjoying some sort of FCC licensure and/or priority status? In turn the provider could guarantee cross-media emergency message alerts and other efforts at fact-based public issue ascertainment, response, and documentation of service. Is there any life left in the old public service model or would any such regulatory proposals be considered too "Big Brother" by millennials?

There is much innovation and inspiration to be found in these early research projects. It may be too late to save legacy television network program executives from the nefarious influence of *Dr. Horrible's* insidious *Sing-Along Blog*, but taking the time to review the work of developing communication scholars may represent a useful antidote to some of the dizziness, angst, and dyspepsia induced by the swiftly morphing visage of the new media Hydra.

13

CHANGING PARADIGM?

Mitchell Shapiro

As the respondent to the second panel of competitively reviewed research papers, a pattern through these studies became noticeable to me. It made me think back to earlier days and ideas, specifically one of the seminal concepts that Marshall McLuhan put forth—the notion that through the evolution and advancements of media technology the world is becoming more of a "global village." His notion is that through technology the physical and cultural distances between the peoples of the world are shrinking and that a common "global" culture is emerging. People from formerly vastly different cultures are now increasingly sharing experiences, events, and ideas almost instantaneously.

In American society, from the beginning of electronic mass media with the development of radio broadcasting in the 1920s, mass media have gone through a continual evolutionary process fueled by technological advancements. These advances force the earlier technology to either adapt to a new function or become obsolete. Television's adoption by society a few years after World War II forced radio to change if it was to survive. Aided by newer technology that allowed radios to become smaller and more portable, radio evolved into a background medium as television became the predominant mass medium during the 1950s. Once regulatory constraints were removed, cable television (as we know it today) grew up in the late 1970s and 1980s. This allowed homes to receive many more television signals than broadcast would allow, and also brought a better quality picture into the home. This period also brought the video-cassette recorder (VCR) into the picture, thus allowing the receivers of the content to have some control over when they would view it—prior to this the sender had absolute control over when the receiver had access to view the content. The late 1980s introduced the small home satellite dish, the widespread growth of remote controls, and CDs. The 1990s brought the computer, internet, and DVDs, thus making it easier for the sharing of mass mediated content within and between cultures. The first decade of the twenty-first century brought with it a revolution in both large-screen and digital high-definition pictures and sound; as well as digital video recorders (DVRs), cellular telephones, and portable computer devices that allowed users to receive and record video and audio material at their convenience. This decade also saw the mushrooming of social media. Applications such as YouTube, Facebook, and Twitter take advantage of the current state of technology to allow users everywhere to have even more control over their communication.

The traditional research paradigm regarding the impact of mass-mediated content on individuals and on society at large has tended to focus primarily on "differences." Researchers in our field for the past 50-plus years have focused on: how differences among and between people manifest as a result of exposure to mass-mediated content; how different people are affected by the same content; and how different cultures react to and/or are affected differently by content issues.

The three research presentations that comprised this specific panel were very good examples of the popular paradigm. Each of them was well thought out, was executed in the proper manner, and provided some keen insight to the specific questions each addressed. Fei Shen, Zhi'an Zhang, and Mike Z. Yao (Chapter 4) conducted a national survey about uses of broadcast and new media channels in China; Michael D. Bruce (Chapter 5) examined the visual structure of content on several different transnational Arab news channels; and Peter B. Seel (Chapter 6) provided a wonderful presentation of the history and evolution of visual displays.

While each of the studies on this panel presented findings that focused on differences, for some reason that I can't fully explain, nor understand, I was drawn to the similarities involved. I noticed how new media use in China was strikingly similar to the way American audiences use new media; in Bruce's study I was drawn to the similarities that existed between the different Arab news channels; and in Seel's presentation it became evident that the different iterations of "television" screens all seemed to go through similar transformative processes, facing similar economic and technological concerns.

We have learned a great deal over the past half century about such differences—this doesn't mean we can't learn more about these issues. However, maybe it is time for a change in the direction of our research. Maybe it is time to start focusing on the similarities that exist among and between "different" audiences. After all, might not such knowledge provide us with a fuller understanding of the role and impact of mass media and its messages. Maybe, we are truly entering into McLuhan's global village.

14

IMMERSION

Implications of Wearable Technologies for
the Future of Broadcasting

John V. Pavlik

Introduction

Wearable digital devices such as the experimental Google Glass are poised
to transform traditional broadcasting media. Among the implications are
new methods of video production, shifts in storytelling, increases in public
engagement, and realignments in the structure, management, and funding
of the broadcasting industry.

Television and radio have long been the staple technologies of the
broadcasting industry. Only a generation ago, television sets were rectangular boxes that displayed video via heavy cube-shaped cathode ray tubes
(CRTs). Viewers generally sat in front of their TV sets and watched as
mostly third-person narratives played out on the screen.

Principally devoted to audio playback, radio sets have tended to be
smaller, lighter, and more mobile than TV sets. While in the early part of
the twentieth century Americans often sat around large radios built from
vacuum tubes and positioned as elegant pieces of wood-cased furniture,
the transistor fueled major changes in the technology. Miniaturization
characterized much of the change in radio sets for the latter half of the
twentieth century, with wearable radios and other music playback devices
becoming common along with the car radio.

Radio and television, whether in the form of sets, cameras, microphones,
or systems of distribution, were analog in format (i.e., not computerized)
for most of their twentieth-century history. Viewers and listeners relied
on analog sources of audio and video delivered over the air, via cable and
satellite, or played back audio or video from analog recording devices such
as the videocassette recorder (VCR).

Digital technology ushered in a wide spectrum of changes in the world of broadcasting. By 2014, finding a CRT TV set became almost as rare as spotting a rotary phone or eight-track cassette player. Flat-screen TV sets have become the norm. Radio sets not only have shrunk further in size, but they also are convergent devices that can display visual information about songs, artists, and stations as well as provide user navigation capabilities via voice or touch command. The broadcasting distribution system has undergone similar sweeping changes as digitization has introduced compression of signals, server-based on-demand services, and competition from phone companies and other fiber-optic broadband carriers as well as direct-to-user satellite transmission.

The Emergence of Wearable Technologies

Wearable technologies are positioned to exert further and fundamental changes to broadcasting in the twenty-first century. Whether in the form of a wristwatch, sunglasses, a Walkman with headphones, or ear-buds connected to an iPod or smartphone, consumers have already demonstrated a fondness for wearable devices, including media. Wearable media devices are especially popular among the young, who seem to have a high level of attraction to the personal, customization, and on-demand continuous entertainment, information, and communication capability they afford. It takes little imagination to envision a future where consumers widely adopt lightweight, powerful, convergent, and wearable media devices. It's this logic that has inspired major digital enterprises such as Samsung, Google, and Apple to devote enormous resources to the development of wearable digital media technologies. Google is not alone among commercial enterprises to have developed head-worn digital devices. Meta's SpaceGlasses (Meta, 2014), Vuzix's M100 (Vuzix, 2014), and Epiphany Eyewear (Epiphany Eyewear, 2014) are available in 2014 in the commercial marketplace. In September, 2014, Samsung introduced a new smartphone equipped with a virtual reality (VR) headset (*CBS This Morning*, 2014). Moreover, today's youth have already demonstrated close ties to their personal communication devices. A recent study by the Pew Research Internet Project shows, for instance, that nearly two-thirds (61 percent) of persons 18–24 sleep with their smartphones next to their heads (Smith, 2012), almost three times the rate for those 65 and older (22 percent).

None of this necessarily implies everyone will be walking around wearing digital devices on their heads or as eye-wear, although analysts forecast 500 million wearable devices will be sold in the next four years (Pogue, 2014). Some digital wearables on the market in 2014 come in the form of wristwatches, such as the Samsung Gear and Gear Fit smartwatch (Samuel, 2014). This device can discreetly take photographs, make voice phone calls or receive text messages (via a smartphone wirelessly linked to the device). Samsung reports selling at least 800,000 units of the Gear smartwatch worldwide by November 2013 (Samsung, 2014; Tofel, 2013). As research shows that many users of mobile devices look at their smartphones up to 100 times a day, wrist-worn digital devices can be time savers (Pogue, 2014). Google has created the Android Wear operating system for wearables and developers have already created more than 300 apps for smartwatches (Android, 2014).

Critics have accurately noted that the first generation of the Gear smartwatch is still very much a work in progress. It has a variety of flaws or limitations, both in the design of the user interface and in functionality (Hessman, 2013). For instance, Gear relies on the user's smartphone to communicate or access the internet. Similarly, Glass has significant limitations in its current 2014 form. The author has tested his Glass extensively, and has found that the device overheats within about 30 minutes of continuous video use, forcing the system to automatically shut down. The device is warm to the touch, though not dangerous to the user. Yet, this limited time-use capability severely limits what the device can do or how the user may engage it. Still, it should be recognized that Glass, like other wearables, is in the early stages of development and will likely advance dramatically in the coming months and years. Moore's Law, which since the 1960s has shown that digital technology decreases by half in size every 18 months or so, underscores this likelihood (Wikipedia, 2013).

Some companies are developing or have already introduced a wide spectrum of other types of digital wearables, many of which take the form of fashion pendants or other jewelry (Goldin, 2014; Wood, 2014). These devices are sometimes more about emotion or making a social statement, such as "I'm hip," than about function. Still, some of these devices offer sophisticated functionality. For instance, some wrist-worn devices have sensors that can collect health data and then record or transmit the information to a remote device or via a wireless network. Some wearables are also capable not only of gathering health information; the "bionic pancreas" links to the user's smartphone and can automatically administer prescription drugs such as insulin in customized dosages (CBS News, 2014). Some wearable gadgets are waterproof and can be worn while swimming, providing health monitoring while the swimmer or other athlete exercises. There are head-worn devices that can monitor the user's brain activity in terms of EEG (electroencephalogram) signals, which can be useful in stress management (e.g., Muse and Melon; Pogoreic, 2014). Apple has announced the Apple Watch, a wearable device that will provide health, fitness, and similar capabilities, monitoring body temperature, heart rate, and the like, as well as providing communications capabilities when tethered to an iPhone (Covert, 2014; Swider, 2014). A planned Apple digital ear-piece may provide improved hearing as well.

Some wearable technology may be woven directly into clothing, making it even less obtrusive. In development are contact lenses with retinal displays that one day may have all the functionality of a head-worn device such as Google Glass (Eisenberg, 2009). Google has even patented a contact lens design with a built-in Glass camera, ostensibly for persons with vision disabilities (Moran, 2014). Also in development are digital bio implants (Monks, 2014). One project involves a digital compass coated in silicon and titanium and embedded under the skin, giving the human host an embedded direction finder. Other devices being developed by so-called bio hackers include memory chips, temperature sensors, and virtual passwords. Down the road may be video cameras or other sensors embedded directly into the retina, first for those with visual impairment, and later for potentially anyone. Ethicists will have much to debate.

GoPro HD (high-definition) wearable cameras are also poised to fundamentally transform the video production process. With the company's 2014 IPO, a growth in the use of this wearable camera is increasingly likely (Fiegerman, 2014). GoPro has sold more than 10 million of the wearable cameras to the public (Evans, 2014). A high-quality point of view (POV) action camera is set to transform video reporting on a wide spectrum of events, from everyday life to extreme sports.

Computer-synthesized environments known as virtual reality (VR) have been rapidly moving from the realm of research in room-based environments to the mainstream wearable consumer marketplace. An early entrant into this arena is the Oculus Rift Virtual Reality display (Oculus Rift, 2014), which utilizes a relatively compact head-worn display. Designed for VR games, Oculus Rift gives consumers a powerful immersive form of interactive 3D video media. Reflecting the commercial potential of this emerging technology, in March of 2014 Facebook purchased Oculus VR for $2 billion (Ember, 2014).

An area of concern with any wearable technology involves possible unintended, adverse consequences, particularly on the wearer's health. A case in point is a recently introduced wearable device called "Fitbit Force" (Rosman, 2014). San Francisco-based Fitbit is a company that markets wearable devices designed to promote physical fitness by tracking the user's exercise, sleep, and nutritional patterns. The Fitbit Force is a wristband that performs such functions and synchs wirelessly with the user's smartphone or tablet. Unfortunately, a substantial number of users have reported developing a rash where the device contacted their skin. In February 2014 the company issued a recall and stopped selling the device, explaining it is likely the users are experiencing an allergic reaction to materials in the Fitbit Force. Yet, by June of 2014 a second generation of smart wristbands entered the marketplace, including the LG Lifeband Touch and the Samsung Gear Fit, both of which link fitness bands with smartwatches. They not only monitor user health-related information (e.g., physical activity, heart rate), but also deliver communications and information, such as text messages and music (Fergusson et al., 2014).

Four Influences on Broadcasting

Given the likely level of consumer adoption over the next decade, wearable technologies are apt to make significant inroads into the American marketplace and beyond. In this context, there are at least four ways that wearable technologies may influence the broadcasting industry. Among the implications of wearable digital devices are (1) new methods of video production, (2) shifts in storytelling, (3) increases in public engagement, and (4) realignments in the structure, management, and funding of the broadcasting industry.

Transforming Production

In the near-term, the most immediate impact of wearable digital devices, especially head-worn technology such as Google Glass, is on the production methods of television and radio. As one of 38,000 Google Explorers, the author logged more than two dozen hours wearing his Glass. As of January 14, 2015 Google concluded the Explorer program, continuing the program as an internal research operation. Forecasts are for Glass users to reach 21 million by 2018 (Sacco, 2014). One of the things any user of Glass quickly becomes accustomed to is the prompt, "OK Glass," which appears on screen and can be spoken by the wearer to initiate an action, such as taking a picture, making a video call or conducting a Google search on the internet. After this prompt, taking a photograph or shooting a video using Glass is as easy as simply looking at something and stating that command or tapping the top or side of the head-worn unit. Glass can provide a nearly continuous record of what the wearer sees, hears, interacts with, or commands, with time, date, and location stamped on to the image or video. Through the wireless network connection (either cellular or Wi-Fi), all this content can be seamlessly uploaded to the cloud or shared with friends, family, or the public.

For broadcast production, either professional or amateur, Glass can empower the creation of continuous video and audio recording. Anywhere the wearer goes, anything she or he sees or hears can be recorded. While much of this video recording may be of little newsworthiness, the potential vastness of coverage both in time and space or location by thousands or perhaps millions of Glass users makes it likely that there will be occasional nuggets of news produced. And these nuggets will quickly make their way through the social media food chain on to the news agenda, including the broadcasting realm. Importantly, this video will be shot from a first-person perspective or POV, in contrast to the standard third-person perspective of most broadcast news.

One journalist who has already purchased her own pair of Glass is Caroline Lowe, a newsroom manager for KSBY in Santa Monica, California (Nevius, 2014). Her reason for spending $1,500 of her own money is for the potential of Glass as a reporting tool during breaking news events. Had she been equipped with Glass during the heavy rains that pounded southern California in the spring of 2014, Lowe said, "I could have stood under an umbrella and shown what I've seen from the storm." Reporters, or anyone else, can use a free app from Livestream to broadcast live video shot with Glass (Bloomberg, 2014; Shteyngart, 2013). In fact, Vice News has already used this capability to transmit Glass-enabled first-person perspective live video coverage of the 2013 protests in Istanbul, Turkey, and elsewhere (Pool, 2014). Moreover, other news media including KTLA in Los Angeles broadcast live coverage via Livestream.

A journalist using Glass might also be able to provide live virtual experiences for others wearing Glass. In other words, in real time a remotely located individual wearing Glass (or using another type of wearable device) could journey virtually through the same venue as the journalist also wearing Glass. Because Glass is network enabled, the reporter could in real time engage audience members through social media as well.

The convergence of Glass, citizen reporting, and first-person POV converged in early 2014 when a San Francisco woman wearing Glass entered a popular bar (Bloomekatz and Wells, 2014). After an initially friendly exchange, some patrons became upset about her wearing Glass and potentially video recording them. Like many critics skeptical of the benefits of wearable computers, these patrons were concerned about the threat of Glass to personal privacy.

Passions often have run high during debates about Glass. "Glasshole" is the term some critics have coined to describe persons wearing Glass in public places or spaces where anyone not wearing Glass may be (Gibbs, 2014). On January 26, 2014, the popular television animated series *The Simpsons* aired a satirical episode poking fun at some of the potential drawbacks of Google Glass and augmented reality (AR) (Groening, 2014). After donning his "Oogle Goggles" one character gushed "finally I'm not a slave to my stupid human eye-balls." Meanwhile, the company's unscrupulous owner later reveals his true motive in buying the AR specs for his employees as holiday gifts was in fact only to spy on them.

In the case of the San Francisco bar, an accosting of the woman wearing Glass allegedly occurred, and was recorded while it happened, from the woman's first-person POV via her Glass. The woman posted the video to YouTube and it has fueled an ongoing debate as well as police investigation (NewsAttackNow, 2014). The potential of Glass as a reporting tool, POV-enabling narrative device, and crime recorder is well illustrated in the event. Underscoring this potential, the New York City police department is testing Glass for use in the field (Carte, 2014). A related wearable application is the introduction of body cameras for police. Taser International, a company better known for its electric stun gun, manufactures a leading body camera, The Flex, used by police (Hardy, 2012). The body cams capture both audio and video, weigh about 3 ounces, and cost about $500. Police are already, in 2014, testing such systems in a growing number of US cities, including New Orleans, New York, Oakland, and San Diego (Goodman, 2014; Johnson, 2014; Kramer, 2014). One trial has indicated police body cameras have substantial positive impact on policing. In particular, citizen complaints against police for excessive use of force have declined dramatically after police have started wearing body cameras. In a trial in Washington, DC:

> The camera-wearing officers were involved in dramatically fewer incidents involving the use of their batons, pepper spray, stun guns or firearms. Behavioral changes were so striking—both in the officers and in citizens they encountered—that complaints against the cops wearing cameras declined by nearly 90 percent.
>
> (*The Washington Post*, 2014)

In addition, the United States border patrol is launching a test of body cameras for its 21,000 agents. Such law enforcement body cameras will no doubt prove an important source of video for crime- or immigration-related news.

The potential for first-person reporting via Glass is already happening, although often more in the form of citizen reporting than professional news gathering. In one case, a zookeeper at the Phoenix zoo in Arizona has donned Glass to enable visitors, whether on hand or remotely located, to get an up-close and narrated view of animals in the natural enclosures (Phoenix Zoo, 2014).

The author first observed a person wearing Google Glass in public on March 14, 2014, in a Starbucks on the corner of W. 15th street and 9th avenue in New York City. In this case, no one objected to the young man wearing Glass.

Beyond first-person reporting, another way that wearable technology is likely to impact broadcast production involves the convergence of geo-location, drones, and Glass. In a broadcasting context, geo-location refers to the embedding of geographic location information into each frame of video. Geo-location information is typically obtained from the global positioning satellite system (GPS) with location tagging added into the meta-data for each frame of video. As such, it provides a precise tagging of the altitude, latitude, longitude, time, and date at which the video was shot. This time, date, and location information, along with the identity of the journalist who shot the video, can provide a strong digital stamp or watermark. Geo-location is already in wide use in photography, and is emerging as an important tool in video. It has particular value in journalism. Geo-location information can help to authenticate or establish the veracity of video, providing an independent measure of where and when the video was shot. This can prove especially useful when the video may document something that an individual or organization in power wishes to deny or distort, such as a political protest, refugee movements, environmental destruction, or human rights abuses or killings. During the author's recent year (2013) in the Middle East, TheGuardian.com provided video documenting human rights abuses of imported workers in the region, and some authorities denied the truthfulness of the video, alleging it was not shot when or where the reporter claimed. Had the reporter added a geo-location tag to the video, it would have been much harder to deny the truthfulness of the video. Geo-location tagging video can also help professional news media assess the veracity of video obtained from citizen reporters.

Strong watermarks establishing time, date, location, and provenance of video can also help protect the intellectual property rights of freelance journalists or citizen reporters.

Video shot via drones is increasingly capable of including a geo-location stamp obtained via GPS. As such, geo-located drone video is of increasing reliability and value to news broadcasters. Drone video can provide important aerial views of terrestrial news events or developments. Such was the case in the political protests in late December, 2013, in Bangkok, Thailand. Journalists used drones to obtain video of the protests and provide an independent means to estimate crowd size. With geo-location-enabled video, it was particularly difficult for authorities to question the veracity of the video. Having an independent measure of geo-location in drone video is especially important since drones are remotely piloted and do not have a human on board to directly verify what was observed.

Although in prototype form as of this writing, Google Glass is capable of providing piloting ability for those operating a drone. In the case of Paris-based Parrot AR.Drone 2.0, the company's drone piloting software has been developed as of 2014 for use on handheld devices such as smartphones and tablets (Parrot, 2014). Hackers, however, have already modified the software to run on Google Glass (Huya-Kouadio, 2013). This permits a person wearing Glass to pilot the Parrot AR.Drone 2.0 equipped with two HD cameras and GPS tracking directly through Glass control, including simple movements of the head, such as a tilt left, right, forward, or back.

For those producing video for broadcasting, having the ability to pilot a drone in a hands-free mode has significant implications. By operating hands-free in the field, a reporter could focus on watching the video being captured, using hand-held devices to record notes, communicate with remotely located sources or colleagues, or search online for related information. During breaking news or live events, this could be especially valuable.

On April 10, 2014, Google announced it would begin selling Glass to the public by the end of April of that year, although it wasn't clear how many of the units would be available (Kelly, 2014). Still, it suggests the potential for wide consumer adoption. Industry forecasts expect wearable device sales will reach at least 64 million worldwide by 2017, up from just 3.1 million in 2012 (Orlov, 2013).

Reinventing Storytelling

Shifts in storytelling will also likely emerge from the use of Glass and other wearable devices. As broadcast content producers begin to explore the use of Glass, it will be immediately apparent that the first-person POV will open new possibilities for innovation in the ways stories are told. For instance, it will be possible to give viewers a more empathetic level of engagement in the story by letting them virtually see or hear something for themselves. In contrast to the third-person narrative model, which adds a conceptual layer of separation between viewer and storyteller, a first-person narrative can eliminate that layer of detachment. From a production point of view, it's worth noting that, for the videographer, Glass shoots video of whatever the wearer sees. In other words, it's not necessary to point a hand-held camera at the subject. Instead, the videographer need only look at it.

Augmented reality also presents an opportunity for broadcasting innovators to transform storytelling via wearable technology (Höllerer et al., 1999). In the context of broadcasting, AR refers to the use of wearable technology to layer multimedia on to a person's view of the real world. AR can be especially powerful when geo-location is utilized to provide a location-customized story or view of the world. For instance, a person wearing Glass standing outside the World Trade Center site in 2014 might see a view of the WTC before 9/11 layered on to the scene. A reporter using AR might use wearable technology to provide a location-customized first-person narrative or account of 9/11. Such capability holds the promise of delivering interactively what legendary broadcast journalist Edward R. Murrow provided in his award-winning 1950s' TV program *See it Now* (EmmyTV, 2013). Murrow's program "interwove historical events and speeches with Murrow narration" and is still in 2014 the quality standard by which broadcast journalism is judged.

Because the Glass display is relatively small, and it overlays high-resolution images and video, it is "the equivalent of a 25 inch high definition screen from eight feet away" (Glass Specifications, 2014). Because of this perspective, the Glass user interface is described as "glanceable" rather than immersive as in a VR headset. In other words, the user is expected to glance at the display rather than watch it as she or he would on a hand-held or desktop device.

Google Glass currently features two AR apps, both of which are potentially relevant to broadcasting. First is Word Lens. It enables the wearer to look at any printed text and have it automatically translated in near real time to or from English and five foreign languages, including French, Portuguese, and Spanish (Glassappsource, 2014). It works via optical character recognition, and also runs on hand-held devices. Real-time text translation could be helpful to a reporter in the field in a foreign country, for instance. The second AR app on Glass is Field Trip (Glassappsource, 2014). It features content produced by 100 local publishers, which is overlaid on to local views and sites where the wearer finds him- or herself. It is essentially an AR-driven tour guide. For example, standing before the historic Bale Grist Mill in the State Historic Park in St Helena, California, the wearer sees overlaid visually adjacent to the mill itself textual and graphical information about the background of the mill. This same technology could be used to tell stories about recent or historic news events (Pavlik and Bridges, 2013).

Future generations of AR technology may also utilize mobile holographic displays now in development (Welsh, 2013). Mobile holography would involve the projection of 3D imagery in front of the individual. Such technology would mean the user could experience AR without the need to wear anything on or near her or his eyes. For many, this unobtrusive AR format might be the catalyst to actually using the technology. The timetable for the development of mobile holography is unclear, and likely years away. However, researchers at the MIT Media Lab are reportedly developing holographic television sets and expect them to be available to consumers within a decade (Bost, 2013).

Moreover, Glass has a sophisticated and reliable voice interface. The wearer can speak commands, prefaced by "OK Glass," such as "record a video" or "take a picture." Further, the wearer can write text simply by speaking it. This dictation capability offers a journalist a number of advantages, including the ability to create real-time field notes without having to pause to look down at a notepad, taking his or her eyes off a subject or news event as it unfolds.

Researchers at the University of Southern California are experimenting with techniques employing Glass to create interactive storytelling in journalism (Grossberg, 2014). Approaches include VR and 3D models.

Engaging the Public

Media scholar Marshall McLuhan (1964) and his mentor Harold Innis (1951) developed the notion that the media of communication act as an extension of the human senses. For instance, television can act as an extension of our eyes and ears. Few people have personally met world leaders such as US President Barack Obama, Russian President Vladimir Putin, or German Chancellor Angela Merkel. Yet, vast numbers, perhaps even the majority, know a great deal about such leaders, how they look, what they sound like when they speak, and perhaps even what they have done in their leadership roles. By and large, the members of the public know what they know about these individuals through the media, including television, which is still for most persons the leading source of news (Pew Research Center, 2013), although social media are fast becoming a primary news source for many.

McLuhan's notion of the media as extensions of the human senses offers much to how we understand wearable technology and what it means for the individual's media experience. Consider Steve Mann, the developer of the wearable computer and wearcam in the late 1970s (Mann, 2013a). Mann has been a human cyborg for more than three decades, wearing his self-designed head-worn computer and communications system for nearly four decades. Now a professor at the University of Toronto, Mann has used his wearcam to produce first-person news reporting and documentaries, including documentaries about privacy in an age of increasingly ubiquitous surveillance cameras. Mann's wearable computer has become for him virtually an extension of his own biological senses of sight and hearing. For him, a wearable computer, camera, and microphone are second nature. As a case in point, after 9/11 Mann was traveling across the international border from the US into Canada. Ordered by customs agents to remove his wearable technology, he subsequently became disoriented and fell, injuring himself and his expensive technology (Mann, 2013b).

Certainly the average wearer of Glass or any other technology may not develop the intimate connection Mann has with his wearable devices, but it is likely that, for many, a digital device that can capture sight, sound, or other information is apt to serve as a potentially powerful data collection and communication system. Some suggest Glass may signal the beginning of a new age of ubiquitous surveillance, a mobile panopticon (Foucault, 1995; Packer, 2014). It's quite likely that people who make extensive use of their wearable devices may find them becoming second nature, as well. Even today's hand-held technologies are proving a test case for the close connection that can develop between user and digital device. It's increasingly common to see even a toddler who has used an iPad or other digital device unsuccessfully try to use the same touch skills with the pages of a printed magazine (UserExperiencesWorks, 2011).

The extraordinary level of connection users are likely to develop with their wearable digital devices presents a unique opportunity for broadcasters to engage their audiences. It's also likely that wearable devices will utilize increasingly sophisticated artificial intelligence (AI) to support the user experience. Natural language is a branch of AI already being utilized, and Apple has advanced a popular AI user interface called Siri. As voice and AI systems converge in a wearable environment, the user may enter an even closer connection with the technology. The potential for this user–device connection was dramatized in the 2013 blockbuster film,

Her (IMDb, 2013), which in 2014 earned Spike Jonze an Oscar for best original screenplay (Opam, 2014).

Realigning an Industry

Wearable technologies also portend realignments in the structure, management, and funding of the broadcasting industry. For most of its history, television has been a medium experienced by a stationary viewer on a time-scheduled basis controlled by broadcasters. The advent of high-capacity, inexpensive digital storage, high-speed or broadband networking, and mobile digital technology has given rise to a frequently mobile consumer of video content who consumes media more on demand and less on schedule. A primary exception is during live events, such as sports, with substantial social capital, but advances in mobile media are still reducing the demand for fixed-location viewing. Breaking news is another important domain where mobile media will play a particularly significant role, especially linked to social media (Sonderman, 2014).

Although radio, music, and other forms of audio content have long been experienced by a frequently mobile consumer, often using a wearable device, video has been slower to follow this path. Wearable technologies are likely to facilitate considerable growth in the mobile consumption of video. Moreover, wearable users are likely to produce their own video for sharing via social media. Combined with geo-location, video that is tagged to locations will take on greater prominence in the mobile user video experience. In addition to news and information that is locally tagged, advertising and marketing video content will exploit geo-location tied to the mobile user of wearable technology. The combination of location-based advertising, and mobile and interactive video prosumers (persons who consume and produce video) operating via networked wearable technologies, is apt to lead to a restructuring of broadcasting. One fundamental shift is to move away from place-based delivery and consumption of audio and video controlled by broadcasters, toward a user-centered system of interactive and on-demand delivery and production.

A second shift is in the likely mechanisms for funding broadcasting in a wearable media age. While some generic audience advertising is still likely, an increasing portion of that commercial messaging is likely to be highly targeted in terms of user customization. This customization is apt to take the form of both location awareness and adaptation to individual characteristics and interests. Targeted advertising is likely to develop for broadcasters in combination with advances in advertising exchange systems utilizing real auctions as developed by digital media enterprises such as Google and Facebook (Khan, 2013).

One major question about the funding of content in a wearable marketplace is the likely role of paid content. Since the 1970s, consumers have spent an increasing portion of their disposable income on paid media content, particularly pay TV and telecommunications services. As these systems converge in a mobile, wearable, network-enabled twenty-first-century system, the potential for paid content is significant. Yet, traditional broadcasting organizations face uncertainty in this future. While cable, satellite, and fiber-optic systems have built substantial paid content businesses, the rise of network-based content providers such as Netflix and Amazon is reshaping this environment. The potential growth of interactive wearable content production and distribution may add more fuel to the fires of economic uncertainty for twenty-first-century broadcasters.

Beyond these shifts are possibilities raised by digital funding developments including crowdfunding and Bitcoin, a provocative new digital currency. Crowdfunding through online resources such as Kickstarter and Indiegogo offers funding opportunities to independent entrepreneurs who might be interested in starting their own digital initiatives in the realm of wearables and broadcasting (Indiegogo, 2014; Kickstarter, 2014). Projects launched on Kickstarter or Indiegogo, both international efforts, generate their funding from contributions from the public who find the new undertakings engaging and worthwhile. Kickstarter has grown dramatically since its launch in 2009 and, as of March 2014, had raised more than $1 billion in funding for creative projects. Many Kickstarter projects deal with video-related initiatives such as digital documentaries.

Bitcoin is a new digital or crypto currency, launched as an open-source platform in 2009 (Steadman, 2013). It is based on peer-to-peer exchange, and has seen its value against the US dollar rise and fall dramatically. As of this writing (March 8, 2014), a Bitcoin was worth about $627, about half its value of six months earlier. For broadcasters, entering into the Bitcoin realm opens new possibilities to engage a high-tech audience likely also drawn to wearable technology.

Yet it is vitally important to temper with skepticism any expectations of potential economic, social, or political benefits from emerging technologies such as wearable devices. The potential benefits of emerging media technologies have been hotly debated for decades (Pool & Schiller, 1981). Some scholars have outlined the negative impact of the internet and related developments on journalism (McChesney & Pickard, 2011). Others have pointed to the potential positive economic, social, and cultural influence networked technologies may exert (Castells, 1996; Kuznets, 1955). Morozov (2013) has cautioned against relying on technological solutions to a wide spectrum of social, political, or economic problems. Many anticipate that technology-fueled innovation such as the widespread use of wearable technologies will lead to economic growth, and it may. However, data suggest economic growth may also produce an increasingly unequal distribution of that wealth, an issue of increasing concern in the US and internationally. Piketty (2014) presents an analysis based on three centuries of data for

20 countries. Piketty has found that, since the eighteenth century, when the rate of return on capital exceeds the rate of growth on income and output, wealth inequality grows. Such was the case in the eighteenth and nineteenth centuries, and preliminary trends suggest strongly that it will be the case in the twenty-first century (Piketty, 2014). How these patterns will shape media economics is a key question for future research.

Related here are some of the legal and ethical issues swirling around Glass. Among the issues in the US is the intersection of two constitutional issues, the First Amendment, protecting freedom of speech, and the Fourth Amendment, protecting privacy. These two rights often come in direct conflict with regard to Glass both in the US and around the world. Reports indicate that Glass is already banned in at least a half dozen venues in the US, including hospitals (for patients or visitors, not medical staff), casinos, Guantanamo Bay, many bars and restaurants, at live performances, and in strip clubs (Low, 2014).

Table 14.1 summarizes the emerging issues surrounding wearable technologies and the media. In the near-term, wearable technologies will prove especially valuable for media producers as a hands-free method of producing content, including photos and video. Moreover, providing an easy method of GPS watermarking will be immediately useful. Content or storytelling opportunities include producing live, POV streaming audio and video content as well as glanceable content ideal for audiences with short attention spans. There will be immediate social media connections to engage the public. Regulatory frameworks will largely be local in the near-term, but gradually national or international frameworks will emerge, especially around the issues of freedom of speech, privacy, and security. In the far-term, wearable costs will fall while the devices become increasingly

Table 14.1 Wearables and Media: Emerging Issues

Issues	Methods of Production	Content and Storytelling	Public Engagement	Economic and Regulatory Frameworks
Near-term	Hands-free, GPS watermarked, expensive	Live, POV, "glanceable" content	Growing social-media connection	Local regulation
Far-term	Ubiquitous, continuous, falling costs	Immersive, VR narratives	Citizen reporters	Global, First and Fourth Amendment/ privacy battleground, new revenue models

ubiquitous. Wearables will provide a near continuous source of media content. Formats will become increasingly immersive with corresponding new narrative forms. Citizen reporters will provide much content, especially in an international arena. Over time, new revenue models will emerge to tap into the live and immersive potential of wearable media.

Concluding Reflections

Wearable digital devices represent the next generation of mobile media. Wearables signal an era of increasingly mobile, geo-located, and personal audio and video consumption, production, and distribution. As such, wearable digital technologies bring both challenges to, and opportunities for, the future of broadcasting. These changes are likely to emerge in at least four areas: (1) methods of production used in creating video content, (2) the ways stories are told, (3) the level of engagement with the viewer or public, and (4) the structure, management, and funding of broadcasting as well as corresponding legal and ethical considerations.

Each of these four areas represents directions for future research on wearable technologies and broadcasting. Combined, they outline an agenda for investigators interested in how wearable technologies may redefine the nature of broadcasting in the twenty-first century. Considering the unintended consequences of wearable technologies, including health effects, privacy concerns, and other unexpected and potential negative political, social, and economic impacts, should also guide this research.

As consumers begin to embrace wearable devices such as the experimental Google Glass and the Samsung Galaxy Gear smartwatch, investigators and broadcasters alike have an opportunity to innovate, experiment, and evaluate. This exploration should be guided not only by financial incentives, but also by ethics and a commitment to the highest standards of journalistic and broadcast excellence. While promoting the values of freedom enshrined in the First Amendment, those who employ wearable technologies should maintain a respect for personal privacy as established in the Fourth Amendment, as well as security in a time of globally networked data, communications, and surveillance.

A half century ago Murrow admonished broadcasters in a famous speech that the medium of television "can teach, it can illuminate; yes, and it can even inspire" (Murrow, 1958). But achieving those laudable goals would happen only when people use the medium to those ends. Otherwise, television would be "nothing but wires and lights in a box." Murrow's words might equally well apply in today's digitally connected world. Except, rather than wires and lights in a box, there are electrons, chips, and bits in a wearable computer. Whether they help to illuminate, teach, and inspire will depend on how humans put them to use.

References

Android. (2014). Android Wear. Online at www.android.com/wear/ (retrieved March 24, 2104).

Bloomberg. (2014). Livestream your world with Google Glass app. *Bloomberg Business*, April 14. Online at www.bloomberg.com/video/livestream-your-world-with-google-glass-app-9KhdbTr6SKmVgT8hHUrxgQ.html?cmpid=yhoo (retrieved April 16, 2014).

Bloomekatz, Ari, & Wells, Jason. (2014). Google Glass-wearing woman posts video of alleged S.F. bar attack. *LA Times*, February 26. Online at www.latimes.com/local/lanow/la-me-ln-google-glass-attack-video-posted-20140226,0,3398634.story#ixzz2uiLvxagW (retrieved March 1, 2014).

Bost, Callie. (2013). MIT researcher says holographic TV could debut in next 10 years. *Bloomberg Business*, June 19. Online at www.bloomberg.com/news/2013-06-19/mit-researcher-says-holographic-tv-could-debut-in-next-10-years.html (retrieved March 4, 2014).

Carte, Brandon. (2014). Police departments have their eye on Google Glass. *USA Today*, February 22. Online at www.usatoday.com/story/tech/2014/02/12/us-police-consider-google-glass/5341597/ (retrieved March 3, 2014).

Castells, Manuel. (1996, 2nd ed. 2000). *The rise of the network society: The information age: Economy, society and culture, Vol. I*. Cambridge, MA; Oxford, UK: Blackwell.

CBS News. (2014). Bionic pancreas uses smartphone to control blood sugar. *CBS News*, June 16. Online at www.cbsnews.com/videos/bionic-pancreas-uses-smartphone-to-control-blood-sugar/ (retrieved June 15, 2014).

CBS This Morning. (2014). Ahead of the curve: Samsung unveils new phones, virtual reality device. *CBS This Morning*, September 4. Online at www.cbsnews.com/videos/ahead-of-the-curve-samsung-unveils-new-phones-virtual-reality-device/ (retrieved September 4, 2014).

Covert, Adrian. (2014). Apple's wearables will be for fitness. *CNN Money*, February 21. Online at http://money.cnn.com/2014/02/21/technology/innovation/apple-wearable/ (retrieved March 3, 2014).

Eisenberg, Anne. (2009). Inside these lenses: A digital dimension. *The New York Times*, April 25. Online at www.nytimes.com/2009/04/26/business/26novel.html?_r=0 (retrieved March 3, 2014).

Ember, Stanley. (2014). Facebook's $2 billion deal for Oculus. *The New York Times*, March 26. Online at http://dealbook.nytimes.com/2014/03/26/morning-agenda-facebooks-2-billion-deal-for-oculus/?_r=0 (retrieved March 27, 2014).

EmmyTV. (2013). See it now. *Archive of American Television*. Online at www.emmytvlegends.org/interviews/shows/see-it-now (retrieved March 3, 2014).

Epiphany Eyewear. (2014). Online at www.epiphanyeyewear.com/ (retrieved March 24, 2014).

Evans, Carter. (2014). GoPro CEO reveals new POV action camera. *CBS News*, September 29. Online at www.cbsnews.com/videos/gopro-ceo-reveals-new-pov-action-camera/?utm_source=feedburner&utm_medium=feed&utm_campaign=Feed%3A+cbsnews%2Ffeed+ (retrieved September 29, 2014).

Fergusson, Rebekah, Perez, Vanessa, & Ruiz, Melinda. (2014). Next-generation fitness bands. *The New York Times*, June 18. Online at www.nytimes.com/

video/technology/personaltech/100000002947823/the-next-generation-fitness-bands.html (retrieved June 19, 2014).

Fiegerman, Seth. (2014). Lights, camera, IPO: Gopro goes public. *Mashable.com*, June 26. Online at http://mashable.com/2014/06/26/gopro-ipo-3/ (retrieved June 26, 2014).

Foucault, Michel. (1995). *Discipline and punish: The birth of the prison.* New York: Vintage Books.

Gibbs, Samuel. (2014). Google Glass advice: How to avoid being a glasshole. *The Guardian*, February 19. Online at www.theguardian.com/technology/2014/feb/19/google-glass-advice-smartglasses-glasshole (retrieved March 3, 2014).

Glassappsource. (2014). Online at www.glassappsource.com/listing/word-lens-for-glasses (retrieved March 28, 2014).

Glass Specifications. (2014). Online at https://support.google.com/glass/answer/3064128?hl=en (retrieved October 1, 2014).

Goldin, Melissa. (2014). Designers aim to bring high-tech fashion to the average shopper. *Mashable.com*, February 22. Online at http://mashable.com/2014/02/22/wearable-tech-fashion-show/ (retrieved March 4, 2014).

Goodman, J. David. (2014). New York police officers to begin wearing body cameras in pilot program. *The New York Times*, September 4. Online at www.nytimes.com/2014/09/05/nyregion/new-york-police-officers-to-begin-wearing-body-cameras-in-pilot-program.html?ref=nyregion (retrieved September 5, 2014).

Groening, Matt. (2014). "Specs and the City" episode of *The Simpsons* on Fox. *Fox.com*, January 26. Online at www.fox.com/watch/140254787683 (retrieved March 5, 2014).

Grossberg, Josh. (2014). Digital journalism: Your Sunday newspaper will never be the same. *USC News*, September 25. Online at http://news.usc.edu/68433/digital-journalism-your-sunday-newspaper-will-never-be-the-same/ (retrieved September 26, 2014).

Hardy, Quentin. (2012). Taser's latest police weapon: The tiny camera and the cloud. *The New York Times*, February 21. Online at www.nytimes.com/2012/02/21/technology/tasers-latest-police-weapon-the-tiny-camera-and-the-cloud.html?pagewanted=all (retrieved August 21, 2014).

Hessman, Agnus. (2013). Galaxy Gear smart watch from Samsung has drawbacks. *Live Tech News*, November 20. Online at www.livetechnews.com/galaxy-gear-smart-watch-samsung-drawbacks/ (retrieved March 3, 2014).

Höllerer, Tobias, Feiner, Steven, & Pavlik, John. (1999). Situated documentaries: Embedding multimedia presentations in the real world. In *Proceedings of ISWC 99 (Third International Symposium On Wearable Computers)*, San Francisco, October 18–19, pp. 79–86.

Huya-Kouadio, Fredia. (2013). Flying AR Parrot drone through Google Glass. *YouTube*, September 23. Online at www.youtube.com/watch?v=Y7wM0dD9rpI (retrieved March 3, 2014).

IMDb. (2103). Online at www.imdb.com/title/tt1798709/ (retrieved March 3, 2014).

Indiegogo. (2014). Online at www.indiegogo.com (retrieved March 8, 2014).

Innis, Harold. (1951). *The bias of communication.* Toronto: University of Toronto Press.

Johnson, Kirk. (2014). Today's police put on a gun and a camera. *The New York Times*, September 27. Online at www.nytimes.com/2014/09/28/us/todays-police-put-on-a-gun-and-a-camera.html (retrieved September 28, 2014).

Kelly, Andrew. (2014). Google to sell Glass to public next week. *Reuters.com*, April 10. Online at www.reuters.com/article/2014/04/10/us-google-glass-idUS-BREA391YM20140410 (retrieved April 11, 2014).

Khan, Farrha. (2013). Google partners with Facebook to sell more ads: More targeted ads are on the way. *techradar.com*, October 21. Online at www.techradar.com/news/software/applications/google-to-start-selling-ads-on-facebook-1191354 (retrieved March 3, 2014).

Kickstarter. (2014). Online at www.kickstarter.com (retrieved March 8, 2014).

Kramer, Marcia. (2014). WCBS-2 6pm newscast, August 21.

Kuznets, Simon. (1955). Economic growth and income inequality. *American Economic Review, 45*(March), 1–28.

Low, Cherlynn. (2014). Google Glass banned! 7 places you can't wear them. *Tom's Guide*, March 18. Online at www.tomsguide.com/us/pictures-story/663-8-google-glass-ban-places.html (retrieved April 17, 2014).

Mann, Steve. (2013a). Wearcam. Online at http://wearcam.org/ (retrieved March 3, 2014).

Mann, Steve. (2013b). My "augmediated" life: What I've learned from 35 years of wearing computerized eyewear. *IEEE Spectrum*. Online at http://spectrum.ieee.org/geek-life/profiles/steve-mann-my-augmediated-life (retrieved March 3, 2014).

McChesney, Robert W., & Pickard, Victor (Eds.). (2011). *Will the last reporter please turn out the lights: The collapse of journalism and what can be done to fix it.* New York: The New Press.

McLuhan, Marshall. (1964). *Understanding media: The extensions of man.* Cambridge, MA: The MIT Press.

Meta. (2014). Online at www.spaceglasses.com/ (retrieved February 14, 2014).

Monks, Keiron. (2014). Forget wearable tech, embeddable implants are already here. *CNN*, April 9. Online at www.cnn.com/2014/04/08/tech/forget-wearable-tech-embeddable-implants/index.html (retrieved April 11, 2014).

Moran, Lee. (2014). Google patents smart contact lens system with built-in Glass camera. *New York Daily News*, April 15. Online at www.nydailynews.com/life-style/google-patents-smart-contact-lens-system-article-1.1756554 (retrieved April 15, 2014).

Morozov, Evgeny. (2013). *To save everything, click here: The folly of technological solutionism.* New York: PublicAffairs.

Murrow, Edward R. (1958). Speech to the attendees of the RTNDA convention. Radio Television Digital News Association, October 15. Online at www.rtdna.org/content/edward_r_murrow_s_1958_wires_lights_in_a_box_speech (retrieved March 28, 2014).

Nevius, C. W. (2014). Google Glass can be useful, but mind the distractions. *SFGate*, March 5. Online at www.sfgate.com/bayarea/nevius/article/Google-Glass-can-be-useful-but-mind-the-5291870.php (retrieved March 6, 2014).

NewsAttackNow. (2014). Online at www.youtube.com/watch?v=XT1rAPXVTso (retrieved March 3, 2014).

Oculus Rift. (2014). Online at www.oculusvr.com/ (retrieved February 14, 2014).

Opam, Kwame. (2014). Spike Jonze wins best screenplay Oscar for "Her." *The Verge*, March 2. Online at www.theverge.com/2014/3/2/5464740/spike-jonze-wins-best-screenplay-oscar-for-her (retrieved March 3, 2014).

Orlov, Laurie. (2013). Shipments of wearable technology devices will reach 64 million in 2017. *Age in Place Technology Watch*, October 4. Online at www.ageinplacetech.com/pressrelease/shipments-wearable-technology-devices-will-reach-64-million-2017 (retrieved November 10, 2013).

Packer, Jeremy. (2014). Such a perfect day: Digital augmentation and media technologies of the self. Presentation at Social Media and Psychosocial Well Being: A Symposium, Rutgers University, New Brunswick, NJ, April 18, 2014.

Parrot. (2014). AR.Drone 2.0. Online at http://ardrone2.parrot.com/ (retrieved February 21, 2014).

Pavlik, John V., & Bridges, Franklin. (2013). The emergence of augmented reality (AR) as a storytelling medium in journalism. *Journalism and Communication Monographs*, 15(1), 4–59.

Pew Research Center. (2013). How Americans get TV news at home. Online at www.journalism.org/2013/10/11/how-americans-get-tv-news-at-home/ (retrieved March 3, 2014).

Phoenix Zoo. (2014). Google Glass gets you up close and personal at the Zoo. *USA Today*, May 5. Online at www.usatoday.com/videos/tech/2014/05/05/8718971/ (retrieved May 7, 2014).

Piketty, Thomas. (2014). *Capital in the 21st century*. Boston: Harvard University Press.

Pogoreic, Deanna. (2014). Multineurons is developing head-worn sensor & iPad app to monitor patients with brain disorders. *MedCity News*, March 24. Online at http://medcitynews.com/2014/03/multineurons-developing-head-worn-sensor-monitor-patients-brain-disorders/ (retrieved April 18, 2014).

Pogue, David. (2014). All on the wrist. *CBS Sunday Morning*, March 23. Online at www.cbsnews.com/news/smartwatches-eat-your-heart-out-dick-tracy/ (retrieved March 23, 2014).

Pool, Ithiel de Sola, & Schiller, Herbert I. (1981). Perspectives on communications research: An exchange. *Journal of Communication*, 31(3), 15–23.

Pool, Tim. (2013). Tim Pool live streaming from Istanbul. *Vice News Livestream*, June 14. Online at www.vice.com/read/tim-pool-live-streaming-from-istanbul (retrieved October 1, 2014).

Rosman, Katherine. (2014). Fitbit to stop selling and recall its Force wristband. *The Wall Street Journal*, February 21. Online at http://online.wsj.com/news/articles/SB10001424052702304275304579397250102593142 (retrieved March 4, 2014).

Sacco, Al. (2014). How many people actually own Google Glass? *CIO*, June 4. Online at www.cio.com/article/2369965/consumer-technologyow-many-people-actually-own-goo/consumer-technology/how-many-people-actually-own-google-glass-.html (retrieved September 4, 2014).

Samuel, Ebenezer. (2014). Review: Samsung Gear Fit watch is sleek and small— and perfect for the gym. *New York Daily News*, April 11. Online at www.nydailynews.com/life-style/review-samsung-gear-fit-watch-article-1.1753446 (retrieved April 14, 2014).

Samsung. (2014). Galaxy Note 3 + Gear. Online at www.samsung.com/global/microsite/galaxynote3-gear/ (retrieved February 14, 2014).

Shteyngart, Gary. (2013). O.K., Glass: Confessions of a Google Glass explorer. *The New Yorker*, August 5. Online at www.newyorker.com/magazine/2013/08/05/ o-k-glass (retrieved September 22, 2014).

Smith, Aaron. (2012). Part IV: Cell phone attachment and etiquette. Pew Research Internet Project, November 30. Online at www.pewinternet.org/2012/11/30/ part-iv-cell-phone-attachment-and-etiquette/ (retrieved March 6, 2014).

Sonderman, Jeff. (2014). Unlocking mobile revenue and audience: New ideas and best practices. American Press Institute, June 10. Online at www.americanpressinstitute. org/publications/reports/white-papers/unlocking-mobile-revenue-audience/?utm_ source=TBR&utm_medium=email&utm_campaign=20140610 (retrieved June 10, 2014).

Steadman, Ian. (2013). Wary of bitcoin? A guide to some other cryptocurrencies. *Ars Technica*, May 11. Online at http://arstechnica.com/business/2013/05/wary-of-bitcoin-a-guide-to-some-other-cryptocurrencies/ (retrieved January 10, 2014).

Swider, Matt. (2014). Apple Watch release date, news and features. *techradar. com*, September 9. Online at www.techradar.com/news/portable-devices/apple-iwatch-release-date-news-and-rumours-1131043 (retrieved September 9, 2014).

Tofel, Kevin C. (2013). Samsung says Galaxy Gear smartwatch sales hit 800k: What's a "sale"? *Gigaom*, November 19. Online at http://gigaom. com/2013/11/19/samsung-says-galaxy-gear-smartwatch-sales-hit-800k-whats-a-sale/ (retrieved March 3, 2014).

UserExperiencesWorks. (2011). YouTube, October 6. Online at www.youtube. com/watch?v=aXV-yaFmQNk (retrieved March 2, 2014).

Vuzix. (2014). Online at www.vuzix.com/augmented-reality/products_m100ag/ (retrieved February 14, 2014).

The Washington Post. (2014). Putting cameras on police officers is an idea whose time has come. *The Washington Post*, May 12. Online at www.washingtonpost. com/opinions/putting-cameras-on-police-officers-is-an-idea-whose-time-has-come/2014/05/12/4674b3b6-da20-11e3-8009-71de85b9c527_story.html (retrieved August 19, 2014).

Welsh, Jennifer. (2013). Soon we'll get to view holograms on our phones and tablets. *Business Insider*, March 26. Online at www.businessinsider.com/portable-holographic-displays-on-your-phone-2013-3 (retrieved March 4, 2014).

Wikipedia. (2013). Moore's law. Online at http://en.wikipedia.org/wiki/ Moore%27s_law (retrieved June 9, 2013).

Wood, Molly. (2014). Wearables: Beyond the wrist. *The New York Times*, March 6. Online at www.nytimes.com/video/technology/personaltech/100000002753176/ wearables-beyond-the-wrist.html (retrieved March 6, 2014).

INDEX

The Journals of the Broadcast Education Association

Editor:
Zizi Papacharissi
University of Illinois at Chicago

Journal of Broadcasting and Electronic Media

Tandfonline.com/hbem

Published quarterly for the **Broadcast Education Association**, the *Journal of Broadcasting & Electronic Media* contains timely articles about new developments, trends, and research in electronic media written by academicians, researchers, and other electronic media professionals. The Journal invites submissions of original research that examine a broad range of issues concerning the electronic media, including the historical, technological, economic, legal, policy, cultural, social, and psychological dimensions. Scholarship that extends a historiography, tests theory, or that fosters innovative perspectives on topics of importance to the field, is particularly encouraged. The Journal is open to a diversity of theoretic paradigms and methodologies.

Editor:
Phylis Johnson
Southern Illinois University Carbondale

Journal of Radio and Audio Media

Tandfonline.com/hjrs

The *Journal of Radio & Audio Media* is a semiannual publication designed to promote scholarly dialogues generated by various disciplinary and methodological points of view. The Journal welcomes interdisciplinary inquiries regarding radio's contemporary and historical subject matter as well as those audio media that have challenged radio's traditional use. Scholars are invited to submit articles pertaining to any area of radio and audio media. Areas of interest include, but are not limited to, formats and programming, new technology, policy and regulation, rating systems, commercial and noncommercial networks, radio history, management and innovation, personalities, popular cultures, uses and effects studies, propaganda, social movements, advertising and sales, market concentration, Internet and satellite radio, podcasting, alternative formats, diversity, gender and international radio.

IN THE US CONTACT:
Taylor & Francis
Call Toll Free: 1-800-354-1420, press "4"
Fax: (215) 207-0046
customerservice@taylorandfrancis.com

BROADCAST EDUCATION ASSOCIATION
Educating for Tomorrow's Media